William Steele, PsyD, MSW, Founder, The National Institute for Trauma and Loss in Children: Chasing Lilly is "a remarkable, richly detailed journey into what matters most in the lives of severely traumatized children . . . This should be required reading for anyone caring for or treating traumatized children . . . What a wonderful story. Thank you for allowing me the opportunity to endorse such a meaningful and insightful work . . ."

Foster W. Cline, M.D., is an internationally renowned child and adult psychiatrist, as well as co-author of Parenting with Love and Logic. He has served as a consultant to school systems, pupil personnel teams, and hospitals around the world: "Just quality writing in general: descriptive, interesting, enticing, and leads me to smile in an understanding way. I have read your fascinating book, Chasing Lilly. I found it to be so enlightening, and hope it becomes a classic reference work for prospective foster and adoptive parents."

Bryan Sawyer, LIVE! with Kelly Top Teacher Award recipient: "Chasing Lilly is an eye-opening look into the world of mental illness from the prospective of a parent. Her harrowing tales make it easy to forget that Lilly is a real girl. As an educator, I would recommend this book to anyone who works with individuals with emotional disturbances."

———————————

Also Available By Nealie Rose:

Chasing Lilly
Curriculum and Discussion Workbook

This workbook is designed for studies in counseling, clinical psychology, psychiatry, and intervention. Available for Kindle and other devices.

Nealie Rose

Chasing Lilly

Nealie Rose

Nealie Rose

• Printed by CreateSpace, An Amazon.com Company
• Available on Kindle and other devices

Dedicated to Lilly Angel, who still makes me smile,
and has a solid place in my heart.

Nealie Rose

PROLOGUE

I waited on my porch for the three guys to corral and catch seven-year-old-Lilly. I knew it wouldn't be easy. A maroon van speeding down the street caught my attention, and I was surprised as it turned in at my house and shot up the driveway. A short, chubby lady quickly got out of the driver's side and slammed her door shut. As she hurried toward me, I recognized her as a woman who lived across from Lilly's kindergarten school. She had waved to us many times on our walk home the previous year and was once again waving her arms, but she wasn't happy.

Marching up to me, she asked with gritted teeth, "Do you know what your little girl did?"

Bracing myself, I asked, "No, what?"

After taking a deep breath, she glared at me and said, "Well, I saw her running all over and that your husband was trying to find her, so I thought I'd help and said to her, 'Hey, you look thirsty. How about a nice cold drink?' She said yes and came up on my porch. I got her a glass of water and brought it out, and she took some big gulps and then she yelled, '*Fat bitch!*' and threw the glass of water at me! Then she ran down off my porch. Do you *believe* that?"

I certainly did believe it, but she was too mad to listen to anything I might have to say.

Stomping back to her van, she got in, and peeled out of the drive.

I'm not sure why I thought it was so funny. Soon I heard tiny-girl cussing sounds coming my way, and my mind drifted back to how we got entangled with the little girl in the first place, and I had to smile again.

This is a true story. Names and places have been changed to protect privacy.

Nealie Rose

CHAPTER ONE
Eighteen months earlier

In mid-March the phone rang and it was Doris Champion, who along with her husband, John, headed The Center for Helping Children, a nearby Peoria foster care agency. She said they were trying to find a place for a "very disruptive" six-year-old girl to stay for the upcoming weekend.

As relatively new foster parents, we said yes immediately. A couple days passed though and we heard nothing from her about the little girl. I assumed they must have found another home. Doris had sounded desperate when we talked, so the possibility of that happening didn't seem likely.

Doris called again three days later. "Would you be available first thing in the morning to meet with me and this little girl's therapist?"

Somewhat startled, I asked, "She has a therapist? At six years old?"

"Yes. We'll need a home for her for about fourteen days. That's the estimated time frame for a bed to open in a residential institution near Chicago."

"OK, we can be there in the morning. What time and where?"

"Oh, good. Nine o'clock at the Child and Adolescent Services (C&A) Building on Fourth Street. I'll wait for you in the lobby."

My husband, Bruce and I wanted a little foster girl, and it looked like it was going to happen. Before she got off the phone with me though, I just had to know the name of the institution-bound young girl.

"What's her name?"

"Lilly."

I paused, then asked, "And her last name?"

"Angel. Lilly Angel."

Something about her name caused goose bumps to rise.

Sometimes it's better not to know what's coming. There are easier ways to ruin your social life than foster parenting, but none are quite so satisfying. Before Lilly entered our lives, I had been at home with my kids for years, and got it in my head that I wanted to foster a little girl. My parents had fostered for a while when their nest was empty, and I had noted with interest that foster parents can change lives for the better.

Before Lilly Angel came, Bruce said that as long as our daughters didn't object, he had no problem with fostering. Torie and Joy were fifteen and eighteen respectively and always on the go. Heck, they didn't care. They tell me now that they were all for it because they had hoped our attention radar would be on someone other than them. Their theory proved correct because who cares about a "C" when you have rows of teeth marks on your arm?

So we had checked out different foster agencies to find one that was a good fit for us, because there were lots to choose from, and we spoke to a few people who had gone before us. That's how we'd settled on The Center for Helping Children (CHC). They were the first choice because they had an excellent reputation under the management of John and Doris Champion, and it was in our town of Peoria, Illinois. We began the necessary paper work, followed by twelve weeks of training classes every Tuesday. All of this had to take place before we would be the foster parents who ended up taking on Lilly.

Some folks we knew were curious as to why we wanted to embark on this new endeavor, especially when our girls were almost grown. Others wanted to know for their own personal information, as they, too, had considered fostering but had never followed through.

"Watch that you don't get attached." We heard that more than once.

One acquaintance looked steadily at me as she said, "I heard about a foster child who poisoned her foster parents. Be careful."

Wow, I really needed to hear that.

Bruce and I looked forward to our Tuesday class because Tana was an awesome trainer. She was a tall, stately African American woman who had been in the trenches. She regularly challenged our thinking and one night in particular asked our class, "What determines a person's culture?"

There were eighteen in the class and hands began going up. The answers were all similar: "your race" and "ethnic background" seemed to be the general consensus.

Tana silently looked over her class before responding. "Wrong," she said. "Your culture is how you were raised. I was a Black girl, raised around Whites. My culture was White. Culture is not defined by your skin color."

I can't say that I didn't know that was possible, but when I heard it put that way, I began to see people differently. *Thank you, Tana, for teaching me something.*

Tana's dark eyes were slightly sad but gentle, and she knew well the subjects that she taught from working at The Center for Helping Children (CHC). She had seen firsthand the abandoned children, the abused children, and the kids whose lives were shattered because of parents' addictions or prostitution. Once those kids landed in "the system," agencies like CHC would take them into their foster homes as beds became available.

There were some people in our class who were pretty creepy looking, with dirty hair and nails, or scowls and hard stares coming from their faces. I wouldn't have wanted to visit their home much less sleep in their bed. There were also those who acted bored and didn't participate. As the weeks went on more and more chairs were empty as people dropped out.

I was often relieved to see a particular chair vacant because I would have felt sorry for *their* future foster child. I had to keep reminding myself that everyone would get a background check, reference check, and be finger-printed. The process also included a home inspection, fire inspection, and CPR certification. That part was easy because of my medical background as an X-ray technologist, and Bruce's years as a police officer. One day the mail brought us a paper certificate stating: State of Illinois,

Department of Job and Family Services Treatment Foster Home, Bruce and Nealie Rose, 1408 Lawndale, Peoria, Illinois 61604.

We were official. When I thought about being a foster parent I felt strongly that John and Doris Champion and all their staff would be there for us when we needed them. It's good they didn't know then just how *much* we'd need them.

When we arrived at the C & A Building the morning after the call from Doris, she was standing in the lobby wearing a red winter parka. She had a brown purse on her arm and a folder clutched to her chest. She gave us a hopeful smile and a quiet "hello" and led the way.

I really liked her. She wasn't gushy or loud, but radiated a determined optimism without saying anything more. I felt a kindred spirit because I, too, am a quiet optimist.

We eventually came to a tiny office with an open door. Therapist Kathi Beadle got up from a cluttered desk and greeted us with handshakes. She was about thirty five and thin with an earthy-artsy look to her. The office was so small that after we all sat down we were almost knee-to-knee. Looking at each other I think that all four of us somehow knew that it was a very important meeting.

Thinking back to that day I can still feel the hope and concern for the little girl, Lilly Angel, coming from those two women. (And looking back, had we changed our minds, how would her life have been different?) They hardly knew where to start, and as Bruce and I sat and listened, we soon found out why.

She had been at another CHC foster home for four weeks. As we spoke, she was in the Psychiatric Ward at Columbia Children's Hospital for the second time in two weeks. Apparently she had tried to kill the foster parents' three small dogs by choking them. They were rescued and she was admitted.

After discharge she was returned to the foster home, but nothing had improved. Lilly broke the dining room chairs (How does a little girl do that?) and tried to get a car to run over her by lying down in the street. She had twice wielded a knife in a threatening manner at the foster mother and threatened to burn their house down as well.

I listened and thought how nice it was of those two women to take the time to really inform us when it was only going to be for fourteen days.

Doris shocked me when she said, "It would be great if it worked out to have Lilly staying at your house, because then maybe she'd be able to live with you permanently."

Bruce and I looked at each other and he said, "We want to help her. We'll take her for the fourteen days until her name comes up on the waiting list. For any time longer than that we would need to have a family meeting to see if everyone is in agreement with it."

We were both feeling that we should proceed cautiously because how would taking the girl into our home affect the safety of our family members and two cats? I silently wondered if Lilly really was as dangerous as we were hearing.

Kathi had asked if we had any pets. We knew where that was going. Bruce told her we had two cats, Baler and Peek. He also said we could put them on another floor of our home to keep them safe.

Honestly, as we left, our heads were spinning. But we knew we could do anything for fourteen days. Couldn't we?

CHAPTER TWO

As soon as Bruce got home from work the next day we headed to Columbia Children's. While he drove we tried to review and recall everything we'd been told the previous day. If we knew all the information well, then we would be more prepared for what was ahead.

I purchased a booster seat for our car earlier in the day, and it was in the back seat even though we knew Lilly wouldn't be coming home with us yet. She had been at the hospital for eight days and wasn't ready to be released, and we planned on visiting her daily until she was discharged into our care.

While she was still in the hospital, we had hurriedly painted a main floor room yellow. We chose it because it was by the kitchen, and our bedroom was across the hall from it. It seemed the most logical location for keeping an eye on the little "angel."

All those plans and nervous thoughts were coming out in our conversation during that thirty-minute drive to the hospital. After the car was parked, we took an elevator to her floor where we were granted prior clearance to gain admittance. We walked into a large room that had lots of stuffed green chairs in groupings, and a handful of people visiting their much older children.

We would soon find out what Lilly looked like, but it crossed my mind how we would appear to her. At the time I was forty-two and Bruce was forty-six. I'm of medium build with brown hair and glasses and Bruce shaves his head, is six feet tall and weighs about one hundred eighty pounds. I hoped that we would appear likeable to Lilly and reminded Bruce to smile.

It was easy to figure out which child in the ward was the one we had come to see, because she was the only little girl there. When I first saw her she was running around in a rumpled set of blue hospital-issued pajamas. Someone had wound white cloth tape around and around her waist over the pajamas. The nurse explained that the tape was required because she would strip naked without it. *Whoa.* As we settled into a couple of once-beautiful upholstered chairs we observed her.

She looked as if she should have been in preschool -age four maybe, but never six. *Such a little figure in a psychiatric ward.* Her tiny body looked sturdy, and she had hair almost the same color as mine. It was just below her chin and very tangled, covering some of her face. She sucked on her thumb and crawled under the tables and flitted about the room. We noticed that she would pause occasionally and bite her fingernails *and* toenails. She glanced over at us only a few times that night.

The second, third, and fourth days visiting her were easier on us because we were not as nervous. Lilly spent most of her time crawling around the large room while pretending to be a cat. She would go up to just about anyone and "meow." Right after the meek mewing sound she would let loose with an authentic, sinister-sounding snarl, startling anyone nearby who had never heard it before, and she would get great pleasure at their surprise.

With each visit she would look at us a bit more and I noticed her eyes were an intense blue, yet somehow dull looking. We'd smile and try to interact with her, but her behavior was distant most of the time. Finally on the third visit she came up to me and stood there in the wrinkled and taped gown with her thumb in her mouth. Those empty eyes were locked on mine as she removed the thumb and asked, "Are you going to be my Mommy?"

I smiled and answered "Yes," and she was gone before any more could be said.

What a mess of a little kid.

That was when I first saw a few freckles across her little cheeks. I was starting to feel like her mother in a small way, and the thought of working with the little urchin intrigued me.

Before we left for our fifth and final trip to the hospital, we put Baler and Peek in the basement. It was roughly furnished and was to become their second home. The space had an area rug and plenty of light coming in so we felt it would be a great place to keep them safe. *Yikes! While we're trying to save the life of a little girl we also have to save the lives of our cats.*

I looked once more into the little bedroom by the kitchen. The fresh new paint was an inviting shade of butter yellow. There was an off-white day bed with a pretty pink and white comforter on it, a four-drawer chest, a white-wicker toy box, and lace curtains on a large 4 x 5 foot window. It had a roller blind at the top to pull down in the evenings. I'd painted the unfinished wood floor cream, and we placed a light-colored area rug in the center. On one of the walls, I hung a couple of white-framed pictures that had cute little Beatrice Potter bunnies, matted in purple. The room was adorable and I couldn't believe that we had done it in less than a week. We were ready for Lilly Angel.

When we got to the nurses' station, they had her belongings ready behind the counter. A worker brought her out to us already zipped to the chin in a purple heavy winter coat. There was a plastic bag in Lilly's hand that held art-therapy papers and a red, green, and yellow stuffed parrot. Another plastic bag was handed over the counter to us. It contained clothing items, toiletries, and some wrinkled cut-out magazine pictures of animals and junk foods. Bruce took five prescriptions that needed to be filled at the hospital pharmacy before we could leave.

We signed some paperwork and left that floor with two bags and a new fourteen-day daughter who was very quiet, sucking her thumb, and acting as if she didn't want to let us out of her sight.

She chewed on her fingernails during the twenty minute wait at the pharmacy. I smiled at her and reassured her that we'd soon be on our way, and I saw that her nails were bleeding in places, and she was obviously very warm from wearing her zipped coat indoors.

I bent toward her and gently asked, "Lilly, would you like to take your coat off until we are ready to leave?"

She looked at me briefly and shook her head once as she put her thumb in her mouth and turned her head slightly away from me.

Suddenly very tired, I straightened up and walked over to some chairs and sat down. I could have cried right then and there if I had not willed myself not to. *What kinds of things must have happened to this six-year-old to make her afraid to be left behind by people she didn't even know?*

We finally left the hospital and went to the car where Bruce buckled her into the new booster seat. Her bags were placed beside her, and we began a nervous drive home. I put Disney sing-a-long music in and Bruce began whistling and singing in a gentle, calming way. I don't know if it helped her or not, but it sure calmed me.

After the thirty-minute "forever trip" we pulled in our driveway. My heart was pounding and I told myself that she was probably more scared than I was. We got out in the garage and Bruce handed the bags to me as he went around and unbuckled her.

I went into the kitchen from our back door first, with Lilly following, but not too closely. Bruce shut the door and walked on through the kitchen to let Torie, our youngest daughter, know that we were home. As soon as the slim, blonde teen came into the kitchen to greet us, Lilly ran in fright into the nearby den. I looked at Torie and shrugged my shoulders. "It's okay," I said, knowing Lilly could hear me. "This is Torie, one of our daughters."

Torie understood the timing wasn't right and turned to leave the room. "I'll see you later, Lilly! I'm leaving now."

As soon as she left, Lilly came out of the doorway she scurried into and put that thumb in her mouth again.

I got down on my knees in front of her and said, "Here, let me help you get your coat off. I'll hang it in your room on a hook. You can see it in a minute." I removed her coat, picked up the bags, and led the way the short distance to the yellow room. I placed the bags on the floral comforter and hung her coat.

She followed and was scanning the room with those lifeless eyes. She still had not spoken.

I took out the parrot and asked, "Would you like to put this on your bed?" When she didn't answer I placed the parrot on her pillow. "What's his name?" The thumb came out of her mouth and she picked up the parrot.

"Her name is Polly," she said as she examined the small room looking at everything with those eyes that seemed full of nothingness.

Or maybe numbness?

She bent over the wicker toy box and rifled through the odds and ends of toys in it. There was a plastic model horse, a few Boyd's Bears wearing clothes, four brightly colored foam balls, an Etch-a-Sketch, and other interesting playthings we had gathered up.

Bruce put a keyed lock at the top of the staircase to the second floor. Our new visitor didn't need access to the three bedrooms and a bath, until we felt she could be trusted. Likewise for obvious reasons she would not be shown the basement. It also had a door at the top of the stairs and a hook-lock at the top.

It was getting late and bedtime was approaching so I led her on a tour of the main floor: bathroom, living room, our room, the kitchen and den, all mostly decorated in different colors of blue and white with white lace curtains.

Afterwards I went into her room and got the foam balls. "Lilly, come play with me in the living room."

Following, she returned my smile as I got on my knees and tossed a ball to her. She missed the catch but giggled and went after the green ball. We tossed the balls back and forth, getting sillier with each toss and catch.

Lilly seemed to be enjoying herself, so I decided to try a bit closer contact by putting the orange ball in my shirt. "Hey, would you like to put that yellow ball inside your shirt and belly-bonk me?"

She did it right away and I walked on my knees quickly toward her and smacked my foam belly into hers. She laughed with delight and got me back as I pretended to fall over.

During our play I was able to see that she had all her baby teeth, and quite an overbite, which was probably from sucking her thumb.

I was getting worn out fast playing that game, and my knees were taking a pounding. To see the game to a successful close, I announced, "I'm too tired to cook tonight so I'm going to get you a bowl of Cocoa Puffs if you're hungry."

Lilly jumped up quickly and ran to the kitchen table. She gobbled up three bowls and swallowed her three evening medications using the chocolate-flavored milk left in the bowl. She seemed exhausted too, and so I took her to the bathroom to get ready for bed.

"Here are some pretty pink pj's with balloons on them, and I'll go get your toothbrush and toothpaste out of your bag."

I left to get them and a pull-up from a package that I had purchased a few days before. We had learned in training classes that some children in foster care needed to wear pull-ups, and she was among the small group that did. I decided that she would not have any bathroom privacy at our house. Doris and Kathi had warned us to keep an eye on her every minute so bathroom duty fell to me. I helped her get the pull-up on and buttoned the pajama top.

She slowly brushed her teeth at the sink, too short to see herself in the mirror above the counter, so I pointed out a full-length mirror on the door. Lilly glanced at it but continued where she was. After rinsing her toothbrush she placed it on the counter, and lifted her sleepy face to mine.

I put my hand on her shoulder and said, "Come on, I'll tuck you in."

We walked to her room and I pulled down the covers. Clutching Polly, she rolled away from me onto her side. The thumb went in her mouth and her eyes closed.

I said a short, "Now I lay me down to sleep ..." but she was asleep before I finished. Leaving the room I glanced back at her for a moment. Nestled in the bed and sucking her thumb, she looked so very sweet and peaceful. *Was it possible that this lovely child had tried to do serious harm to pets?*

CHAPTER THREE

During our classes at CHC, we had been cautioned about bombarding children with house rules and information. Tell them the things that they needed to know over time, in order to ease their introduction to your home as much as possible.

The first evening Lilly wasn't told we had a basement (or cats), and that she wasn't permitted to wander into our bedroom without an escort or go outside on her own. She also didn't know we had put a motion-sensor alarm on her door lest she get up at night and leave the room.

It was several weeks before we showed her the upstairs bedrooms, one of which belonged to Torie. (Joy had just moved in with friends.) We didn't want to have to be looking all over for her, and our time was usually spent on the main floor anyway. There were far too many potential situations she could get herself into if we opened everything up to her.

Over the years to come she would never be out of our sight without trouble of some kind happening. Things would often happen right under our noses. But I'm getting ahead of myself.

We were required to fill out a critical incident report for any incident that involved unusual violence, theft, runaway, hospitalization, injury, sexual assault or misbehavior, harm to pets, self-harming, or destruction of property. That's a lot of categories, but we did not have to file a report for something as "harmless" as ripping a coloring book to shreds and breaking every crayon. Before fostering that would have counted as a big deal. With Lilly, that was small-time, baby.

The first year she was with us we had to turn in over three hundred critical incident reports. I couldn't possibly mention every one that occurred, but that gives the reader an idea of all the excitement that was going to follow the first night she spent with us.

The first couple days went pretty well, and I began to relax. On the third day Lilly was finishing a kids' video and she held up the next one she wanted to watch.

I said, "No, only one show. We'll find some other things to do."

She threw the video on the couch, walked up to the television and punched the OFF button before stomping to her room and slamming the door. I heard her in there yelling, "I hate you! You are not my mother! You are a FAKE mother!"

Though difficult to translate in this story, she had a speech impediment that I found delightful at times, because her pronunciation would take the edge off the mean things that were being said to me.

Although I'd never heard the term "fake mother" before and found it amusing in a way, she'd probably had a number of other fake mothers and there was nothing funny about that.

I waited until she stopped yelling inside her room before I loudly said, "I'm going to rock in the rocking chair. Sure wish I had a little girl to rock, but since I can't find one, I guess I'll just rock all by myself." The downstairs floors were all hardwood so I went to the living room rocker and started to rock, knowing that she would be able to hear me.

Within thirty seconds her door opened, and she dashed across the hall and pinned her little body against the staircase wall barely out of my view. Lilly hugged the wall while she slowly and stealthily crept toward me until she reached the main post of the staircase. Peeking around it she softly said, "*I'm* here."

I smiled at her and patted my lap. "Come on, let's rock."

She ran over to me and jumped in my lap. I wrapped my arms around her fairly bursting inside with (fake mother) love for that little girl. I knew then that I wanted to keep working with her.

Nealie Rose

The day that we'd been in Kathi Beadle's office with her and Doris Champion, they had said that Lilly's main diagnosis was Reactive Attachment Disorder, or RAD. We were taught in training that RAD occurs when a child has suffered severe loss and lack of attachment with a lasting parental figure in their lives. It involves a huge fear of *more* hurt or loss if they become close to or attached to another parent figure.

I really didn't understand RAD other than that the definition seemed to make sense. I wanted to help her, but did I want to have her attached to ME if I wasn't always going to be in her life? Then I, too, would seem to be part of the problem wouldn't I? That background thought fueled my determination to keep working with her, even when in future days it may not have seemed the wise thing to do.

CHAPTER FOUR

Lilly had been in a pre-school program while she was at the previous foster homes, but it was decided by everyone involved to keep her out of school and allow her time to adjust to our home before introducing her into another new environment. Even though Doris had mentioned early on that it would be great if she could stay with us longer than fourteen days, we still thought that CHC might yank her out and send her to the Chicago institution. It was as if nobody really knew much about how things might pan out.

Bruce was working six days a week, and Torie was in school, while I focused on trying to bridge a gap with Lilly and keep a watchful eye on her as well. That proved to be an interesting and exhausting task.

The day after the video incident, she and I were home alone, and she was playing with some toys. I realized that I hadn't eaten my own breakfast yet, so I sat down to eat a bowl of granola at the kitchen table. I had just picked up my spoon when the phone rang, so I got up and answered, talking only briefly because I don't like to eat soggy cereal.

I went back and sat down and was surprised to find there was no cereal in my bowl, however there was a drippy trail of milk leading from the bowl through the kitchen and into her room. It led to her dresser. I wasn't sure where she was, but I opened the top drawer to find my wet granola in a pile on top of her pink pajamas.

We had learned in fostering classes about kids who hoarded food because they hadn't always had a regular source of food. Tears sprang to my eyes as I lifted the wet pajamas out of the drawer to clean up. I figured she might be hiding because she was afraid, and went ahead and wiped up the milk trail and decided to start over with my breakfast.

When I was almost done, Lilly appeared near the table and looked at me.

Even though she'd had her breakfast, I asked, "Would you like some granola to eat?"

She put her thumb in her mouth and shook her head no, and I didn't mention the discovery because I was pretty sure she already knew.

Later on while she was occupied playing, I called Doris. She said that Lilly had been found scavenging for food in garbage cans at about age two. Doris also said she was sending a social worker by that day with bags of clothes, shoes, and toys that had been at the last foster home.

When the worker got there, Lilly was thrilled to see her things and began digging through the three large black garbage bags looking for favorite toys. She asked about a few items she wanted but weren't in the bags, and I knew nothing about. I told her I would ask Doris.

The story we got and later found to be true was that Lilly often destroyed items, and they would have to be discarded, and that had been the fate of some of the missing things. We were getting her history in just bits and pieces with some coming from Doris and part from Kathi Beadle. It seemed that nobody knew the whole story because she was too young to tell it when she was taken from neglectful and abusive teen-age parents.

Lilly's mother was seventeen when she was born and at least a third generation foster child herself. The father was eighteen. She had been exposed to many different people coming into and leaving her basement "home" at odd hours. As an infant she had been left alone in her crib for up to three days at a time with nobody home, and there were marks on her consistent with cigarette burns.

No wonder she had Reactive Attachment Disorder. How could she have attached to someone who neglected even her basic needs and caused her physical injury on top of that? I couldn't dwell on that without coming to tears. The abuse was somehow reported to authorities, and the initial police and Children's Services intervention took place. Eighteen months later she was found alone in the street in February.

About that time I found out she had a sister, Tina, who was fourteen months younger and they shared the same parents. I am not sure exactly what Tina's circumstances were but they must have been similar in some respects. The girls went into permanent foster care after Lilly was found in the street. She was two at the time, and Tina was ten months old.

Doris had also told us that she had learned from the county that Lilly had had a habit of banging her head on the floor between the ages of two and three. She would bash her head with the intention of hurting herself. To protect her, previous foster parents had been instructed to put a special helmet on her until she stopped. Only a history of unbearable pain and misery could have prompted a toddler to do that.

When she was five a family in a nearby town, Anne and Marty Wells, had tried to adopt the girls. They kept Tina, but were unable to keep Lilly for reasons yet unknown to me. We would be meeting them because she was to begin visits with her sister in the not-too-distant future.

CHAPTER FIVE

The next noteworthy thing that happened soon after Lilly arrived followed closely on the heels of the cereal heist. She switched videos on me, and put in one that I had told her she wasn't allowed to watch. When I discovered the switch, I turned off the TV and took out the video right in front of her.

She defiantly yelled, "Yes I CAN, you stupid bitch!"

So much for the six-year-old angel.

I waited outside until she decided to come out, and then stood and blocked her path and firmly said, "You are not leaving your room."

She went back in and proceeded to rip all the linens off the bed and throw them along with other things all over the room.

When she finished, I said, "If you want out of this room, then you have to clean up. Start with the toys, and when you get to the sheets I'll help you." I knew that Lilly would never be able to get the sheets back on the mattress by herself.

Breaking down crying, she began to pick everything up and put it where it belonged. Once the toys were back in their wicker box, I went in and helped her put the sheets on the bed like I had promised.

When everything was back in its place, she said, "I'm sorry."

Lilly was a very active little girl. Later on the same day, she found a dry-erase board and markers in a closet. It puzzled me as to why she was in the closet, because I knew where she was and what she was doing every minute, or so I thought. (She was quiet as well as elusive and it was hard to relax.) She asked if she could draw on the board with the markers.

When I hesitated, she promised to "write only on the boyd."

I loved the way she spoke, and when she said that she would make a picture and to, "Close your eyes because it a surprise," I gave in. Stupid me.

Soon I heard her say, "Okay!"

Opening my eyes, I saw that she had made a simple rainbow on the board as well as colored all over her face, eyelids, arms, and hands.

I calmly put the board and markers away without any reaction at all.

Stomping to her room, she said, "I'm angry!"

Boy, did she look silly with marker scribbling all over her face.

The day wouldn't have been complete without a third and last bit of excitement. Torie needed to be picked up from school, and I would have to take the little troublemaker with me.

We were warned that she had a long history of getting loose in the car, and that the CHC workers had refused to transport her alone. Bruce had rigged up what he called a Houdini-proof booster seat. I put my marker-scribbled "kid of many colors" in it, and off we went.

Fifteen minutes later we picked up Torie, and on the drive back she got a smack in the back of the head from the stuffed Polly the parrot.

Looking back at Lilly, I told her that if she hit Torie again, I would take Polly away from her.

She did.

I reached back, snatched Polly, and tossed her onto the seat next to Torie.

To get even, Lilly unbuckled her seat belt, but was surprised to find herself with the booster seat still stuck around her backside. Infuriated, she started kicking the back of Torie's seat as hard as she could.

I reached my right arm back while driving and grabbed at her little feet to stop the kicking. Teeth bit down on my forearm more than once, but thankfully we were only about a minute from home.

Torie helped me get her into the house, and as we went into the kitchen, I locked the deadbolt.

Strangely enough, a bug saved the day.

Lilly spotted a black beetle on the kitchen floor and forgot instantly that she had been trying to get away from us. All of her attention zeroed in on that little black beetle. She said, "I want to let him go outside."

Because she had calmed down, I said okay.

While she was letting the bug loose just outside the kitchen door, Torie's hazel eyes looked and at me and narrowed as she crossed her arms over her chest.

"Did that really just happen? I got beat in the head with a STUFFED PARROT and the back of my seat kicked, while you drove with one hand on the wheel and the other hand trying to grab that kid's feet? What was that about? Is she *nuts?*"

Before I could respond, Lilly came in the back door with her thumb in her mouth and her eyes carefully checking out the kitchen floor for the possibility of another amazing beetle sighting.

"Torie," she said as she looked up at her, "if you find any more bugs, tell me." With that, she walked through the kitchen and turned right to go into her bedroom as if the car fiasco had never happened.

My gaze followed her and then I looked at Torie. Her mouth hung open and her eyebrows were up. She ALWAYS had something to say, but at that moment she was speechless.

I was left wondering what would have happened if Lilly hadn't had that big bad booster seat still strapped to her butt after she unbuckled her seat belt.

Later that night as we all sat down for dinner, I asked Lilly if she wanted to say a grace.

Without any hesitation, she said "Yes," and then folded her little hands and closed her eyes and said, "Dear Father, thank you for letting me be here. Amen."

Where did she learn that? After that wacko day, I thought our new little angel was a perfect little heathen.

Later on down the road, I would learn that there had been loving and caring foster families who had worked hard to help her. Some good had been sown into her life, but not enough to make up for the horrendous neglect and abuse of those first years.

In our classes Tana had tried to help us understand with a very helpful illustration. She asked everyone in the room to close their eyes and picture an empty swimming pool.

I obeyed.

She said, "Now, take a bucket of dirt and dump it on the dry bottom of the pool. That dirt is "the bad" in a neglected or abused child's life. Next, add buckets of water over and over. With each addition of good (or water), the bad (dirt) is diluted. Your job as foster parents is to dilute the dirt with so much love and caring, that the children can eventually begin to live empowered lives with self-worth and healing. Yes, the dirt has still happened, but let the healing water help it not to matter so much."

I would think about that example many times over the years. There would be days I felt as if I myself had added to the dirt in Lilly's life, because of my own impatience and anger at times with her behavior. But most days we were able to add at least a cupful of wonderful diluting water, and those have been some of the most meaningful days of my life.

CHAPTER SIX

When we decided to be foster parents we hadn't considered that along with your foster child comes parental or sibling visitations. In Lilly's case she came to us with Tina, Tina's adoptive parents (Ann and Marty Wells), her therapist (Kathi Beadle), a therapeutic play therapist we hadn't met, a psychiatrist who prescribed her medications, a registered nurse who monitored those medications, a county worker whom we hadn't met, a CHC worker who helped Doris by visiting our home regularly, and a court-appointed guardian ad litem that would be coming to check on her. Whew!

After she had been with us about four days I called Ann Wells to set up a time for Lilly to see her sister. I was curious to know more about their lives.

Answering the phone, Ann seemed very glad to hear from me. She was friendly and open, saying that she and Marty hadn't been able to have children and someone had told them that there were two little sisters in foster care who could be adopted. They went through fostering classes with the county and were assigned to Tim, who was the sisters' social worker.

Right before the sisters were placed with them, Ann discovered that she was pregnant, but they decided to go ahead and foster-to-adopt the girls. The first two months went reasonably well, but then Lilly's behavior became frighteningly violent and angry. She attempted to kick their dog and cat, urinated and defecated on carpets, and threw shoes and other items at them when angry. She also stole jewelry, household cleaners, makeup, checkbooks, and anything else not locked up. Then there was the night-wandering looking for the cat, and threatening to kill Ann and the baby when it was born.

All this at five years old.

Ann said that caseworker Tim wouldn't take them seriously because he felt that the Wells were doing something wrong. After all, they had never been parents before.

Lilly's actions escalated to the point that she actually *bashed in* the Wells' sliding glass doors going out to their sunroom.

Ann said that she and Marty were desperate, so they pleaded with Lilly's pre-school principal and therapist Kathi Beadle to write letters on their behalf about things they themselves had seen with her behavior. They agreed, and the two letters went off to Roberta Smith, Tim's supervisor.

Marty tried to record on video a long episode of violence to help get the county to believe them.

Ann went on to tell me that the straw that broke the camel's back was when Lilly kicked her in the abdomen. She was already a high-risk pregnancy, and the kick started vaginal bleeding. A call to the county that Ann was en route to the hospital finally resulted in Lilly being picked up and placed back in the foster home where she had lived before the Wells' house.

Their unborn child survived, and approximately six weeks after this incident Ann gave birth to her daughter, Sarah.

"The Visit" was set up for April 7th at CHC. The sisters would get to see each other for the first time in six weeks, and I would get more information from Ann. I had an intense desire to find out everything I could about Lilly.

In the meantime we needed to figure out a way to get through her violent outbursts without her getting hurt, injuring either of us, or destroying our home. From what Ann had told me, we had only seen the tip of the iceberg and more would certainly come.

CHAPTER SEVEN

In class we had learned approved restraining techniques for children who posed a risk to themselves or others. One such restraint was called a basket-hold. The problem with the maneuver was that the person you were "basket-holding" was able to kick backwards to strike you in the shins, or slam their heads backwards into your face or chest, and Lilly did both.

A basket-hold sounds kind of cozy, but the name was most incongruous with the reality of having her in one. (Just try to keep a fighting wildcat in a "basket.") We talked with different people about the restraining problem and cautiously I came up with the idea to use a small velour blanket to wrap around her when she was way out of control.

We planned to roll her middle up tightly in the soft blanket with shoulders and head free at one end, and shins and feet free at the other end. The "blanket-wrap" as we came to call it, would immobilize her arms against her torso and keep her safe. (We are not recommending this to any readers, as it can be deadly if implemented improperly.)

I purchased a twin-size, navy blue velour blanket and cut it in half to downsize it. We put it on her bed and explained that she'd be wrapped up like a tortilla if she became dangerous and unwrapped as soon as she settled down.

Lilly was totally fascinated with the idea and wanted to try it on for size. We demonstrated with a willing participant and felt it really would be helpful. She seemed fine with the idea, but I knew that the little wheels in her head were turning.

Now, when I look back on those blanket-wrap days as a whole, I remember them as some of our most difficult, because those were the days that she was off-the-charts to begin with and the wrap was not easy, but it seemed to be our only option.

Nobody knew what to do with Lilly. She told us that the hospital would give her a shot when she was "bad" and "put me to sleep."

What? That shocked me. I could hardly believe stuff like that really happened. What option did a family have? That was why a child as violent and destructive as Lilly would be passed from home to home. If we hadn't had the blanket-wrap, I don't know how long she would have lasted at our house. We'll never know.

We have since heard about an incident out West where a child was suffocated by being inside a blanket-wrap gone awry. We were careful to NEVER allow it near her face, and her safety was ever-present in our minds. I don't think any other CHC or county parents were permitted to use a blanket-wrap, or even knew that we did. Then again, nobody else had a kid like Lilly.

By that time, we'd been spit on, kicked, and bitten. Oh, and I was repeatedly notified while being cussed out that I didn't care about her; I was not her real mother but fake, and she hated me.

Well, this fake mother got her all fixed up for a portrait session at Sears. She seemed pleased and allowed me to fix her hair in an up-do and dress her in a red print dress. She is beautiful when she's all cleaned up and loves dresses and skirts to this day. Getting her to wear the dress was easy, and I added a plastic flower necklace. She looked like a princess.

Soon I was alone in public with what looked like a four-year-old, who except for the blue eyes, was a near duplicate little image of me. I was very aware of the fact that if there was an incident of some sort, people would naturally assume that I was her birth mother, not a fake mother. I wished then that we did not resemble each other. We sat in the photo area waiting room with other people and I sweated bullets, praying nothing embarrassing would happen while we were there.

I needn't have worried because it went off without a hitch. Lilly hammed it up for the girl taking pictures, and afterwards I quickly herded her out of Sears and into the car, hoping that the spell would not be broken until we got to our scheduled therapy appointment with Kathi Beadle.

She behaved well in the car on the way there, and it was as if she knew she was too beautiful to misbehave. She seemed to be happy to see Kathi and looked forward to the one-on-one play therapy during sessions.

Kathi picked up two little stuffed cats and Lilly chose a plastic tiger from the small stash of toys in the office.

I sat and watched as Kathi had one cat be the mother to the other cat. She'd hold them and talk while the mother cat "licked and protected" the baby cat.

Meanwhile, the tiger in Lilly's hand would stalk them and pace around them and roar at the little stuffed cats.

Kathi always protected them from the mean tiger that wanted to cause harm. She especially had the mother cat on guard, watching out for her kitten. The therapist surrounded the little cats with pillows to protect them from the angry tiger. She was trying to demonstrate what a mother is *supposed* to do, because Lilly's mother was anything but protective of her.

It was exhausting trying to act interested as I continued watching the play that never changed much. But I understood the necessity for the play activity, and the bond of trust that Kathi was working to form in their relationship, as well as between the toy characters.

After many of those sessions, I'd find myself fighting to stay awake. This fake mother had seen enough aggression at home, and the cat play-therapy would weary me.

Kathi had wonderful skill and endless patience as she worked with Lilly, and she continued to be her therapist for about three years.

That particular day she said she had never seen the little girl so relaxed and content, which gave me a smile of motherly pride –fake mother, though, I reminded myself with a grin.

CHAPTER EIGHT

The arrival of nice spring weather always brought children to a nearby park. That particular spring was different for us though, because we had a little girl who would stand in our breezeway-porch and call out to any kids walking by.

Lilly would shout, "I like your bike! I like your hair! I like your dog! Can you play with me?"

She had some success from time to time, because I'd be cooking or cleaning in the kitchen and would see a youngster mosey up to our porch to talk to her. We had a few neighborhood children who were also lured to the porch.

It didn't take any of them long to realize that she was not your average six-year-old. She would usually start playing "cats" by growling deeply and pretend to lick her paws. If the new playmates wouldn't stay and play that with her, she would yell after them as they escaped, "Get off our property!" or "Get out of here, you M-F-er!"

That was not exactly the way most little girls burned their bridges. The first time it happened, it really rattled me, and I immediately whisked her indoors. I couldn't believe it. *What would the neighbors think?*

Sometimes she would be successful in her playing, as the day I looked out and saw her on our porch with a boy about seven, and a girl a bit older. I recognized them as kids I'd seen in the neighborhood but did not know their names. The three of them were huddled together on their knees in a circle talking quietly and looking at something in their midst.

I went out to investigate and discovered that the girl had found a dying bird and named it "Karina."

The three children watched as Karina breathed her last. Then they decided to dig a hole behind the garage and bury her.

I watched from the door as the kids dug with sticks before placing the bird gently in the hole. They covered it up with dirt, and the girl pierced a ragged little slip of paper with a twig and asked me for a pencil. She wrote the bird's name and the date on it. They were so solemn and reverent, and I was very pleased that Lilly had been part of a group activity even if it had been a funeral.

I thought that the threesome had disbanded afterwards because I saw the boy leave.

Ten minutes later I heard the girl scream.

I ran out the back door and there she was, standing open-mouthed with her hand on her chest and her eyes popping out of her head. I quickly looked in the direction of her gaze, and there on the porch was Karina the dead bird, all propped up like she was taking a nap.

Standing off to the side, Lilly was intently admiring her creature-resurrection.

I started to laugh and couldn't stop to save my soul.

The girl looked at me, then at the bird, then back at me and started laughing, too.

Lilly began to chuckle deeply, and soon the three of us were doubled over holding our sides.

After so much stress the previous two weeks, the laughter was like a refreshing rain falling over me, and I was so thankful for it.

CHAPTER NINE

When we arrived the next day at the CHC building to meet the Wells family, Kathi told me she would also be there to monitor the girls, and it made me feel we weren't in this alone.

I had only told Lilly that morning about the upcoming visit and she was overjoyed to learn that she would soon see five-year-old Tina. They hadn't seen each other for "way-too-long" in her opinion!

When we got there, Kathi met us in the small entry and took us back to the same large room where our fostering classes had been held. We walked in to see the Wells family was already there and waiting, and the pretty girl who we knew must be Tina had reddish hair and brown eyes.

As soon as their eyes met, they flew into each other's embrace.

We had been told that the girls shared the same parents and had assumed that there would be some resemblance, but we couldn't have been more wrong.

Lilly squealed as she hugged Tina then abruptly ran over to Ann and Marty. She shouted, "Mommy! Daddy!" and as they bent down and hugged her, I noticed a baby carrier on the tabletop beside them.

Lilly saw it too and went over to it and said, "Oh, Sarah!" She evidently knew the baby. Her attention went right back to Tina and the snacks that Ann had brought for the sisters to share.

At that point we were able to say hi to Ann and Marty and shook hands with the attractive couple in their early thirties. The four of us sat down on some metal folding chairs off to the side in the big room, while Kathi was clear across the room sitting near the girls while they ate their snack.

The Wells seemed to be so very pleased to meet us, and we spoke in hushed tones about how things were going for each of our families. We didn't take much time for pleasantries because it wasn't about us, it was about the girls.

Ann handed me three letters that she said documented Lilly's behavior while with them. She said that if we read them, some of the questions we had would be answered, and we would better understand their journey with Lilly.

I tucked them into my purse to read later. We could have spent hours with them because they were so likeable and pleasant. Ann was a part-time accountant and Marty was the vice president of a local company. They exuded sadness and seemed to feel guilty that they had to send Lilly away from their family, separating the sisters.

We certainly didn't see that they had a choice in the matter, given the attack on Ann that had threatened to end Sarah's life. I wondered how they lasted the three or four months that they had, trying to make things work. Most people wouldn't have continued once their carpet was soiled or their checkbook taken.

Kathi had told us ahead of time to keep the visit to forty-five minutes, so the time went by pretty quickly. As it was winding down, I noticed that Lilly appeared to have lost all interest in her sister and had started to roam the room looking for something, but I didn't know what. I would learn that was just something she did everywhere we went.

When it was time to go she became agitated, and went to Tina and grabbed her in a fierce hug. Then when she looked at Ann and Marty she began whimpering and crying, "Mommy, Daddy."

I had heard Lilly call them Mommy and Daddy twice in a short period of time and it was a bit disconcerting, because I had started to feel that I was Mommy. I wondered how many others had also tried to fill those extraordinarily battered mommy-shoes.

She was quiet on the ride home, and I didn't break into her thoughts because I was struggling with my own. I had gone from feeling as if I were an important part of Lilly's picture to feeling like just a blip on the screen of her life. I needed to get a grasp on things because blip or not, I had a job to do in somehow helping her.

The following afternoon she kept asking to talk to Tina on the phone. I decided to call Ann to see if they could talk for a minute or two. After a short phone call with very little dialogue, Lilly said goodbye.

It was only minutes before she erupted into an extremely foul mood and started screaming, "I hate you! I hate Tina! I hate Ann and Marty! I hate the stupid baby! I am going to kill myself!"

She grabbed and threw each one of her shoes and books across the room, and then she went to the wicker toy box and threw the Etch-a-Sketch at the wall. It hit with a loud crash, and that did it for us, because we thought her window might be next.

Bruce and I struggled to get her into the blanket-wrap with him near her shoulders and me at her knees. She was so strong that we could barely hang on as she screamed and fought.

I was certain that she was grieving.

After a while she began to sob, crying puddles of tears as the fighting slowly subsided. We waited until she was done with the anger before unwrapping her. Lilly let us hug her momentarily, then closed her eyes and rolled away from us onto her side with her thumb in her mouth.

Bruce left the room and I tearfully rubbed her back until she fell asleep.

While she had been crying, my heart had just about broken in half for her. To be so young, and to have experienced such loss, hurt, and grief was incomprehensible.

While she napped I filled out an incident report. We took them very seriously and it would be turned in to CHC for review before they faxed it to social workers Tim and Kathi. Everyone on Lilly's team would always know what was going on with her.

Then I sat down to read the letters that Ann had given to me. The first one was from the preschool principal:

Nealie Rose

To Mrs. Roberta Smith (Tim's supervisor)
From Peter Starey, MS School Psychology
re: Lilly Angel

I have known Lilly for three years. She was a preschooler at Havila Primary where I was the building principal. My concern is not just for Lilly, but also for her sister, Tina. Lilly has exhibited the following behaviors:

• Refusal behaviors (acts as though she doesn't hear) when simple requests are made of her, such as 'put on your shoes, sit down, put on your seatbelt, etc.' Screaming, kicking, hitting when made to comply with these requests.

• Pretending that her finger is a gun and shooting another child in the head (between his eyes no less), without any obvious provocation.

• Will walk around very quietly until she finds lotion, nail polish, or a spray bottle and proceed to empty it and smear it on everything in sight.

• Does not initiate play with her sister, or if Tina begins to play, Lilly will intervene until Tina walks away. Her play generally involves some kind of destruction such as hitting the dolls or throwing them, breaking anything that Tina has made, turning herself in circles while screaming, or taking the object being played with. On outings Lilly would wander off by herself and show little interest in her surroundings. Animals are the one exception. She shows little caution around them and will want to poke their eyes or examine their ears.

• When on the playground, Tina will invite Lilly to join her on a piece of equipment. Lilly will go off by herself, and if there are any other children on something she will avoid that equipment until they leave.

• Lilly is very interested in anything with which she can associate death. On one occasion men were working on water lines in the street and Lilly stated it was because 'it could kill you.' Another time we had to slow down in the car because lines were being painted and Lilly spoke up that 'someone had crashed and died.'

• Of particular concern to me is Tina's response to Lilly's behavior. Typically she will relinquish anything to Lilly rather than stand up to her. When Lilly is out of control, Tina will seek a lap to sit in or crawl up on a chair. Often she will cry silently.

Based upon reports from Lilly's preschool teacher for the school year, and my own observations, it is very apparent that Lilly is in need of intense, long-term therapeutic intervention. Lilly needs help now!

The letter was very sobering, and I went on to read the letters written by Ann and Kathi. They mirrored the first letter almost exactly, and I was three times reminded of the seriousness of Lilly's problems.

CHAPTER TEN

I began reading more about Lilly's main diagnosis of Reactive Attachment Disorder so that I would be able to understand better what was going on with her.

By working with a number of professionals and reading educating materials, I have learned some basic information about the disorder. My understanding is that RAD is a rare but extreme condition that happens when a child's bond with the main caretaker in his life fails to develop properly and is severely damaged. The damage is done during the first three years of life and can occur from neglect, abuse, or from being separated from their main caretaker, either emotionally or physically. A trust issue results and these children do not trust anyone, and they feel as if they have to be in control of everything.

I also learned that there is a deep-seated rage inside these children due to unfulfilled needs at a very young age. Experiences affect brain development and serious problems arise when a young child does not receive proper care and stimulation.

Lilly's situation fit that description to a heart-rending "T." Most of the other children in foster care had more than their share of heartache, but they did not have RAD. So, if you're a foster parent or thinking about becoming one, keep that in mind when you read this book, because the vast majority of children in foster care are kids who just need someone to be there for them with a home, hugs, and support.

Lilly's diagnosis or condition prevented her from accepting those hugs, that support, and a home. She trusted nobody near her, but she would be overly friendly to total strangers because they posed no bonding risks to her. That was also typical of the condition.

When I learned these things, I was really discouraged until I read that Helen Keller also had attachment disorder. Helen Keller overcame because she had someone who went the distance for her, and I wanted to go the distance for Lilly.

Before we knew it, the deadline had passed and we hadn't heard anything from CHC about the residential placement possibility. I thought it would be sad to see her go. Having Lilly with us had certainly flip-flopped our entire world as we knew it, but we felt as if we were making a difference and that made it worth it.

There were so many circumstances that would arise because she had come to live with us. Sometimes they would creep up on us, and other times they would hit us at one hundred miles an hour. We were constantly planning strategies, sometimes hourly, alternating between defensive and offensive tactics. Being one step ahead of her was difficult because she was sneaky and always up to something.

If she needed to be disciplined for something that she did such as writing on the walls with crayon, we'd try a timeout first -either in a chair or in her room. We also tried to have her take some responsibility for anything she destroyed or messed up.

The blanket-wrap was to be used only when she was a danger to herself or others. It was no fun using it anyway because it was so much work getting her "tortilla'd" (as we'd come to call it).

It didn't take long for Lilly to begin urinating when she was mad at us. That would usually follow a timeout that she refused to take. We would send her to her room, but while in there she would pee on her area rug to get even.

We decided to wise-up and have all in-room timeouts with an open-door policy, meaning the baby gate would be up in her doorway. She could have easily jumped over it, but it was a reminder to stay put in her room for the duration of the timeout.

Before we started using the baby gate in her doorway, she had pulled the fiberfill out of her bedspread, bent the bed frame (yes, the frame), and destroyed toys. When the gate was in her doorway she couldn't close her door, and we would have continual visual surveillance because her room was situated near the center of our main floor.

Once we were expecting dinner guests who were people we'd recently just met. Lilly did everything she could to keep our home in turmoil that day. I had made an apple pie for desert and had it cooling on the counter. At some point in my preparations, I walked by the pie and noticed that the entire top crust was missing. She had taken a large coffee cup and skimmed the crust off into the cup and ran to hide and eat it.

When discovered under her bed with the piecrust, she erupted with profanity.

Shortly thereafter, she wrote on some wicker furniture with crayons.

We made the decision that Lilly would not eat with us that evening. She would be fed her dinner first before company came and then spend the time during their visit behind the gate in her room.

When she found out what her consequence was going to be for the terrible behavior that afternoon, she began spitting on everything in her room and then leaned over the gate and spit on the floor in the hallway. (Sometimes it was hard for me not to see Lilly as one big germ.)

Our guests, Mr. and Mrs. Garth, sat down at the table in the kitchen after greetings which included introducing them to the little girl in her room behind the baby gate.

Lilly smiled happily and waved, and then she sweetly asked, "Are you all going to eat now, Mommy?"

I answered yes and smiled as I got the guests settled around the table.

Mr. Garth looked at Bruce and me and asked, "Isn't she going to join us? If she's not eating, then I don't want to eat."

He looked over at Lilly again and she tipped her head to one side and looked sadly at the four of us seated at our table. She was acting perfectly the part of a rejected puppy!

I was shocked that Mr. Garth, a new guest in our home, would start the evening with an ultimatum like that.

Bruce set his jaw and answered, "Lilly will not be joining us at this meal."

I gritted my teeth and began dishing out food as though it were the most enjoyable of evenings. Inside I was ticked off at Mr. Garth, Lilly, and myself for being in the unbelievably ridiculous situation to begin with.

There were many, many days with Lilly that no amount of income from fostering would be payment enough. Yes, money from being Lilly's foster mother enabled me to be able to stay home with her, because I could never have had her in my home and held down another job. But it went beyond, far beyond the money issue.

We stuck with her because we felt we should, although at times it was trying, unpleasant, and socially lonely. We continued because it was the right thing to do. We instinctively knew that we were Lilly's last chance to have a family, and to experience healing and love.

Bruce and I normally had frequent dinner guests and often went to our many friends' houses in return. All that screeched to a halt when Lilly came, because every friend we had owned pets, and we couldn't relax for thirty seconds if we took her to someone's home. I must also add that the invitations became few and far between.

Speaking of pets, Doris Champion had given us some incident reports from Lilly's last foster home. One dated just six weeks earlier said, "Lilly tried to choke one of the three small dogs in the house. She said she wants to kill them. She tied the little dog to her bed with her jump rope trying to choke her. She put another dog in a dresser drawer and wouldn't let her out. She spinched and hit the dogs. She pulled the bird's tail and threw objects at it."

What was up with so much access to animals?

German theologian and philosopher Dr. Albert Schweitzer said, "Anyone who has accustomed himself to regard the life of any living creature as worthless is in danger of arriving also at the idea of worthless human lives."

That made me wonder who else out there did terrible things because of Reactive Attachment Disorder?

We hoped and prayed that we could work with Lilly to foster respect and caring for animals and not harm them.

One day, we felt it might be safe to visit some relatives who didn't have any critters. Lilly used their bathroom and came out with red lipstick wildly scrawled over her lips. Upon further investigation in their bathroom, all lipsticks had been turned up into their lids effectively ruining them. It was just easier to stay home most of the time.

CHC knew that we had to have some downtime, so they started looking for a foster family suitable to do two day-respites each week for us.

The dictionary says a respite is temporary relief. That's what we needed after only two weeks with her, and we looked forward to that first day-respite as if it were a two week Caribbean cruise rather than just four measly hours of childcare.

CHC asked the older couple from our training classes, Roger and Mary Stevens if they would do it for us. They agreed to until school started, assuming things went okay with Lilly, the two foster boys they had living with them, and their two small dogs. Mary said she'd never leave her alone with the boys or the dogs, and I believed her.

They were such nice people and seemed to be more like grandparents. Lilly warmed up to them and enjoyed going to their home. During those respites I kicked up my heels and went grocery shopping or lunched with a friend. If Bruce was not working we shopped together and ate out. Oh, how we looked forward to those breaks. CHC paid the "babysitters" for which we were grateful.

Those respites kept us going that crazy, exhausting first summer.

CHAPTER ELEVEN

I have a niece who is a year older than Lilly, and Cookie came to play one day early in the summer. She brought a new model horse along to show it to me.

The girls played well enough, because Cookie didn't mind the "cat play," and expanded on it (to Lilly's tremendous delight) by making a veterinary clinic of the yellow bedroom and allowed *her* to be one of the cats in the clinic. That really made Lilly's day! Dr. Cookie wore a stethoscope and patiently tended to the menagerie of stuffed animals and the very large yowling "cat." Ace bandages were in high demand for wounded paws, and they played for a long time.

When it came time for lunch Lilly became overly silly and began saying repeatedly, "Kiss my butt!"

At first Cookie's eyes widened, and she pursed her lips and stifled a giggle, but she understood that it was inappropriate.

We tried changing the conversation and ignoring it, as well as giving warnings, but she just wouldn't quit! After the second warning and the tenth, "Kiss my butt!" I lifted her out of her seat and explained that she was done being at the table with us.

Cookie finished up quickly and asked to go out to play. Lilly asked to go out with her but I said no because she definitely had some table-sass left.

She appeared very disappointed and asked Cookie nicely, "Can I play with your horse when you're outside?"

Cookie hesitated a moment before agreeing, then handed over the horse and headed outside.

I checked on Lilly in her room just a few minutes later, and she had pulled the horse's mane loose, removed the brown beaded eyes, and torn up the soft plastic saddle and bridle. I was stunned! She had been so quick and secretive about it.

When Cookie came in and saw the demolished horse, I regretted not seeing it coming. Cookie burst into tears, and Lilly didn't show one ounce of remorse and seemed totally unmoved by Cookie's heartbreak.

I waited about a minute to see if she would apologize or change her nonchalance. When it didn't happen, I said, "Cookie, Lilly destroyed your horse and as a consequence I am going to send her favorite toy home with you."

I immediately went looking for Polly the parrot but couldn't find it. Knowing things needed to be over quickly, I picked up Lilly's new Cabbage Patch doll and handed it to my niece and said, "You must take her home with you to replace your horse. The ruined horse is hers now, and you'll have a new horse as soon as possible."

Cookie and I had been standing outside Lilly's doorway, and she slammed the door in our faces. We went to the kitchen table, and I reassured her that the horse would be replaced and that the doll had to go home with her to teach Lilly a lesson.

A few minutes later a changed girl came slowly out of her room. She was carrying the doll's bottle and the box it had come in. She handed them to Cookie. "Here, you will need to have her bed and brush. Take care of her and bring her back, okay?" She accepted the situation with solemn blue eyes, and I was jubilant inside because I felt she was making progress.

The very next day Lilly took an entire bag of chocolate cookies and ate them under her bed. The evidence was all over her mouth. How she got them I'm not sure, because I had learned to keep sweets well-hidden.

When I told her to go sit in the timeout chair she yelled, "No!" and tried to bite my arm and then took off running. I caught her and did a basket-hold sitting down because the standing ones usually ended with me getting head-butted and kicked in the shins. I had lots of bruises to testify to that.

Lilly in any basket-hold or restraint wasn't much fun. She began spitting on my pants and arms as I sat Indian-style wrapped around her (pretending to be a nice and cozy basket). After a while she agreed to the timeout chair and I was so relieved.

Once in the chair though, she began making faces at me and yelled, "I hate you! I'm going to kill myself!" She kicked at anything within reach of the chair and soon gave that up and took off, which meant I had to capture and restrain her again until she settled down.

Back in the chair, because she finally agreed to take the time out, Lilly put her fingers down her throat and vomited all over her clothes in an apparent attempt to "show me." Those lovely blue eyes were smoldering with defiance.

I stayed calm and told her, "It's sad that you're gonna have to sit there like that until your timeout is finished."

She didn't believe me because her next announcement was, "There, I peed!"

When she saw that I didn't seem to care that she was sitting in urine and vomit, she became enraged and stripped naked and threw her clothes on the floor, but remained in her timeout chair. Thankfully nobody else was home or it would have been a circus!

I calmly told her, "I have to do the dishes now, but I sure hope Daddy or any company doesn't come in because you'll be very embarrassed if they do, being naked, you know."

She silently put her soiled clothes back on while I had my back to her, doing dishes. After sitting quietly in the chair for the allotted five minutes, the timer went off, and I dried my hands and gave her some wet paper towels to wipe the vomit off the chair, then I put her in the tub and bathed her. She was very subdued during the bath and didn't say much or play. Afterward we rocked in the living room rocking chair, and I hugged on her. That would become a routine after incidents were resolved, whenever Lilly would allow me to. There were times when she wouldn't allow such bonding time in the rocker, and she chose to stay moody and angry.

On days like that I was always thankful for her evening medications because they usually helped her relax and get sleepy. Then I'd be able to approach her with a good-night backrub and some loving words.

Once I had her evening pills in one hand and my vitamins in my other hand as I prepared to give her the bedtime meds. I inadvertently swallowed hers instead of mine, and realized my mistake immediately. I wished then that I knew how to make myself vomit like she could.

I told Bruce what I had done, and he took over while I went into our room, crawled into bed, and waited to be knocked out. It didn't take long.

CHAPTER TWELVE

I talked to Ann Wells weekly on the phone, and we were becoming good friends. They continued to be involved with Lilly even after she was removed from their home. This included taking Lilly to therapy and doctor appointments to help out foster caretakers, which was an amazing commitment. Ann also told me that we were the third in a recent series of foster homes after Lilly had left their house.

She said the family who had Lilly before us had quite a time with her. The foster mother had called Ann crying and said Lilly had poured chocolate syrup all over the inside of their baby grand piano, then went on to say that she now was on nerve pills because of all that had happened while Lilly was there.

As terrible as some of these stories were, I found them funny sometimes. That must have been because they hadn't happened to me.

The second visit with her sister was at our house and went well, so it started a pattern of visits there. Occasionally if I was feeling brave, and Lilly was behaving, we'd meet at McDonald's play-land for about an hour because that was about as long as she could successfully handle.

Lilly had talked to us about Ann's father, Grandpa Morey, with much affection. According to Lilly he was the person who loved her most and understood her.

Once while Ann and I were sitting at a play-land table, I asked her about her father. She spoke about him amid the cold French fries, drinking cups, and paper wrappers on the table while we watched the girls play. He did indeed sound very lovable, and I wondered what he'd done to win Lilly over. Unfortunately, Grandpa Morey went to Heaven not long after Lilly came to live with us, and I never learned his secret.

Lilly Angel had been with us about a month before Bruce and I took her to church. We talked about keeping her with us in the pew, as well as putting her in a classroom with other kids, and decided not to attempt a classroom setting at that time because it was a scary thought.

I dressed Lilly in a frilly light-yellow ruffled dress, yellow socks and white patent leather shoes. Her hair was pulled up into a pretty bun on top of her head, and she was all into getting ready because she was so excited about going to church and getting out of the house.

When we arrived, we took three seats but needn't have, because she spent the whole hour either in our laps, wrapped around our necks, or on the floor (my guess was looking for purses). She had loud hiccups, blew kisses, and waved to anyone watching her production.

That night as she closed her eyes for her bedtime prayer, she said, "Dear Father, thank you for Tina. Thank you for me. Be with Ann and Marty. I hate church."

Oh, that girl could make me smile. To this day she will always include, "thank you for me" in any prayers. That used to surprise me because she so often said that she wanted to die or that she hated herself. But that "thank you for me" always seemed to bring her full circle to the gift that she really was.

I couldn't help thinking about what Anne Frank had said, "I don't think of all the misery but the beauty that still remains."

There was something deep inside Lilly that knew she was worth loving.

ER THIRTEEN

ts up to Torie's room on the top floor, so Lilly
mini-trampoline.

During those times, Lilly was no different than any other six-year-old, but when she'd had enough or been told no to something, she would swear at me and say, "You hate me! You don't care about me!" Oftentimes she'd shove the Big Wheel across the basement or throw the toys, trying to smash and break them.

She was better -behaved with Bruce most of the time. My understanding is that children with RAD typically are unconsciously angry with the caregiver that did not protect or care properly for them, and that was usually a female. I represented that female so Bruce was preferred to me, but he was often at work fifty-plus hours a week.

Fifteen-year-old Torie was busy, too, but when available, she was a big help. Lilly admired the pretty Torie, and found out that at times she could be as tough as nails with her if needed. I was always thankful for her support and for not running out on me when I needed help. If I ask Torie now if she ever resented Lilly's presence, her answer is always the same. She says that given Lilly's back-story, she knew that Lilly needed us, and the attention demanded from us by the little housemate gave her more freedom as a teenager to do what she wanted.

Joy didn't seem to have an opinion either way, because she was living life as a free young- adult in an apartment with a friend. She was basically out of the picture, with other things to think about.

I kept a journal of some things that went on in our house, and many entries included events about the two of them. I came across a spot in my diary from that first year that read, "I get tired of dealing with Lilly, but it is very rewarding. It's a good thing, or I doubt I could keep up the pace. I keep on believing that we are training and helping her, and she'll be okay someday. But part of me is afraid it may all be in vain. I guess that's where faith and love come in."

By the start of that first summer, Lilly had been with us about six weeks. Cold weather and spring rains had kept most of the crazy incidents invisible to the neighborhood. I knew neighbors could see her when she was standing in the big picture window looking out, because they told me that she'd line up her small toys on the windowsill and frantically wave at every passing person who glanced her way. It was reported that she would give the middle finger to anyone going by who didn't smile back at her.

There was an older, three-story brick mansion that faced her bedroom window. It had been made into apartments, and our friends -the Smiths- had the large downstairs flat. They had two teens, a girl and a boy. The upstairs apartment belonged to Ingrid, who I only knew a little. She had a German accent that was pleasant to listen to, and she was a thirty-something single professional with no children.

Ingrid was quite intrigued by the little brown-haired girl who called out to her whenever she entered or left her apartment. The first time they actually met, I was gardening on a hill sloping down from my house and speaking with Ingrid, who was standing on the sidewalk below me.

Lilly spotted her and ran straight down the hill at her without slowing down and jumped into her arms. Ingrid was surprised and startled, but pleased. Just as quickly, Lilly wanted down.

That was the start of a long-term relationship between them. Lilly would use her to get pieces of "shockalot" (chocolate), as Ingrid would say with her accent.

One evening not long after, we gave Lilly a flashlight just as it became dark outside, so she could stand on the porch and shine it out into the darkness. Our daughters did that when they were younger, only I don't remember them ever standing out there barking like a dog for thirty minutes straight.

From across the street I could see Ingrid throw open her second-story window and lean out. The streetlights were on, and she looked down at the six-year-old on our porch. In her accented English she called out, "Lilly what are you DOING?"

Lilly stopped her barking and motioned with her flashlight. "I am talking to that dog over there."

Ingrid paused a few seconds before responding, "Oh, okay. I was just wondering when I heard all your barking."

The window closed, and the tireless "Woof! Woof! Woof!" continued into the darkness.

CHAPTER FOURTEEN

We've all seen T shirts for kids with funny sayings on them, like Trouble is My Middle Name and similar stuff, but Trouble seemed more like Lilly's first, middle, AND last name. If we were in tuned to her mood and attitude changes, trouble had a chance of being avoided. A slim chance, but we tried.

One day Lilly was on the porch and I looked out the kitchen door to check on her. She made a nasty face at me. *Ah, there's an attitude change.* Opening the door, I told her to come inside. Glaring, she turned and jumped off the porch and started running.

There were so many streets in our neighborhood, and I was afraid she'd run with abandon if I chased her, and possibly be hit by a car, so I went inside and watched from the window to see what she'd do. Peoria is flat, and I could see her as she went past houses.

She continued to wander farther and farther away, so I decided to go out and circle around the back of our property and try to intercept her in the area where she seemed to be headed.

There must've been eyes in the back of her head because she started running faster and flew across two streets without even a glance for cars.

Scared, I picked up speed and overtook her while running so fast I didn't think my legs would stop when I did. Scooping her up football-style under my right arm, I hung on for dear life, knowing people were watching as I carried my cussing, fighting football home.

As soon as I put her in her room, she peed on her area rug before I even had a chance to catch my breath. Bruce and I had just told her that she'd lose her carpet if there was any more peeing on it, so I went in and rolled up the rug and carried it out without saying a word.

Then I brought in the cleaning supplies and sat cross-legged on her floor while she scrubbed the soiled area, complaining at the same time, "I'm gonna find another family. I hate this place! I hate you! I want to die."

I told her, "Sorry, you're stuck with me."

It was interesting watching Lilly clean, because she did a very careful job cleaning up what she had just soiled. Didn't that tell me she really didn't like to be around urine? I was still a long way from understanding so many things.

The next day seemed to be going well, so I decided to take a risk and go to Kmart with her, without Bruce. While we were there, I had her sit in the front seat of the shopping cart because she was tiny enough to fit in it, and it would keep her out of trouble. Having that issue under control, I confidently went about my shopping and allowed her to pick out a large purple ball for herself.

Things went so well at the store that I felt it was safe for us to stop at a garage sale that we happened by on the way home. What could it hurt? She was on a good-behavior roll.

After parking in the driveway on our return home, I went around to unbuckle Lilly. I did a double-take when I saw sticky blue dribble all over her mouth and hands. She'd stolen candy at Kmart.

I was so ticked, and as I unbuckled her, I notified her that the purple ball was going back to the store because she took the candy. With that announcement came a chomp on my forearm and a brush of brown hair across my face as she leaped from the car and took off running down the center of the street.

Once again I kicked myself for telling Lilly a consequence while outside the containment of our house, and sprinted after my teeny look-alike.

I caught up with her about a minute later and grabbed the back of her red knit top to stop her. She hissed and spat on me while slapping wildly, but my adrenaline was flowing and Super Mom kicked in as I held on, not caring who was looking.

Just six or seven weeks before, I wouldn't have been caught dead wrestling with a little girl in public. But I was dragging one home as she loudly screamed, "You M-F-er! You bitch! Let me go! I hate you stupid bitch."

Bruce heard Lilly screaming before we got to the house, and he almost collided with us on his way out to help as she and I tumbled into the kitchen.

Lilly snatched a glass of water from the counter and threw it at Bruce. It hit him in the chest and neck. Dripping, he picked her up and put her in a kitchen chair for a timeout.

She screamed, "I will pee!"

"Fine, but you'll have to sit there until you settle down for the timeout," Bruce said.

Looking from him to me, she didn't say or do anything.

Was it over?

Then Bruce left me in charge of the timeout while he went to pick up Torie and her friends. Lucky guy.

As soon as he left, Lilly stood up in the chair, which was wet from urine, and stripped off all her clothes. She had a sticky blue face, the hair from her once-pretty ponytail stuck out all over her head, and she was totally nude.

I casually mentioned to her that Torie's group of friends would be there soon.

She didn't bat an eye at the thought of being caught naked and blue. Glaring at me, she squatted in the chair with her legs spread showing her genitals, just waiting for them to arrive.

Oh, great, just great. Panicky inside, I knew Torie would never forgive us if her friends walked in on THAT.

I've always been an "idea person," and one hit me at that moment. I picked up the chair with Lilly in it and awkwardly carried it out of the kitchen and down the hall to the bathroom. Through the doorway we went, and I set the chair down and closed the bathroom door.

But once in the bathroom, Lilly wouldn't stay in the chair for her time-out. She jumped off, grabbed the glasses from my face, and wildly threw them, and they clattered into the bathtub.

I planted her back on the seat of the chair. I wasn't about to attempt a basket-hold on a naked kid, so I improvised and did a basket-type hold from behind the chair with the back of the chair between us.

Finally she calmed down and agreed to put clothes on to finish what she needed to do: a lousy five minute quiet time-out. (Was that asking too much?)

I set the timer for five minutes as she sat there obediently. While it was ticking I drew bathwater for her, and she knew to get in the tub when the timer went off. After the battle-sweat was washed off, I helped her dress.

We rocked in my chair in the living room as she relaxed and cuddled in my arms.
After a few minutes she looked into my eyes and asked, "Am I stuck with you?"

I smiled a little bit wearily and replied, "You certainly are stuck with me."

Lilly smiled a crooked little smile, put her thumb in her mouth, and said, "Good.

After she was in bed for the night, I went downstairs to put her dirty clothes in the washer. As I did, something metal clanged into the empty washer drum. I frowned and reached my arm down to feel around the bottom for it. My fingers found a sparkly blue ring that had been on display at the garage sale.

CHAPTER FIFTEEN

Lilly's obsession with our cats never left during the time she was with us, although it did lessen to some degree over the years. We were always watchful, making sure that her interaction with them was short and would not be considered negative by her, Peek, or Baler.

The routine with the cats was always the same: they had free run of the house during the respites as well as during the day, after she was placed in kindergarten that first fall. All other times they were safely put away, and the cats seemed to totally "get it."

If Lilly would urinate when angry, she wouldn't see them that day or even the next day if she was in a "mood."

We were learning what signs to look for when trying to make a decision regarding the state of her psyche. Pacing, increased thumb-sucking, her head lowered toward her chest, and trying to control everything that happened were subtle signs that all was not well. And then there were the obvious signs such as hurling objects and bared teeth.

Sneakiness was Lilly's MO for getting control of things that she wasn't allowed to have. We had to lock up everything considered dangerous such as medicines and knives, as well as my cosmetics, purse, mouthwash, candy, cereal, peanut butter, cookies, and crackers. The list went on and on. We put a lock on the pantry door, but always had fresh fruit out for her if she was hungry between meals.

Back in the early days I had a problem with Lilly drinking from my glass of Coke whenever I'd leave the room. It took me a while to catch on but when I did, she was warned to leave my glass alone. That didn't work, so one day I figured out a way to teach her a lesson.

Pouring water and ice cubes into my glass, I added a large amount of soy sauce to it. It looked just like Coke and I was so excited I could hardly stand it. I placed the counterfeit Coke on the kitchen table, left the room, and stood just out of sight so I could listen.

It took about five minutes before I heard choking and coughing.

"Caught you!" I appeared laughing.

She was mad at first, but when she saw I couldn't stop laughing, she feigned great indignation and she said, "How dare you."

From the signature, crooked little smile I could tell that her respect for me had gone up a notch.

On the flip side, we had many days that were not so funny and wondered if we would ever make it through till evening was over. One I remember well was at the two-month mark with Lilly. She woke up that morning angry and in a dark mood. Knocking her chair over at breakfast, she said that she wasn't going to eat and could get her own food. She also refused to get dressed and screamed, "I hate you, you Wicked Step Mother! Damn you to hell!"

Damn me to hell? That's an interesting saying. I wonder where she heard it.

Then the screaming, door-slamming, and throwing things began.

I was glad to have Bruce around the early part of that day, because he helped me with a restraint and then later a blanket-wrap.

We called Kathi Beadle, and she came over to try to calm Lilly down with some play-therapy. It helped some, but after she left and Bruce had gone for the day, I was alone again.

Then the time came for me to pick up Torie and her friend Josh at a Dairy Queen. Lilly seemed glad to be going somewhere in the car, but I didn't feel so glad to be taking her. My finger had a bite mark on it and I had some bruises from the first part of that day.

Not long after getting into heavy rush-hour traffic, she announced, "Ha, Ha! I figured it out! That damn booster seat was easy to get off!" She reached behind me and grabbed my right upper arm and scratched at it, all the while kicking the back of my seat.

As my "Tazmania-mobile" pulled into the Dairy Queen, Torie and Josh could see that I was in trouble and quickly jumped into the car. The teens put Lilly back in her booster, and we took off with all seeming calm to the next destination.

As soon as the kids were dropped off and I pulled out onto the road, Lilly unbuckled again and then took off her shirt and threw it into the front seat.

Grabbing her left ankle, I tried to hold it and drive.

That sounds crazy, but what alternative was there? If I didn't keep moving she might figure out how to jump out of one of the car doors or windows. Even if I had pulled over, I would've had to let go to call for help on my cell phone. She would have bolted into traffic while I was dialing. No wonder the social workers refused to be in a car alone with her!

When we got home, I pulled into the garage and managed to wrestle her into the house and deadbolt the door.

Lilly ran to her room and proceeded to throw every item in it and tore down the curtains, the rod, and the window blind.

Twice I went in and did basket-holds while sitting on the floor. Each time she seemed to give up, only to start up again with a vengeance. My arms felt like rubber.

Deciding that I needed to somehow stop the supply of items being thrown and re-thrown, I started placing everything in garbage bags and removed them from her room. Her screaming reverberated through the house as she slammed the bed into the wall and door, eventually cracking the wooden door itself.

I went in again and was bitten several times. While all this was going on, I worried about her smashing out her big picture window. I kept going into the lion's den because I had visions of Lilly kicking out the Wells' sliding glass doors going through my mind.

Bruce got home at seven p.m. and took over for me because the demolition was still in full swing. I wondered aloud to him, "Does she ever

give up? This is the worst we've seen so far and it began at breakfast."
(Lilly had been with us two months.)

We thought that maybe the next day's scheduled visit with her
sister Tina might have something to do with what was going on, but other
times Lilly would have days like this with no plausible explanation.

Surprisingly, the next morning with Tina was uneventful. It was as
if the previous day had not happened. Ann brought Tina and the two played
while we talked. Getting together with Ann was something I looked
forward to because she'd seen Lilly in action and understood what we were
going through. Relating was easy because we were both soldiers in a war of
some kind, trying to help kids.

I know that she would agree with me if I said you get to a point in
this struggle when people inevitably judge you, and you don't care what
they think, because you know it's about saving a life and not what they
think. I was developing toughness because I was determined to win, for
Lilly.

CHAPTER SIXTEEN

One day Joy came to me and mentioned she knew a nineteen-year-old girl who needed a place to stay. We had the room -I wondered if she would be able to help us with Lilly. Bruce and I figured that even if "Hannah" couldn't help, there would be one more set of eyeballs in the house, and eyeballs were a good deterrent for trouble. Hannah was able to move in after a background check and fingerprinting. She soon became part of our family, but was gone quite a bit because of school and work.

By the end of our third month as Lilly's foster parents, there was a training class we simply had to attend because we had to get in a certain number of educational classes each year to keep our license. CHC had a few trained workers that could be used occasionally to watch her in our home so we could go to a class, because they realized we would never find a qualified ordinary babysitter.

Any prospect would have to be interviewed, finger-printed, have a background check, CPR, and restraint training. Who would go through all that to baby-sit for one evening a month?

Katie came to us from CHC to baby-sit for the first class and arrived early so she could check out our house layout and get instructions for the evening. She was a beautiful, heavyset, brown-skinned woman who arrived with a smile and exuded a calm confidence. While Bruce occupied Lilly out of earshot, I nervously gave her the game plan.

We would enjoy those evenings out because they provided needed, ongoing training while allowing us an opportunity to rub shoulders with other foster parents in the same boat. (Actually, I don't think anybody had a boat like ours. Remember, most of the children in foster care don't have Lilly's issues.)

We had a great time that night, and on the way home, I said we needed to stop at the market and get a bouquet of flowers for Katie as a thank you even though she was being paid by CHC. I was so grateful to be able to get out for a while, knowing Lilly was in good hands.

We got home all smiles and refreshed after Lilly's bedtime, and I handed Katie the flowers as she sat down wearily at the kitchen table.

"You may not thank me after you find out what happened," she said as she propped an elbow on the table and rested her face in her hand while the other one held the flowers.

I looked at her and noticed that the smile and confidence seemed gone, and her pretty face looked tired and drawn.

Katie sighed and told us Lilly had heard music coming from an ice cream truck going down our road and had dashed out the back door. Katie had to chase her up and down the streets and alleys alternately yelling, "I have ice cream!" and talking to her supervisor on her cell phone while running.

Lilly finally ran up to a house and rang the doorbell, and an unsuspecting person answered the door. She pushed past and ran inside, and that's how Katie caught her. The first time, that is.

She went on to say that right after she got her back into our house, Lilly escaped again, so she called her supervisor to come help chase her down. It took both women running this way and that while communicating by cell phone to locate and close in on her. She was eventually captured and dragged back to our house, given her meds, and put to bed.

That evening's events made history as they were discussed in the offices and halls at CHC. We were definitely "The People to Watch," and although no paparazzi followed us, thanks to Lilly we had more attention than we wanted.

By then it was toward the end of June, and school was two months away. Since we'd home-schooled Joy and Torie, I never understood the comments from fellow parents about looking forward to fall, so they could get a break.

Until Lilly came, that is. Then we dreamed daily about school starting.

I have to say we were very thankful for the two weekly day-respites at Roger and Mary Stevens and those were going well, but the four-hour segments always seemed to be over before we could blink our eyes.

One evening, p.m. medications didn't kick in and make Lilly drowsy as usual. She stayed up all night and didn't fall asleep until five a.m. Bruce stayed up monitoring lest she get into trouble, so he was pretty tired. Imagine our despair when it happened again the next night. She seemed wired and became increasingly active until she was absolutely wild. She was throwing things, kicking, slapping us, and running through the house on rampages. We tried corralling her, blanket-wraps, basket-holds, and gave her the Benadryl the hospital had sent home with us.

She didn't sleep until six forty five a.m. and only slept about three hours, and afterward she seemed unaffected from staying awake both nights but I can't say the same for Bruce and me.

The third night the meds worked and we all got to sleep. We were totally baffled about the cause of the sleeplessness.

The next day she became angry with me over not getting chocolate milk so she slammed her left hand through the glass on our back door.

I couldn't believe she'd done it.

She began to scream and cry as a gash on her hand dripped blood. It was obvious the wound needed attention so I took her to a nearby hospital for stitches. We bonded more during that hospital trip because she was my injured little girl, and I was her mom.

During those early months Lilly had met my sisters and their children. My youngest sister, Tibby, was planning her oldest daughter's birthday party and we'd been talking on the phone and making plans for it to be special. I was looking forward to going and taking Lilly to the party with all of her new "cousins."

Two days before the party, Tibby called and said her husband didn't want Lilly to come. He thought things would go better if we just got a babysitter and came without her.

"Oh yes, just get a babysitter! Impossible!" I was so angry and frustrated that I hung up on her and cried. That wasn't like me. Anyone who knew me knew that I never even hung up on telemarketers. We wouldn't have allowed her to ruin the party, didn't they understand that? I had never had words with Tibby before, let alone hung up on her.

I wondered why I was so hurt. I think in retrospect, it was because we'd lost our normal social activities with friends since Lilly had come, but not ties with family. That outlet and network had remained intact until then, and I think it really shook me.

She called me the next day in tears and we made up, but I was still deeply jarred inside, and we were not at the party.

CHAPTER SEVENTEEN

Lilly Angel could be so funny at times but not in the usual, normal little kid way. The things that made me want to smile were some of the names that she would call us. Besides being called a fake mother, I was also called Cruella Deville, and she just loved to call Bruce a bitch.

After I allowed her to watch *My Fair Lady* on television, she started calling me something new when she was angry: "Just you WAIT Henry Higgins, just you WAIT!" It was meant to be a threat, but I think being called Henry Higgins was my favorite verbal abuse. It sure beat the really bad swear words that were in her repertoire.

I'm convinced Lilly heard many of the words in the womb before she was ever born. Research has shown that the unborn can hear music, sounds, and recognize voices.

Only once can I remember a time when she couldn't think of a properly insulting name for me. She was mad about a food issue again after I had refused her dessert because she hadn't eaten her vegetable.

She jumped up from the table, glared at me, and said, "You are very, very, VERY!!!" Then she went into her room and slammed the door.

I took that as a wonderful compliment.

The next day we were sitting on the floor playing "Pound Puppies" and were making our little stuffed puppies talk to each other. I actually enjoyed doing that with her.

She moved her small brown puppy toward mine and squeaked in a tiny voice, "Hey, what's your name?"

My white spotted puppy replied, "My name is Fred."

She put her puppy's nose up to my pup's nose and said in the same small voice, "You're a cute little shit-head."

I blinked and told Lilly, "We don't talk like that!" Truthfully, I thought it was hilarious.

As she got older the swearing took on a less innocent bent, and she was more deliberate in using verbal assaults. We tried various consequences with some success, such as having her put one of her quarters in a jar each time there was a cussing downpour. Nothing ever seemed to work for long. We tried putting a few drops of vinegar on her tongue, and we also tried hot sauce. The hot sauce was no hotter than the average Mexican salsa, but the name "hot sauce" seemed fearsome to Lilly. We never used soap because we wondered about the chemicals in it.

Her liberal use of foul language was *quite* a handicap for all of us wherever we went, because decent speech is obviously an important part of living in the community.

I remember once going to JC Penney with her to make a quick purchase. She started hiding among the racks of clothing and wouldn't come out. The walls in that department may still be blue from what came out of the mouth of my six-year-old girl. I desperately wished I had been wearing a T-shirt that said, "I'm a foster parent!"

Interestingly, Lilly would usually try to control her tongue when around babies and much younger children. She would say, "They shouldn't have to listen to that."

The only other time I can remember when she "kept a lid on it" was when we took her to church. Although she said she hated church, she usually seemed very happy there and loved to dress up and go. We started her out in a pre-kindergarten class in July, and I remember one Sunday getting paged while we were sitting in church.

Bruce left his seat to go check on her. When he got to the class, the teacher told him Lilly was being sent out of the classroom because she had no underwear on under her dress. He brought her to the sanctuary and sat her down between us. I looked over at him, obviously wanting to know what had happened.

He whispered, "You didn't put any underwear on her."

I hissed, "Yes I did!" I clearly remembered her picking out a sparkly pair with a Barbie on the front and putting them on her. She was not happy to be sitting there with us, and before the service was over she urinated on the upholstered seat.

On the drive home I asked her where the sparkly panties had gone. She responded by telling us when they had their potty break she got them wet, so she flushed them down the toilet.

That afternoon I noticed that she'd lined up all of her shoes in a row, and I was standing there admiring what she'd done. Her church shoes were little white patent slip-ons, and my eyes stopped when they landed on them. There was one of my panty liners in each shoe as the perfect-fitting insole.

I looked at her in disbelief and asked, "Have you been wearing your shoes to church like that?"

Her blue eyes met mine and she grinned.

CHAPTER EIGHTEEN

One more month until kindergarten would start, and we were getting giddy just thinking about it. Lilly's CHC team and Kathi Beadle worked together on the best option for school, and it turned out that the neighborhood elementary school actually had a Severe Behavior Handicapped (SBH) kindergarten only twelve blocks away. I started taking walks with her and going by the school so she could get used to the idea.

At some point she would be assessed and tested for an IEP or "Individual Educational Plan." IEP's are done for children who have special learning needs in various subjects. We thought Lilly's needs were huge and wondered about any school being able to handle her, let alone teach her required subjects. And if she were in a class with other kids who had behavioral problems, how in the world would they learn anything?

We still had to wait a month to find out but I kept talking school up to her and would have her do little projects to help get her in the groove of sitting and concentrating.

One sunny afternoon after returning from one of our walks past the school, I showed her a large bag of colorful beads that I purchased for her to string with a plastic cord. She got all excited at the sight of the pretty beads but when it came down to putting the cord through the centers, she quickly lost patience and angrily dumped them all out onto the floor.

I told her she had to pick them up and of course she refused, so I said, "Please have a seat until you decide to clean up your mess." I pointed to a chair.

She started swearing at me and ran to her room and grabbed the velour blanket off her bed and brought it to the kitchen. She held it out and demanded, "Wrap me up! Wrap me up, 'cause I'm NOT sitting in da damn chair!"

Talk about trying to be in control. I told her if she would pick up the beads I would help, so she dropped the blanket and began picking up beads with me. After a few minutes she got frustrated and poured out what we had just collected and threw the bag down the hall. I held onto her until she settled down. Then we worked together until the floor was clear. She was proud of herself when we were finally done.

I had just spent forty minutes intensely working one-on-one with her and didn't have even one bead on a string to show for it. If Lilly required that kind of supervision all day long at school, she'd need to have her very own superhero teacher.

There were many other activities I'd find for her to do besides beads, walks, and "Pound Puppies." I knew she was interested in death, so I thought up a very successful game that would allow me to rest for about half an hour.

The game was called "Playing Funeral," and I know it sounds morbid but you've got to understand that desperate times call for desperate measures. I would lie on the couch on my back with a pillow under my head pretending to be dead, and Lilly would cover me up to my neck with a blanket. She would place stuffed animals and silk flowers all around me as I lay there resting. She put a lot of thought into the arrangement of the grave blanket and decorations, and it was a peaceful and relaxing time for me.

Her most favorite activity was riding a small blue bike on the sidewalk. We set clear limits on how far she could go down each side of our corner property's sidewalks. Lilly managed to wreck about every day, even though the bike had training wheels. Some crashes were serious enough to require incident reports for scrapes or bruises.

When she ventured farther than the designated limits, I'd find a reason to call her in with something tempting. "Come get a Popsicle!" or, "Time for a snack!" Both worked great. Once she was inside (see I was learning), I'd give her the snack or treat and tell her I knew she hadn't stayed inside the boundaries, which meant she wouldn't be riding the bike again that day.

She was usually surprised and would ask, "How do you know?"

My response would be, "I know everything."

She would look at me and wonder if I truly did, because she never seemed to get away with anything.

We'd been given a large bouncing horse on a springy frame for Lilly and put it on the porch. She'd ride it so hard that it would actually travel across the cement patio, and the metal frame would clang over and over on the cement. I cautioned her more than once to be careful but she rode like a crazy woman on that thing.

The momentum once tossed her right off the back of it, and she dented a downspout with her head. Thankfully, she hadn't hit the cement but she was shaken, so she allowed me to comfort her and give her a Tylenol.

One morning the horse was gone. Lilly was so disappointed that someone had stolen her horse, and so were we. It had really helped her to get some energy out.

Soon after, her physical therapist encouraged us to try a crash-bang therapy. The theory was for her to tire herself by falling onto pillows or pounding pillows to get frustrations out. Her interest in those activities was short-lived, but crash-bang was one of many ideas we would try in order to help her.

The countdown to kindergarten continued, and by August we were at the six-month mark with Lilly. One day I had been baking and had made both a pie and a chocolate cake. Susie Smith, the neighbor across the street with the teen boy and girl, stopped in to say hello. We talked a while and I went with her out into the breezeway to say goodbye (forgetting Lilly would be alone with the goodies).

While I was out there, Torie had come into the kitchen and found "someone" had dug into the top crust of the pie, as well as taken several fistfuls from out of the side of the chocolate cake.

When I came back inside, faithful Torie was sitting on the floor with a sticky, chocolate-covered girl in a basket-hold. She told me she tried to have her just sit in a chair but "the punk" wanted to fight, kick, and pinch. I stayed out of it because Torie was doing great, and I was *so* angry. So much for my bakery.

I cannot even begin to count how many food incidents we've had with Lilly. I became more and more careful as time went on, but sometimes opportunities happened enabling her to snatch whatever she desired.

One day I made a chocolate pecan pie and it was piping hot as I took it out of the oven. It was a new recipe, and it looked and smelled glorious. I was certain it was safe for the moment because it was 350° degrees.

Wrong again. That kind of heat was not a deterrent to a sugar-lover hell-bent on capturing a prize. I left the kitchen for five minutes, and she wasn't even IN the kitchen when the pie came out of the oven. When I returned there was steam rising from the chocolate filling, but not a single pecan was on that pie. I went looking and found her in the den quietly watching a video while sitting cross-legged on the carpet.

There was no chocolate on her face and hands, and she appeared innocent but she and I were the only ones home.

I truly lost it and started to yell, "Where are my PECANS? What did you do?! You are sweets-grounded for the week!" We were taught to keep our cool and not come unglued when foster kids gave us a run for our money, but I was so upset.

Lilly stood up and put her hands on her hips and snarled, "I didn't take YOUR NUTS!"

The promised ban on sweets stayed for the week but I didn't find the top of that pecan pie until two weeks later.

Lilly was at a respite, and Bruce and I decided that we'd like to curl up on the couch in the den and watch a movie. It was a bit chilly so I reached for an afghan to cover up with. The one inside edge of the knitted afghan had a glob of chocolate-covered pecans stuck in it, dried and hardened onto the yarn.

We sat there and laughed. Lilly must have forgotten all about it, and I felt better knowing she didn't get to eat her stash of chocolate nuts.

Since we were always going to training classes we would continually try to implement any new and helpful ideas. Looking back, I think the trainers themselves were searching hopefully for any new concept that would help keep the children in their foster homes.

An idea was discussed concerning children who hoarded or stole food, and our ears perked up. It involved overloading the kids with whatever they tried to sneak, so their needs would be more than met in a dramatic teaching manner. As I understood it, if a child stole or hoarded a loaf of bread, give them five loaves to keep for themselves.

The problem was Lilly usually took sweet things and loading her up with *them* didn't seem to be a great idea. (We always had fruit out and available, but that is not the kind of sweet she craved.)

And then there was the honesty-issue about stealing or thieving from people who were trying to be her family. I couldn't see myself saying, "Lilly, it's okay that you've ruined all my hard work, here ruin another pie."

I do remember two occasions where I tried to overload her with goodies and make a point at the same time. One day I found she'd managed to take a bag of M&Ms and hide them. I noticed the unopened bag was missing and found it under her bed after searching for it.

"Come here and eat a bowl of M&Ms! We have lots!" I said, crawling out from under her bed with the bag.

She came running with a dubious look on her face as I pulled out a kitchen chair and poured her a generous bowl of the candy. "You can have all you want but we eat in the kitchen, not our bedrooms."

She smiled and dug in, emptying the bowl very quickly.

When lunchtime came, I sat down to a sandwich and fruit while Lilly had another bowl of M&Ms for lunch. She asked, "Don't I have to eat fruit?"

"No," I answered. "Just what you really, really wanted- the M&Ms."

She ate that bowlful more slowly than the first one she'd had a couple of hours earlier but was still very happy with her good fortune.

When it was time for dinner, Bruce, Torie, and I sat down to eat chicken and mashed potatoes with corn. Lilly loves potatoes and corn and came to the table smacking her lips.

I poured her a bowl of M&Ms instead and said, "In this house if you want a food so bad that you steal it, you will get to eat it all day. Isn't that great?"

She ate that meal very slowly and left quite a few candies in the bowl. It was a long time before another food theft occurred. The next time it was a bag of walnuts, and we repeated the bowls of generosity. Walnuts for lunch and dinner weren't as appealing to her but she accepted her consequence with growing understanding.

CHAPTER NINETEEN

The end of August was closing in and I was shopping for school clothes for Lilly that were cute but dirt-hiders, because she was a dirt collector. She couldn't wear anything white. Dark pants and patterned tops worked best, and her favorites were animal prints and glitzy tops with embellishments. The embellishments never lasted long though because she would chew or twist them off.

The day before school started, Doris Champion sent a social worker over to our house. She was going to walk with us to kindergarten orientation. We had a warm sunny day, and the walk was exciting for me because Bruce and I would soon have part of our lives back.

Her classroom was on the ground floor just to the right of the main entrance, and it had four big open windows that looked out onto the street and sidewalk. Mrs. Firm met us at the classroom door and introduced us to her aide, Miss Coops. The age difference between them was about twenty years, with Mrs. Firm being older, probably in her forties. They introduced themselves to me, the social worker, and a thumb-sucking Lilly.

The classroom roster showed Lilly would be the only girl in a class of ten boys. She stopped to stand in front of the big open windows to see what was outside, and even though they had told her their names, she turned and asked each of them again, "What's your name?"

Mrs. Firm explained the fairly typical class rules while we stood there, and then asked Lilly to remove her thumb from her mouth. *Good luck with that one.* Mrs. Firm seemed to be a seasoned teacher with a game plan for working with the "special behavior" kids who would start the next day in her class.

As we left to make a vacancy for the next child's orientation appointment, I felt relieved for the help that was on the way. I also felt growing concern for Mrs. Firm and Miss Coops and hoped that they had a good game plan.

The caseworker and I talked about the school on our walk home with Lilly, who was quiet and walking about three steps ahead of us. She spotted a discarded bag of potato chips on the sidewalk and snatched them up and began eating.

I quickly intercepted and said, "No! Those are trash, and we don't eat food from off the sidewalk." She was angry and wanted those chips. After all, she was the one who had found them.

The first day of kindergarten she looked really cute in a hot pink shirt that had purple flowers on it and a pair of dark purple knit pants, new pink tennis shoes and a ponytail tied with a purple ribbon. She was a pretty little girl and appeared no different than any six-year-old dressed and ready for her first day of school, except that she was smaller.

The fact that there were going to be ten boys in the class continued to make me uneasy. Maybe her teachers being female would balance things out.

Mrs. Firm met us at the door as I handed Lilly off to her care until two thirty. Miss Coops was sitting at her own desk off to the side, cutting something with scissors. She smiled and waved.

Mrs. Firm had a very clear and precise way of speaking and also had a highly structured classroom with definite rules and consequences. A true warrior, I thought with admiration.

Finally home, I let Baler and Peek upstairs, and the three of us reveled in the carefree life. I breathed deeply and smiled, putzing around the house all day, not doing much of anything. I needed that day to relax and unwind because there were many more to come filled with chores, appointments and busy activity while Lilly was in school, but that day was special, and I savored it.

All too quickly it was over. I sighed and put the cats back in the basement and headed up to the school so I could escort my little girl home.

School was out, but each child still sat in their seat, and Mrs. Firm was at her desk. Miss Coops greeted parents at the door as we waited there. When Lilly's name was called she quietly got her papers and a sticker and left with me. It was all orderly and quiet, almost surreal.

Once out of the room she started calling to other kids also crowding out of the building, asking, "What's your name?" and saying things like, "Ahh, I like your shoes," and "Is that your dad?" Most ignored her, but she was undeterred and kept it up until we were walking alone on our way home.

We were barely in the door after getting home before the pacing and thumb-sucking began. *Oh boy, something is coming.* Her preschool history was filled with after-school fallouts and sure enough, it fell on me. Before I could start crash-bang therapy she became uncontrollably violent and spewed profanity as if a switch had just been flipped.

I added a Benadryl to her afternoon meds but it didn't kick in until after a blanket-wrap following several unsuccessful basket-holds. She screamed and fought to exhaustion before finally falling asleep.

Usually after an episode of that intensity she would wake from her nap as though nothing had ever happened. I, on the other hand, knew it happened because of teeth marks, bruises, sore muscles, and a trashed house.

We had regularly scheduled appointments with the pediatric psychiatrist and a registered nurse who worked closely with Lilly in between psychiatric appointments. The nurse monitored medications, and we kept her abreast of general moods and behavior. Based on what we and her play therapist (Kathi) would observe, her medications would be changed until we had a better combination of them to help her be less aggressive and impulsive.

I won't mention all the prescription combinations, but over the years she has been on Clonidine, Paxil, Geodone, Depakote, Trazadone, Lithium, Abilify, Risperdal, Ritalin, Cogentin, Buspirone, Halidol, and others. Some gave her tremors while others caused sleepiness, depression, and weight gain.

When weight would quickly pile on, it would have to be decided if the benefits to her quality of life surpassed the negativity of the extra pounds. Medications were supposed to be adjusted or changed if she began having hand tremors, but that wasn't always the case. The tremors scared me more than anything.

We went into this horrified at all the medications and their possible side-effects and risks as well as wondering why so much importance was placed on their usage. After all these years I am still wary at times about using them, but see much more clearly their necessity.

On one hand, we could have an unmedicated child who was so uncontrollable and violent that she couldn't go to school and learn, play with other kids, or even live in a family.

On the other hand, you had the risks that came with the medicines, but because of them a child might be afforded the chance to stay in a family setting, school, and the community.

And so you have a dilemma in which some serious consequences exist no matter which path is chosen. I feel we made the right decision to support the medication path because number one, Lilly was always so much happier about herself when she was having success in the community and in our home. Number two, she would have not had even a taste of normal life without them.

CHAPTER TWENTY

The first week of school went reasonably well for Lilly. I never knew what the afternoon and evening would be like at home, though. On the eighth day, school behavior took a dive.

When I reached the classroom doorway to pick her up after school, I could see her sitting at a desk just inside the door. Mrs. Firm called her name and got up to come talk to me as she signaled for Lilly as well. I could see there were scissor-cut holes all over the front of her new black pants.

Mrs. Firm stood and lectured her until I started to feel sorry for Lilly, so I looked down at her and said, "I'll bet you won't do that again."

Her blue eyes narrowed and she looked at me and spat, "Oh yes, I will!"

That did it. I looked right back at her and responded, "Then you can wear those pants to school again tomorrow!"

After a better day at school the next day, I asked her if she'd like to take the pants off and throw them away. She nodded and because the attitude was gone, they went in the wastebasket.

Lilly challenged Mrs. Firm and Miss Coops daily. She'd tear up the school papers she refused to do. She would put her thumb in her mouth, an index finger up one nostril, and blow snot out of the other just to aggravate them. She would remove and throw her shoes, socks, and clothing articles, write on her clothes and desk, and take things out of the teachers' desks whenever their backs were turned. She gave new meaning to the words "special behavior."

At the start of November things in the SBH class were beyond wild, courtesy of Lilly. After running errands one day, I parked my car down the street from the school and walked in to collect her at two-thirty.

All she had on were scribbled-on pants and her ripped-up sleeveless undershirt. No outer shirt, shoes, socks, or ponytail; instead, hair stuck out in every possible direction. The little boys must have been witness to many things, and while some looked amused, others appeared tired and more than ready to go home for the day.

The teachers looked weary and relieved to see me because their classroom had been turned into a three-ring circus. Lilly had taken off her shirt and thrown it, chewed on her undershirt and pulled at it until there were holes, threw her shoes, peed on the floor in several places, blew snot out of her nose, fought with the teachers, and cussed them out.

Miss Coops started to gather up the scattered clothing from the floor as well as a jacket, and she brought them to me. I took the items but said, "Evidently she didn't want to wear these in class, so she won't be wearing them home. It's kind of cold out, but she made her decision."

Mrs. Firm looked awed and said, "You're even tougher than I am."

I marched my little charge down the hall, through the crowd, and outside toward the car. More than a few stared at us and (I'm sure) wondered at the homeless-looking urchin in bare feet, but I was getting used to being Lilly's mother.

I didn't scold her, but asked if she'd like to hold my hand as we walked to the car. At first she said no, but after a few yards, she grabbed my hand and sadly said, "I'm not a good girl."

"Why do you say that?"

"I don't want to tell you," she said with her head down.

"I already know, Lilly, but I still love you."

When we got home I told her that I was going to rock her.

"I don't want rocked," she said.

"Well, I'm going to rock you anyway."

"Why do you have to rock me?"

I looked at her little face and responded, "Because I want you to know that I love you, and I am so proud of you when you are a good girl."

Lilly paused to contemplate that statement, and she then climbed into my lap. We rocked quietly and the only sound was the chair creaking on the hardwood floor.

She sighed and said, "I am so worn out today."

The school situation was quickly becoming a learning disaster for the rest of Mrs. Firm's behavior-challenged class. She talked to the principal and they decided to have Lilly temporarily cut down to a half day, from eight thirty to eleven thirty a.m.

She was more than happy to be leaving early. I thought it was a consequence that rewarded poor behavior, but what else could be done? Suspend her in a sealed capsule from the ceiling during class?

One nice day soon after, we arrived home from school and she asked if she could ride her bike. Looking at her school clothes I said, "Yes, but go put on play clothes and old shoes."

A few minutes passed and she came into the kitchen on her way toward the back door wearing play clothes and shoes on the wrong feet. I smiled at the innocence of that, as well as her purposeful stride through the kitchen.

"Oh, your shoes are on the wrong feet."

She put her hand to the door handle and said, "I know. Someday I'll be normal."

I went over and knelt down, asking, "Who said you aren't normal?"

She looked at me and there was no response, just a passive expression in her blue eyes.

"Lilly, you are normal to me, and I love you. Now go outside and ride your bike, but remember the boundaries."

After she went outside, I stood in the window and watched her cycle up and down our sidewalk. She was wearing a royal blue sweatshirt, jeans, and old beat-up black dress shoes that she loved because they were shiny patent and had a little heel on them. Her hair was blowing with the November breeze. She was happy and that made me happy. Whenever there were peaceful, contented moments with Lilly I celebrated them in my heart, and that day I felt myself flying down the sidewalk with her.

The kindergarten adventures did not change much even with the new schedule. Disruption continued for Mrs. Firm and the building principal, a trim woman who looked very professional in her sharp skirt suits. She was being called to the SBH classroom on a regular basis to help with Lilly, who often tried to escape the classroom and had a good deal of success. The principal and teachers were forced to run in the halls, either trying to find her or chasing her.

One high-speed pursuit was memorable, and school personnel probably still talk about it. Lilly had escaped and started running up and down hallways and stairs, going in and out of doorways and literally had a posse chasing her. She ran into yet another doorway and sprinted across (unbeknownst to her) a stage and into midair, crashing into a heap on the auditorium floor. She was pretty banged up and once again a regular kid who needed to have attention for her boo-boo's.

Another day brought the principal back to the room after Miss Coops went to get help. Lilly had been so disruptive that Mrs. Firm had placed her behind a tall partition about ten feet away from the other desks. While back there, she had thrown her shirt over the top of the partition and followed with her shoes and socks. Then she urinated on the floor in several places, all the while yelling loud, lovely profanities from behind the wall.

The principle was summoned to help and had gotten into a restraint situation on the classroom floor with her. Lilly screamed so loudly that two bicycle policemen going by the building parked their bikes and ran into the school. They found a well-dressed woman wrestling on the floor with a tiny, half-naked little girl who was calling her "bitch," as a classroom of little boys who had severe behavior problems watched.

I came upon the scene a moment after the policemen, because it was time for me to pick her up. She did an about-face when the policemen started talking to her. I stood in the doorway and looked the room over and then at my six-year-old. She had snot on her face and in her bangs, and no shirt or shoes. There was food all over the floor.

She looked at me as if to say, "It's about time you got here." She was ready to leave that place and said, "I hate deez teachers! They make me work, work, work! I hate this stupid place! I'm gonna kill myself! I'm *never* coming back!" She proceeded to collect her stuff and marched over to me to take her home.

All the trouble Mrs. Firm had with Lilly made me feel better because it wasn't just me having problems dealing with her. And I'll wager Mrs. Firm felt better about herself as she watched the school principal wrestle on the floor. There were a couple other times the police were called back to that kindergarten classroom because of Lilly, also giving *them* a run for their money, and I think that must have made the principal feel better about herself as well.

Before we left that day, Mrs. Firm motioned that she wanted to speak to me in private. She crossed her arms over her chest and asked, "Do you know what Lilly says to me when I tell her she'll get a consequence if she does something she shouldn't?"

I looked blankly at her as I braced myself.

Mrs. Firm lowered her voice and narrowed her eyes and said, "She says, 'GO for it, Bay-Bay!'"

I smiled and wanted to laugh because that was one I hadn't heard before. I left there feeling very, very good about *myself*.

CHAPTER TWENTY-ONE

This chapter is dedicated to the glasses. Just before school started, Lilly had an eye exam at our neighborhood optometrist office. They said she needed to have glasses, and that she also had to see a specialist because her right eye was crossing inward.

The eye specialist at Columbia Children's Hospital informed us that Lilly needed to wear an eye patch four to six hours a day and glasses all the time. Wow. As if we didn't have enough problems, now we had to make her wear a patch over one eye and glasses over that.

When Lilly wasn't acting up she was all about her own beauty, and in her mind, the new additions quickly became the ENEMIES of her beauty. The first pair of wire-rimmed glasses lasted nine days before they were twisted and the lenses popped out. She was telling me off before church and refused to wear them.

I decided I'd had enough and went after her as she kicked me with those white church shoes, informing me, "They are very hard! You better watch out!"

I managed to get her in a basket-hold and ripped my dress in the process. (It's amazing the things that people go through before church.)

Day after day we had problems enforcing the eye patch and glasses. She went through several pairs in a very short period of time.

The glasses had what I called "Frequent Flyer Miles," but it had nothing to do with airplanes. Some had more air time than others but they all spent time flying through the air. Sometimes they were stepped on or bent into zigzag shapes, and all had the nose pieces chewed off. I think Lilly had five pair that first year.

When the first pair was destroyed we told her she had to pay for new ones.

She looked at us with real curiosity. "How am I gonna pay for those?"

I told her, "That is a problem, since you don't have any money. But I have talked to the people at the eye doctor's, and they said that you can pay with TOYS."

Her eyes got big and she put her hands on her little hips. "I'm keeping all my toys," she announced firmly.

Bruce said, "If you don't pick out something nice to pay them with, then I will."

Seeing she had lost, she caved in. She started looking for acceptable items and chose her best Barbie doll. We took her up to the eye doctor with her offering to "pay" for new glasses.

They played along wonderfully that time and at least four other times down the road. Over that two-year period they collected several Barbies, books, stuffed animals, and two sequined dress-up dresses as "payment." (Most of the time CHC paid the bill.)

The people at the eye doctor's office saw the problems we were having and suggested that we try sports goggles because there were no metal parts. They consisted of a clear, plastic molded frame held to the head by an elastic strap that was about a half-inch wide. They were far from attractive, but definitely more able to sustain air travel.

We told her those new glasses were very cool, and kids in sports wore them all the time. I had her convinced she looked gorgeous in her big goggles and floral pink dress one Sunday before church. I could tell she almost believed me as she looked at herself in the full-length bathroom mirror.

When we got to church, I walked her down the hall to Mr. Halterman's kindergarten class. As we approached the door to the class, he turned to greet us. Surprised, his eyebrows shot up and he burst out, "Whoa! Ski goggles!"

The goggles came off and sailed across the room.

I wanted to grab his neck and shake him silly.

After about thirteen months of combat over the eye patch, the specialist said our girl was done wearing it. Bruce and I were as thrilled as Lilly was. Sometime later I was reading the tiny print on one of her past medical prescriptions, and it said the neurological possible side effects included crossing eyes.

My own eyes froze on the sentence. Why had no one considered that? We were never even asked if she took medications when she was at Columbia Children's. I realized it was too late anyway because she was off that medication, and her eye wasn't crossed anymore (but she still had to wear goggles because her regular vision was poor).

It took eighteen months of goggles before she was allowed to try glasses again. To this day she feels the glasses obscure her true beauty, and she would rather not be able to see than wear them.

The last pair disappeared after three weeks. I asked her what happened to her new glasses.

"Oh, John has them."

CHAPTER TWENTY-TWO

Joy, our oldest daughter, surprised us with an engagement announcement. We hadn't seen a whole lot of her after she had moved out. Lilly loved Joy because she was very non-confrontational. Joy could just leave and go home when the punk was unpleasant. Hannah had become acclimated to our family but was usually gone or oblivious to Lilly's antics. Torie, on the other hand, was around more, and her help was needed from time to time.

One Sunday that first year, we planned to meet the older girls at a park. Bruce and I were looking forward to it because it rolled back time to the days before everyone was going in all different directions.

Lilly had been very obstinate before we left for the park and almost wore me out before we even got there. But she ran all over the park and had fun once we were there.

We enjoyed the fresh air for a while and decided we'd all go to a hamburger place together to get something to eat. Joy and Torie said they would meet us there and went on ahead.

On the way to the restaurant, Lilly turned nasty again. She kicked the back of my seat and called us stupid while spitting as far as she could, trying to reach us with it. *Yuck!*

Bruce and I believed eating out was a privilege and not a right. So when we got there, we had already decided that after the display in the car she would not be eating at the restaurant, but would eat later at home.

When Joy and Torie arrived we went in and ordered our food, but only water for Lilly. She knew from past experience how we felt about restaurant trips because we had bypassed them before and taken her home to eat. We assured her she'd eat as soon as we got home.

She threw two angry fits, and each time Bruce quickly took our little wildcat out to the car until she was under control, then brought her back in. After the second time, she sat quietly and sipped her water.

That was always how we handled trips to restaurants when she was little. She learned from this how to behave in a restaurant.

One time we were sitting in a booth at an Italian place. She was busy scarfing down spaghetti and had it all over her glasses, mouth, and hands. I was glad I wasn't sitting next to her.

All of a sudden, a woman seated in the booth behind us began loudly yelling at her little boy in a very rude manner.

"Shut up!" she bellowed, "You shut up!"

Lilly stopped eating and leaned forward from across our table towards me and whispered, "Did you hear that mom tell her boy to shut up?"

I could barely see her eyes through the sauce on her glasses. I replied, "Yes I did, shh . . ."

Lilly whispered back at me, "You don't tell me to shut up."

I nodded, "No you're right, I don't."

She looked at me very knowingly and whispered, "She must be his birth mother."

Sadly, she was speaking from experience.

We worked continually with her on the table manners, hand washing after using the bathroom, not sucking her thumb in public, and definitely on not passing gas around others.

One prescription medication gave her problems with the latter, and over and over I said, "Lilly, please don't do that around me. Just leave the room. Thank you!"

One day I was braver than usual and desperate for a few groceries, so I ventured out to the grocery store with her in tow. She was pretty good in the store but as we went toward the checkout I could see the lines were very long, so I told her she could have some chips when we got home if she continued to behave. I know that was bribery.

We waited patiently for our turn with the cashier. When it finally came, I started to unload my cart quickly because everyone in line seemed to be tired of waiting. As I was emptying my cart she slipped quietly to the back of the line of people. I had one eye on her, wondering what she was up to, while I was got my wallet out to pay.

As I handed the clerk my money, Lilly reappeared by my side and looked up at me with her glasses on the end of her nose and said, "Mommy, aren't you glad I didn't toot by *you*?"

At that precise second, an awful odor drifted up from the back of the line.

I wished I'd been wearing a hat and sunglasses.

Speaking of manners and things, the after-toilet-hand-washing training really stuck with her. I always knew she'd wash her hands and that was a sweet, sweet victory.

One day we went to a medical clinic because I had come down with a minor illness.

The staff there routinely performed drug screens using the bathroom and would flip the switch to shut the water off to the sink each time a drug screen was done. They had forgotten to flip the water switch back on, and Lilly asked to use the bathroom.

I waited outside the door while she went in. It was my habit to always inspect any bathroom after she finished, making sure all was in order, and when I went in after her, I noticed there was blue toilet water in puddles on the floor.

"Lilly, why is the blue toilet water all over the floor?"

She shrugged. "There was no water coming out of the sink, so I washed my hands in the potty."

Of course!

CHAPTER TWENTY-THREE

The month of December that first year was an interesting one. Early on, school started improving to the point that Lilly was actually having two or three days a week with passable behavior. She was quite a part of our life; especially mine because almost all of my time was taken up working with her and going to the many appointments. The periods of destructive violence would last sometimes for days on end but the happy times became happier and more frequent.

The last day before Christmas break I went to the school to pick her up and Miss Coops said the day had gone well until a boy in the class named Danny sang a song to Lilly. He was a huge boy with a mop of curly blond hair and almost twice her size. Evidently she felt he was teasing her, so she retaliated by punching him hard in his back. The attack on Danny got her in trouble.

I asked her if she had apologized to Danny, who was standing about ten feet away looking dubiously at us.

Lilly jumped up and ran toward him, and as she neared, his eyes widened with fear and apprehension.

She stopped abruptly in front of him, looked up, and said, "Danny, I am so sorry I punched you in your back!" She said it using a hand motion to swing a pretend punch.

He looked sadly at her with eyes still wide and said, "I'm sorry I *sang* to you!"

We were always having social workers ask if we were adopting Lilly. Up until then I hadn't seriously thought about it, and Bruce was not convinced at all. But when we had four good weeks in a row that December, I must admit I considered it *might* be a possibility way down the road.

We attended a review the county had scheduled and during the meeting we were told that we could adopt Lilly for about $153. I don't know where that number came from. We left there shaking our heads and frustrated.

Why were they pushing us to adopt? It was because she cost the county a great deal of money, time, and paperwork. If she were to go to residential care it would cost at least $200 a day. That money would come from their already strained budget.

If she ever needed to have residential treatment, our insurance would only cover a maximum stay of two weeks. Most admissions would be six months to a year or longer.

I was a little more optimistic than Bruce because I felt time was on our side. Even when Tim, the not-so-popular county worker announced he needed to have a picture of Lilly for their adoption website, I was not too worried. I took the absolute worst picture I had of her, scowling meanly into the camera with glasses on the end of her nose, and I submitted the photo with a big smile.

December also brought the news that Joy was newly pregnant and they'd set a wedding date for March 1, right after Lilly's upcoming seventh birthday.

We told Lilly she would be a seven-year-old aunt. I thought the whole baby thing would be interesting. We couldn't have known then, but the birth of that baby would bring about more healing in her life and forge a bond that she cherishes to this day.

We had eight months to wait for his arrival.

There were a few times during Christmas break that Lilly seemed to *want* to fight with us, and when given a timeout, demanded that she be wrapped in a blanket instead. Talk about turning the tables and being in control.

One time she demanded the blanket-wrap and lay down on the blanket while we, (rather confused as to exactly what to do), wrapped her. Once she was snug, she let loose and fought, screamed, and swore with a vengeance. She was able to free one of her arms in the struggle and bit down on it.

Bruce grabbed the arm and tucked it safely back in the blanket while she shouted, "Why won't you let me bite myself?" This lasted about ten very long minutes and then she was spent. It seemed as if she knew that she'd be safe in that blanket.

Bruce put her in my arms in the rocking chair afterwards.

Over the break, Torie and Lilly got into it one day because she had taken Torie's purse. Torie found out and chased after her shouting, "I'm going to DROP-KICK YOU! You better stay out of my purse!"

Little did she realize, her phrase, "I'm going to drop-kick you!" would be used by Lilly over and over when she threatened Mrs. Firm. It was funny just thinking about it.

During the holiday time we started an incentive where she would be rewarded with a milkshake whenever she had earned ten smiley faces. A chart was placed on the fridge to record progress, and she earned one sticker each time we caught her doing something good.

You might think that would have meant a milkshake reward every other day but sometimes it took days or a week, and that was with us stretching the reason for a smiley face. For instance, if she got mad and only said one swear word instead of ten or twenty, then we would give her a happy face if she hadn't earned one recently. We wanted to try anything that might encourage her.

One day during that time I was sitting on the lid of the toilet in my nightgown with my legs crossed, patiently waiting for her to get dressed for the day. She surprised me with a quick hug and then exclaimed, "Ohh! I think you don't have no panties on!"

She backed up two steps and looked very seriously at me and continued, "People who don't wear panties poop in their bed!"

Indignant, I tried to tell her that simply was not true, but she narrowed her eyes, nodded knowingly and said, "Yes it is. I heard about them."

The next day school sessions resumed, and she was allowed to go for the full day and eat breakfast and lunch there. She didn't care much for the food, and many times it would be thrown on the floor or across the room.

We learned she had been undergoing some tests to see just exactly what she needed in an Individual Educational Plan, or IEP. When she was observed by evaluators she was frequently well-behaved while she was being watched, because she knew something was going on that concerned her, and kids with RAD are usually very friendly towards total strangers.

During that time in her kindergarten year she was on three daytime medications, and still her "Adaptive Behavior Composite" was only in the sixth percentile. She was almost seven, and the testing placed her developmentally at four years and three months.

We wondered if she was disadvantaged because of the early abuse and many homes she had lived in, but I didn't feel she was mentally disabled. After all, she was smart enough to keep us on our toes every minute of the day. At least the assessment would ensure she'd get extra help in her studies, and we were thankful for that.

At that time a couple other good things came about as well. CHC found a great weekend respite family out in the country. Lilly went once a month for the weekend and enjoyed her visits. Bruce and I rejoiced that there was a CHC family who would allow her to spend two nights in a row, AND let her return four weeks later.

We were wowed yet again when we learned about a woman who had a gymnastics studio and had decided to open it up for a few hours each weekend to special needs children -for free. That angelic being even had volunteers lined up to oversee and work with the kids.

It was a wonderful opportunity for Lilly to dress up in pink tights and ballet shoes and be totally "normal." If she gave me any problems in the car during the thirty minute drive to gymnastics, I wouldn't take her the following week.

CHAPTER TWENTY-FOUR

We celebrated Lilly's seventh birthday in February. She had asked me to make her a double-layer chocolate cake covered in walnuts, and we had a few family members over. She wore a full-skirted baby blue dress, and amazingly, it was just a nice little party for a nice little girl.

There would soon be another type of celebration because Joy's wedding was around the corner. We deliberated about ten seconds on whether to allow Lilly to attend the wedding or send her to the country respite that weekend. We had visions of turning our backs for a minute at the wedding reception, only to discover that she had absconded with an entire side of the wedding cake. No, we were going to relax and enjoy our daughter's day.

Lilly was unaware she missed the wedding. We were careful not to speak of it when she was around because we didn't want her to feel left out. She was still very young and as it turned out, she never seemed to notice that she'd missed anything at all.

I was glad to see my little girl after the weekend was over. Bruce and I had danced the night away and had loads of fun, and now it was with happy hearts that we went to collect our little ankle-biter. She had caused a few problems but nothing the respite couple couldn't handle.

Respite parents are paid very little for what they go through. I think they should be paid double because the service they provide is so crucial to children's placements staying intact, but by whom? The foster agencies themselves are stretched to the limit. I personally believe every single levy for these agencies and any special-needs schools or programs should be passed and get our votes.

I would often give extra money to respite workers as a "thank you" to ensure Lilly's return spot with them. You could call that a bribe but we felt it was more of a fair payment for services given if they did a good job, and if we felt good about her returning there.

We never sent her to a respite without first taking her to meet the people and to see the home where she'd be staying. Such was not the case for many of the children. They would sometimes be taken to respite and left for the weekend with people they'd never met.

We didn't always follow through with the respite after our initial visit. I remember one well-meaning couple who CHC had persuaded to take Lilly for an upcoming weekend. We went to meet them the week before, to "see where you'll sleep." The house was clean but it sat close to the street, and every cranny was jammed with knickknacks and collectibles. There was barely room to turn around. We felt taking her there would be setting her up for certain failure, and so we didn't consider them.

Another place wanting to do respite had four young foster children living there already. The mother said she had a teenage son who was always very helpful with the kids. One look at the dirty house and kids did it for me. There was no way she was going there. Of course, we didn't tell those people that we wouldn't allow her to stay there as we pleasantly chatted. We would just have to find a reason to cancel later.

As we were leaving this particular home with Lilly, the sixteen-year-old son came home and we were introduced to him. Just being within six feet of him gave me the chills. Somehow, something was wrong at that house. I relayed how I had felt and what I had observed to my caseworker, and said prayers for those four little kids.

March came, and we realized Lilly Angel had been at our house for an entire year. "We can do anything for fourteen days" had been our motto to ourselves and each other at the beginning.

She knew she had settled into our family and took some comfort from that, but she was still fighting her core belief that the world was bad and so were most people in it. If they weren't bad, then they still needed to be kept at arm's length just in case they turned bad. That was once again part of the attachment disorder and exemplified a lack of trust.

In my mind, that was her policy on survival. For the most part, I don't think she dropped that policy on Bruce and me until she was much older.

Tina was the exception. The love for her sister was fierce in her little heart, but she emotionally and physically abused Tina at times without realizing that what she was doing was even wrong.

The only "sin" Tina ever committed against Lilly was at the tender age of one, when she had accidentally pushed her down some stairs. For years Lilly mentioned that incident to Tina almost every time they got together. I don't know how Tina ever managed to get past her one serious fault and grow up.

She had been behaving tolerably well for most of February and March. But the tolerable soon became intolerable at school. She was given detention time after school from two thirty to three o'clock at the end of March for hitting Mrs. Firm and flipping her own desk over in anger.

Detention was a new concept to this kindergartener, and although it was a good move on the part of the school, it was more work for Mrs. Firm and Miss Coops. Lilly detested detention because she hated to be at school any longer than she had to.

I picked her up after the first detention and on the way home heard lots of words about her stupid teachers. I started on dinner once she settled in and began playing in her room. After a while I went to see what she was up to, and she had taken a safety pin and scraped letters into the paint on the wall.

To me, that was just something a normal kid might do, kind of like peeling wallpaper edges. Not a thing to ignore, but neither one calling for severe consequences. When I asked her why she'd done it, she charged me and punched me in the stomach. I wheeled around and grabbed her as she started to take off, and put her in a restraint.

The attack really surprised me but was a reminder that something I saw as insignificant, she saw as a huge mistake. I held onto her while she struggled and Bruce came in and gently said, "We all make mistakes, and we all have consequences for mistakes. You are not the only one." It did help calm her to hear that.

It seemed that the trouble at home, school, and now respite increased with each passing day until school ended for the year. Lilly began to defecate at home and school in places other than the toilet. One of our professionals pointed out that when a child is left in dirty diapers for days they become used to the presence and smell of urine and feces. Those things became another validation of their pain and misery.

The critical incident reports did not have defecating as a category to check, so I would put a mark by the SUBSTANCE ABUSE box, which was actually intended for drugs and medications.

The "substance" was being smeared on her bedroom walls, door, dresser, clothes, bedspread, and carpet. At least she only did this in her room, but I felt like I was going to lose my mind. After I was done flipping out and sanitizing, I decided we'd have to take radical measures to get it to stop.

We sat her down and said, "If there is any more pooping or smearing, YOU will be responsible to scrub and disinfect the area until it comes clean. YOU will carry dirty sheets and bedding to the washer and then back up again after they're washed. YOU will scrub floors and walls. If you get poop on any stuffed animals, YOU will put them in a garbage bag and carry them out to the garbage can."

She just sat there and sucked her thumb with a glint in her eyes.

Then we waited for "the test."

It came the next day, and my first clue was the odor coming from her bedroom. Sure enough, she'd smeared feces in a few places on her painted floor. I got a bucket of soapy bleach water and rags and started toward her room with them.

She threw a toy my direction and screamed, "I won't! You can't make me, stupid bitch!"

I retreated and put the supplies in the kitchen nearby, then put her gate up and said, "You can eat lunch when you get it cleaned. Just let me know."

"I won't! I hate you!"

Lunchtime came and went as the foul smelling hours marched on. I knew this was where the rubber-hit-the-road, so I'd better stick it out.

When dinnertime came and she still hadn't been allowed out of her room except for two bathroom escorts, she said, "I'll scrub now."

I took the stuff in and she gave a lazy cleaning attempt for about ten seconds and then threw the rag back in the bucket with a splash. "Forget it!"

I left with the bucket so it wouldn't get dumped, and we ate dinner without her while she screamed curses down on us from her room. After dinner she caved in and said, "I'm ready to clean. Then can I have dinner?"

Feeling relieved, I answered, "Certainly."

I sat down on a clean cloth on the floor while she worked industriously until the floor was scrubbed spotless. She worked silently as I quietly watched.

When almost finished, she paused and looked at me. "You didn't put my face in it. Other people did."

I was startled and asked, "What did you say?"

She held my gaze, "Other people did."

When I heard it the second time, sadness flooded over me. A few moments later I told her, "Lilly you will always have to scrub your poop, but we will NEVER put your face in it." I hugged her when she was done.

I'd like to say she never "smeared" again at home. She did, but never again on that scale. It was always just a small area or one or two items in her room that took the hit, and I know it was because she didn't want to have to work too hard cleaning it later.

Lilly was also defecating at school sometimes and had started to strip completely naked in class. Not cool. I decided to use a culotte dress that zipped up the back as her school uniform. It was a little pant-dress that she was unable to unzip to take off, and she had to wear it every day to school during the last part of the year.

I can still picture her purposeful stride in that red-flowered outfit with glasses on the end of her nose, and her thumb in her mouth. She would have her little head tipped down and her dark blue eyes darting from side to side, always vigilantly looking and watching. (I supposed she learned very young to be on guard for danger because she had been harmed in many ways.)

The last month of school was becoming so difficult that I wasn't the only one who wondered if we'd ever live through it. The country respite family had moved to a condo in a vastly more populated area. The condo had just been built and was decorated in white. White carpet, white walls, cream-colored sofa -you get the picture.

CHC staff had taken Lilly to the new location before her respite because we felt it was necessary, and for some reason we couldn't make the trip ourselves. The respite family called us after the first night and asked us to come pick her up early because things were going terribly.

Bruce and I went to get her that evening and walked into the beautiful condo to find her wearing only her underwear.

"She won't keep her clothes on," the respite mother wearily shrugged and then gave us a tour of her living room. There was red lipstick on the couch, curtains, and carpet. There was nail polish and sparkly eye-shadow also on the white carpet, television, and windowsill. A brown feces stain adorned the carpet near the kitchen.

I was speechless at the damage. Lilly had gotten up at night and raided a closet to find all the WMD's (Weapons of Mass Destruction). To somehow make amends, we insisted she leave the favorite stuffed animals she had packed with the family as "payment" for the disaster. She had nothing else to make restitution with.

We commenced to leave with her still in her underwear.

"Her clothes are in this bag, and here's her coat," the woman said matter-of-factly.

I looked down at Lilly and back at the woman and sadly replied, "She didn't want to wear clothes today, so she'll go home in the car just as she is."

The drive home was quiet, and she was learning.

Needless to say, she was not invited back. And to think the family's twenty-four hours with Lilly paid them a whole $52.00. At times CHC would be able to reimburse people for some damages, but not always for the full extent.

Not long after, we heard the family stopped doing respites altogether, and I felt glum to think that we had discouraged them so, because they were wonderful people.

CHAPTER TWENTY-FIVE

"Sticks and stones may break my bones but words can never hurt me."
Lilly dealt with the "sticks and stones" while with her birth parents. Then the words that did hurt happened in the many school and foster care settings.

April was a difficult month. She tried to choke Mrs. Firm, flipped desks, threw breakfast, lunch, and kicked over her "seclusion partition" after throwing poop over the top of it.

Get your umbrella. Picture yourself in that class.

She would have to spend evenings in her room after days like that. I would always try to go in and visit with her if she was hospitable to me. After one super-bad day, I went in and sat on her bed while she lined two horses up on the windowsill. She played very quietly for a while as I watched.

"This one's name is Sugar and that's Blackie," she pointed to the horses. Then out-of-the-blue, she looked at me and asked, "Am I a Christian?"

I wondered where she was going with that, so I countered, "Why are you asking me?"

"Miss Coops said I'm not. She said I have the devil in my heart."

My own heart hurt. I patted the bed beside me and said, "Sit with me."

She climbed up, and I wrapped my right arm around her shoulders and said, "The devil is NOT in you, Lilly. She is wrong. The devil is just like Oscar the Grouch and tries to get us in trouble if we listen, but he isn't in you or me."

Oh," She responded and said nothing more.

I never wanted her to think that again, but the damage had been done. For a long time afterward, when she doubted herself or was having violent episodes, she'd say to us, "The devil is in my heart!"

I was incensed that a *teacher* would make such an ignorant and harmful remark. Bruce was upset as well, so we decided that we'd go together to pick up Lilly after school, and after he left with her, I would stay and ask to talk privately with Miss Coops before she left for the day.

I had no desire to get her in trouble but she needed educating. She was standing near her desk when I approached her.

"Miss Coops, may have a minute with you? Lilly said that you told her that the devil was in her heart. Why would you say that to a little girl?"

Miss Coops appeared startled. "Oh, I didn't realize . . ."

I went on, "You have planted a bad seed in Lilly's already-damaged heart and never should have said that to her."

"You are right, and I am so sorry." She frowned in concern at me.

"You need to apologize to Lilly as well, and tell her that it is NOT true."

She humbly said, "Yes, of course I will. I feel so bad about this."

I do believe she felt very bad, and she did tell Lilly that she was sorry and tried to backtrack, but those words were already out there.

Words really do have an impact on us. We learned a saying in training class that stuck with me: "Say what you mean. Mean what you say. But don't say it mean."

It was easy to get grouchy and retaliate with words. We didn't want to add any more negativity to her many bad memories so I posted that quote in several places in our home as a reminder.

April and May brought thirty-one critical incident reports, an average of one huge incident every other day. Lilly's psychiatrist asked us to consider using soy products instead of dairy, in an attempt to temper the spring downward spiral. Lilly wasn't at all happy with the substitution, and after three weeks of her hating it, we halted the soy. Her behavior had started to improve but we reasoned that it had nothing to do with the diet change and everything to do with school ending.

Everyone on her team knew we'd better be proactive for the summer, so a few things were set in motion to help. One was a new, very experienced respite family. That's what we needed. This family had two slightly older kids in the home. What really excited Lilly about going there was that they had a real Polly-the-parrot.

Bruce and I had met the parents at trainings and we felt fortunate to get the Pancers as our new respite. After doing two months of regular biweekly respites for Lilly, Mrs. Pancer wrote a letter to me, and CHC received a copy as well.

The letter stated that Lilly grabbed their parrot and squeezed it, then she jumped on her daughter and began scratching and attacking her, leaving visible scratches.

Mrs. Pancer's letter also said that Lilly couldn't find her socks and threw a fit that involved attacking her physically, and that Lilly tried to push her down the stairs, bit her wrist and scratched her hand . . .

Lilly told her son that she would grab him by the ears and throw him out of the window and she would watch him die . . .

Lilly yelled that she would push Mrs. Pancer's head through the window and that would kill her, and she would laugh, and that she was going to strangle the bird . . .

A very short time later Lilly said she pooped her pants. She cleaned herself up and then did this two more times in a row. While she was waiting to get into the bathroom, she pelted Mrs. Pancer with shoes . . .

Lilly set off the fire extinguisher!

Mrs. Pancer called all this "a typical respite day," and I was delighted to get the letter, and parts of it made me smile. (Am I warped or what?) It sounded like their time with Lilly was pretty miserable. But it further validated that I was normal, which was what I needed to hear after living such an abjectly abnormal life for the previous twelve months.

CHC also lined up a Monday, Wednesday, Friday YWCA day camp for Lilly to go to for the summer. The teachers there were great, and the program seemed geared to mildly special-needs children. It was called Early Childhood Development Program. They had to request a third teacher for the days Lilly was there because they were at wits' end dealing with her food- throwing and kicking. The other seven children had to sit and wait to get on with the program until she settled down, so the third teacher was brought in to shadow her.

Now just because there was a seven-hour program available doesn't mean I could always get her there. One day for example, Lilly fought me that morning because she didn't want to go, and I went through World War III getting her to the Y. We were over an hour late but I stayed until it looked like she'd settled down and was playing with some plastic blocks.

I left then and took the elevator down two flights and went outside to my car.

Suddenly a second-story window flew open, and the teacher yelled out into the morning, "She's starting up again!"

I went back upstairs to find that she had knocked over a chair and a storage bin, so I took her hand and escorted her back to the car and drove the short distance home. While I was driving she hit the window with her fist and threw her glasses. Once in her room at home, I took out all of her toys so they wouldn't be destroyed or thrown until she settled down.

She said loudly and with determination, "I don't care. I don't need no toys. I can play with my bed! I can play with my dresser!"

I had to smile. What a character.

I had already planned on having a girlfriend come for lunch that afternoon while Lilly should have been at the Y. When my friend arrived, I took a big laundry basket filled with stuffed animals into Lilly's room so she could play with them.

The basket held all her Pound Puppies and cats as well as Polly, and she played quietly while my friend and I ate lunch and visited. I had fed her earlier and either from that or her morning outburst she fell asleep in the basket with the stuffed animals. She was still small for her age and looked totally adorable sleeping in the basket.

After my friend left, Lilly awoke and was wet because she'd had an accident while she was sleeping. I put her in the tub with soapy water and added all the damp stuffed creatures to try to salvage them. We quietly worked on shampooing each one for about ten minutes.

She was soaping up Polly as she said to me, "Thank you for letting me live here with you." She was so serious and calm when she said it and I instinctively knew it was from the heart.

I looked into her blue eyes and smiled.

Then she added exuberantly, "And you are my favorite mom!"

CHAPTER TWENTY-SIX

Ann Wells had warned me early on that Lilly would steal just about anything. I always looked first under her bed, comforter, or pillow when something was missing. One day I almost bumped into her as she was sneaking out of my room with Bruce's shaving kit and a $100 bill. It was as rare for her to be caught red-handed as it was for a $100 bill to be on his dresser. Usually no matter what the evidence said to the contrary, she would stubbornly declare, "I don't have your stuff!"

The missing items were driving me crazy, and after the gum in my purse disappeared I said to her very calmly and innocently, "Lilly, we have a problem in this family. Someone is taking our things, and I don't know what to do about it. Will you let me know if you see anyone taking our things?"

She responded, "Yes, but I never take your things."

I didn't have to wait many days until the perfume from my dresser disappeared. It was found under her comforter, and I put it back where it belonged while she was playing in the basement.

Bruce was down there watching her, so I went in her room and took nine of her ten pairs of shoes out of the shoe holder and hid them in a bag in the garage.

She didn't notice they were gone until the next day and came stomping out of her room wearing a thick, fuzzy pink bathrobe. "Someone STOLE all my shoes!"

I came running over and went in to see the near-empty shoe caddy. I blinked a few times as I looked at it, then turned and commented incredulously, "That's what's been happening to me! Now they stole from you, too. We've GOT to find who is doing this!"

I could tell Lilly was puzzled. From there on out, every time she took something that that didn't belong to her, "That Person" secretly also took and hid one of her toys or something I knew she'd miss.

Eventually she came to see and understand it was no fun when somebody took your things, and although she never accused me of doing it, the thefts at home became much less frequent.

One day she came out of her room and said, "My shoes are back!"

I feigned surprise and said, "Wow, I'm so happy for you!"

She looked steadily up at me for a few very long seconds and then said, "I am going to wear the shiny pair," and went to put them on.

When she emerged from the bedroom she was wearing the old black shiny shoes with little heels, and asked me for a jar so she could catch bugs. I gave her a plastic Cool Whip container and she went outside.

When our perennials were in bloom in the summer, she would try to catch as many bugs near the flowers as she could. She had no fear of spiders, flies, bees, worms, or beetles, and could frequently be heard talking to whatever she caught.

That afternoon I heard her shouting at the top of her lungs, "Dammit! Why won't you let me be your owner?"

I went out to investigate and saw her stomping her feet and cursing into the air.

Frowning, I asked, "What's wrong?"

Exasperated, she fussed, "My fly got away. I had it in my hand and it got away!"

Evidently she wanted to be its owner but it had other plans. I told her she'd find another one and to keep looking, as I chuckled and went back into the kitchen.

Soon I heard her yelling for me to, "Come, see!"

I hurried back outside, and she opened her cupped hands ever so slightly to let me see another fly inside. That one also escaped and flew away, but she wasn't as disappointed as before.

"How are you catching these flies, Lilly?"

"Here, I'll show you."

She hurried over to the upside-down Cool Whip bowl on the ground and bent down and lifted it up. There was a piece of dog do-do under the bowl. When flies would land on it she'd clap the bowl down over them.

The very idea nauseated me, and I had to put an end to it so I bagged the fly-bait left behind by someone's dog, and explained to her that the scheme was very germy.

Lilly looked angrily at me for once again spoiling her fun. She stamped her foot in frustration and then put her thumb in her mouth before I could stop her.

In mid-summer, a much talked-about Therapeutic Behavior Camp began on Thursdays. CHC said Child and Adolescent Service Center had agreed to accept Lilly. We were thankful and very hopeful that this additional day camp would prove helpful, because the very name suggested changing behavior. We also knew Child and Adolescent Service Center employed trained childhood therapists who knew what they were doing, so I didn't think for even one second it wouldn't be a good thing.

The first Thursday she was restrained in basket-holds four different times and ran off into the street.

The second Thursday I had just arrived home after dropping her off, when I was called to go back and get her because she had attacked three other children. At that point she was ironically expelled from further attendance at Therapeutic Behavior Camp. Every program has its limits though, and the entire world didn't revolve around Lilly.

The very next day I completed another critical incident report and called it an "unexplainable behavior day." She screamed almost all day, threw her glasses, escaped boldly from timeouts, and refused to obey even the most basic house rules. All that followed on the heels of a bad day at the YWCA as well.

It was after ten p.m. before she was tired and wanted to go to sleep. I was totally frazzled and exhausted as I put her to bed. As I pulled the covers up to her chest, she asked, "You know why I was bad today?"

I looked at her and my brain was too tired to think or guess, so I sighed and asked, "No, why?"

She pointed at me and fretted, "Because I'm afraid you're going to be LOST from me!"

I told her, "Lilly, I will not be lost from you. You are stuck with me, but this crazy behavior is wearing me out and makes me tired. If it keeps up, you'll have to spend a night at the CHC emergency house so I can rest." I could tell that made her think.

Then, for the fiftieth time that day, she said accusingly, "You don't love me."

After reassuring her all day that I DID, that time however, I said, "Nobody loves me, everybody hates me; guess I'll go eat worms," and left her room.

Within a few minutes I heard her say, "Mom."

I trudged wearily into her room again and she asked, "Mom, will you rock me before I go to sleep?" I agreed even though I *really* wanted to get the day behind me and get to bed myself. As we were rocking she put her hands on each side of my head and looked worried.

I sighed and asked, "What's wrong?"

Her lips trembled as she said, "I don't want you to get gray hair and die!"

I wanted to tell her (but didn't) she wasn't helping me stay young.

Often there was a trigger precipitating terrible behavior, such as when another child teased her or there was a lack of structure that surrounded a weekend or holiday. More often than not it was being told "no" by us or a teacher.

Sometimes she acted up because she felt unable to succeed at something. For example, we might make plans to take her somewhere on Saturday if she had a decent week. Even though she wanted to go, her subsequent misbehavior would disqualify her for the movie or reward. It happened so often that Bruce decided it best not to tell her until we were ready to leave to go somewhere fun, which really helped.

Her feelings of failure often surfaced in connection with any mention of the Wells family. She'd often think about her past failures before an approaching visit with Tina. I coached her not to dwell on it and *instead* think of playing with Tina.

Over that second summer with us she had been able to see Tina almost every week. Ann and I decided that for the first time in eighteen months Lilly might finally be able to handle a visit to their house.

She was overjoyed but very nervous on the way there. I told her it would be an "outside" visit only to play in the yard, because we felt going inside would still be traumatic for her.

She and Tina played for an hour, and little Sarah (who was then walking) added to the fun.

On the way home she was quiet for the first couple miles of the drive, and I wasn't sure what to say, so I said nothing.

After a few minutes she said, "Thank you for taking me."

I tried to engage her and asked, "How did you feel being there?"

She thoughtfully responded by saying, "I felt very comfortable being there. I was happy but I was sad. Sad that I don't live there anymore. They were good parents to me."

Nothing else was said until we arrived home. Then she asked, "Will you rock me?"

While we were rocking I told her that I knew she was sad because she didn't live with her sister, but we were glad she lived with us.

Seeming puzzled she asked me, "Why?"

"Because we love you and need you to be here with us."

Once again she asked, "Why?"

I elaborated a little more, explaining we needed a little girl to love and she was the one.

Relaxing more in my arms, she stared at me and her eyelids wearily drooped down as she said, "If I have to move again, I would cry my eyes out. I would cry and cry. It would break my heart."

CHAPTER TWENTY-SEVEN

The month of August was all that was left of seven-year-old Lilly's second summer with us. She was put on a waiting list at a DD (developmentally disabled) school about ten miles away, but she would have to return to Mrs. Firm's class at her old school until there was an opening. It was a whole month before school would begin, and I thought that might buy her some time to move up on the list. While we waited she continued at the YWCA when I could get her there.

Then came the day our oldest daughter Joy was to have her baby. Bruce stayed with "Aunt Lilly" while Torie and I went to the hospital to be with Joy to witness my first grandchild, Pete, being born.

Joy and her husband lived close to an hour away so we didn't get to see Pete as much as we would have liked. Lilly's first meeting with Pete was happy, and she talked protectively about, "Anybody who tries to hurt my Matthew (she couldn't say nephew), I'm gonna punch their face!"

I believed her.

About that time an old friend sent me a card picturing a perfect-looking housewife holding a mop. The card said, "I get rid of stress by mopping my floor and buffing it to a perfect shine. Then I bang my head on it for a couple hours. How are things with you?"

I had to laugh. If she only knew. I needed school to start soon or I'd be banging my head.

We got word there would be a vacancy at Eastland DD School on September 27th, but she was to start the school year in Mrs. Firm's class again and attend half days there until then.

While we were waiting for that day, September eleven happened, and I don't remember anything between then and school starting. We were in a daze. There was something much more sinister out there than the "war" we had going on daily at our house.

Lilly's last day in Mrs. Firm's class was full of mixed emotions for all involved. I think Miss Coops may have been relieved to see her move on, but I sensed that Mrs. Firm's relief was also mixed with a feeling of partial failure. She was experienced at teaching difficult young children, and I hoped she would have many more successes in the following years. Fortunately the morning went very well, and I picked Lilly up at noon. We said our last farewell and left.

From there we drove to Eastland School for an orientation tour. Eastland had a cheerful atmosphere, and the staff seemed genuinely pleased to be there. They welcomed Lilly with warm smiles and chatter and showed us the school and classroom. The class would have only three boys and three girls, and there was a full-time aide to assist the teacher. The room had a computer and play areas.

After examining everything in the room Lilly seemed to agree that it would be nice, but riding the school bus the next day was what she was really excited about. We found out there would only be four or five others on the bus, besides a driver and an aide.

The next morning she boarded the bus wearing new jeans and a leopard-print top. She had on new light blue tennis shoes and carried her pink Barbie backpack. The aide stood and collected the bag as Lilly stepped up onto the bus, then buckled her in. (Some kids would eat their packed lunches before arriving at school in the morning if the backpacks weren't collected.)

The first two days on the bus went well but after school on the third day, the big bus screeched to a noisy stop at my curb and the bus doors swung open.

Either Bruce or I always had to be down on the sidewalk to collect her and the backpack before she would be allowed off the bus. A one-shoed girl stepped off with a scowl on her face.

The aide handed me the backpack, and the driver said, "She threw her other shoe out the window about ten blocks back. I'll go back and look for it."

I squinted down at her and said to him, "Don't bother. She must not have liked her new shoes so she can wear her old ones now."

His eyebrows went up and he nodded, shut the doors, and drove away.

Lilly had to wear her old shoes until they just about fell apart.

Soon she was unbuckling on the bus trips which resulted in a "four-point harness" being ordered to keep her in her seat. When she was fastened in it, she reminded me of a little bug with glasses stuck in a spider web, because she was sitting there hooked to the seat by the straps and buckles. After all, it was safety first.

Eastland had kids ages six to twenty-one with various disabilities: Down's syndrome, autistic, deaf, blind, mentally retarded -all needing help and special care. A lot of the children were in wheelchairs or used braces to walk, yet it was not depressing because there were many happy faces on the kids.

The school also had two features that the local public SBH kindergarten did not. First, they had a HELP Team. If a teacher was having trouble or an emergency in their classroom, they would press a buzzer and a team of two to four designated HELP workers would come running. They wore protective bite-proof gloves and had walkie-talkies. (This was the big-time.)

The other feature that Eastland had was a "safe room," which is also known as a seclusion room. It was about eight by ten feet and contained absolutely nothing. The only door had a peep-hole so that a HELP team member could see inside. The room was a "last resort" for any child who became a danger to themselves or others, and it could only be used if it was written into a child's IEP. The IEP had to specify conditions that would send a child there, as well as set a time limit for the maximum time a child would be in the room. It wasn't just randomly used.

Some of the kids were adult- size and violent at times. If one of them became angry and tried to harm someone else, the HELP team would be buzzed and escort that child to the safe room if they couldn't help him to de-escalate first. Once there, the child would only be in the room until they ceased to be a danger to themselves and others. Surveillance through the peep-hole allowed staff the ability to monitor and make that call.

Bruce and I were surprised at the existence of such a room and talked a lot about it. We came to the conclusion that if we had a child who could do real harm to themselves or others (and we did), we would rather the child be put in a safe room for ten minutes than taken to jail. Jail wasn't the place for any of those kids, and the room was a safe option.

Lilly did well at Eastland until October sixteenth. A teacher's report sent home in the pink backpack said, "She threw her desk, containers of candy, and broke her glasses. The HELP team had to be called."

The glasses were less than twenty-four hours old. The school honeymoon was over.

Lilly Angel became famous at Eastland. Sure, she had some good days (or should I say hours), and really was learning things. She was getting speech therapy, and the other children in her class did not tease her or make fun of her. Actually, I don't think any of them were verbal enough even if they had wanted to.

She loved the place but had a funny way of showing it. She bit the teachers and HELP team members on a regular basis. When she'd become dangerous to other children in class, HELP would be paged. On one occasion I witnessed the gloved team of four go into the class and each take an arm or leg as they picked up a swearing and shouting Lilly who was wrestling like a captured bobcat.

"Get off me, you damn bitches! I'm gonna kill you all!"

They awkwardly and stoically carried her down the hall toward the safe room as her snapping teeth tried to bite their hands and arms. The halls reverberated with the loudest bursts of profanity ever heard from a fifty-five pound girl. Once there, she would be deposited on the floor as the four people hurried out and shut the door.

Door-kicking and screaming would ensue and sometimes Lilly would strip her clothes off, or throw her shoes up at the ceiling tiles (occasionally hard enough to dislodge them). If they had not had that room,

I doubt Lilly could have gone to school at all. It was a safe alternative to other children being victims of the violent actions and abuse Lilly could generate.

It didn't take long for her to begin urinating and defecating in the safe room to get even because she knew the staff would have to clean it up. What grief she caused the teachers and principal there. I never once detected any of them disliking her, though. And to my knowledge they never planted any thoughtless or mean words in her little heart, only kindness and much encouragement.

I think the biggest joke she ever played on the HELP team was the time she was in the safe room and their view of her through the peep-hole became obscured. The principal smiled wryly when she told that me they had gone in to check it and discovered Lilly had put poop in the peep-hole!

CHAPTER TWENTY EIGHT

That fall I started making a "Life Book" photo album for Lilly because CHC had a requirement that each child had to have one. It was a lot of work but the end result was worthwhile. I used pictures of her and Tina that CHC and Anne Wells had collected and passed onto us, as well as ones we'd taken ourselves.

Seeing them in order and arranged helped her make some sense of who she was, and every time she requested to see the book, I would get it down as long as she was in a good mood. (I wasn't going to risk it getting destroyed.) The Life Book would evoke some good memories but she was the only one who knew the stories behind the photos taken before coming to live with us.

One page showed Lilly grinning with one of her front teeth missing, and I remember clearly how she lost it. We were at my parents' house visiting when she became very aggressive toward me and grabbed my right arm and bit down. A loose tooth dislodged, and she gagged and swallowed it, which startled her so much that she ceased to be a problem. I still tease her about losing her first tooth biting me.

Lilly was about seven-and-a-half then, and most days her bad attitude forced us to keep her inside where we had more control. One Saturday I heard a noise at the back door and turned to see the mini-blind swaying on the door.

Oh, no! She just took off! I darted outside to see her running in the direction of her old kindergarten school a few blocks away.

"Lilly! Lilly! Come back!" I shouted as loud as I could, but she never looked back, which convinced me she knew exactly what she was doing. I ran inside to yell for Bruce, who quickly grabbed his phone and ran out to find her.

She was no longer in sight but he ran toward the school anyway. Next I called the Smith's across the street, because I'd seen them in their yard earlier and knew they would help. Their teenage son was on his bike within a minute, and Mr. Smith was jogging with his phone in his hand a couple blocks behind Bruce.

I called CHC but held off calling the police because I was fairly certain she would be found near the school playground.

As I waited on my porch for the three guys to corral and catch her, a maroon van shot up my driveway. A short, chubby lady quickly got out of the driver's seat and hurried toward me talking loudly. I recognized her as a woman who lived across the street from the school. She had waved to Lilly and me many times on our walk home from school the previous year. She was waving her arms in apparent frustration and her voice was angry.

"Do you know what your little girl did?"

I braced myself and asked, "No, what?"

She took a breath and almost shouted, "Well, I saw her running all over, so I thought I'd help. I said to her, 'Hey, you look thirsty. How about a nice cold drink?' She said yes and came up on my porch. I got her a glass of water and brought it out. She took some big gulps then yelled, '*Fat bitch*' and threw the glass of water at me! Then she ran down off my porch. Do you *believe* that?"

I certainly did believe it but she was too mad to listen to anything I might have to say.

She stomped back to her van and peeled out of my drive.

I'm not sure why I thought it was funny.

Looking down the street, I heard tiny-girl cussing sounds traveling my way. Lilly was draped over Bruce's right shoulder and all I could see were her legs and butt because the other half of her was hanging down his back. Mr. Smith walked beside him, and his son on the bicycle led the noisy procession with a big smile.

I went to put on a jacket for protection from teeth in case she didn't settle down once Bruce brought her back inside. I'd gotten used to putting one on when potentially going into battle.

And so life went. When she wasn't biting, hitting, or kicking, we did allow her outside as much as possible because winter was coming, and we wanted to make the most of the fall weather. After school there would only be a little over an hour of daylight, so she would change quickly and run outside.

One day I noticed she was talking to three little kids who were standing across the street. I watched and picked up on some negative attitudes immediately, so I grabbed my jacket and headed for the sidewalk. But before I got there she had mooned the three kids and then turned and gave them the middle finger.

I looked across to see them with their hands over their mouths. One shouted, "Did you see what she did?" I ignored them and brought Lilly inside.

Will I ever be able to leave her out of my sight?

She told me why she did it, "Because they were mean to me. They said I'm stupid. But *they* are stupid!"

She was upset so I tried a redirection by saying, "Hey, I'll get you a bucket and you can catch some bugs to show Torie. She likes to see your bugs." A big smile spread across her round little face so I went and got a small bucket for her.

I made sure the kids across the street had moved on before I sent her back outside. It didn't take long for her to show up at the back door with a proud grin. She had two slugs in the bucket and had added a couple inches of water from the garden hose. She left the bucket by the back door and came inside to get Torie.

"Torie! I got two slugs in a bucket of water! Come see!"

Torie came bounding down the staircase and into the kitchen and asked, "What did you say?"

Lilly grinned proudly, "I have two slugs in a bucket of water."

Torie appeared disgusted, and one look at her told us she wasn't interested at all.

I started laughing as Lilly stood forlornly with drooping shoulders.

I looked at Torie and asked, "What? You're not interested in two slugs in a bucket of water?"

Lilly's sadness and my laughter loosened Torie up.

"Okay, show me the slugs. Let's get this over with."

CHAPTER TWENTY-NINE

Lilly was edgy her second December with us and seemed unable to get a grip on anything resembling decent behavior. Was it because of the holiday plans that were being made at home and at school? Decorations were certainly going up everywhere and made things look different, but the previous December had been pretty good. There was no sure explanation except possibly a medicine change a few weeks earlier, but maybe that wasn't it at all?

It wasn't easy to figure her out. I tried to send some goodwill her way by giving her a two foot tall artificial Christmas tree to put in her room. We had purchased some plastic drums, stars, and tinsel, and gave her some of my own "safe" decorations to put on the tree. She heaped them together on it just like all little kids usually do and it was cute. But she still paced, and got into trouble at every opportunity.

One time, she tried to stick my hair brush down the toilet. When I noticed her leaving the bathroom, she lunged for me. I was startled and tried to restrain her, keeping my arms away from her teeth.

She announced, "You won't let me bite your arms, so I will bite MY arms!" She bent her head down to her arms that I had crossed over her chest as I held her from behind, and actually left teeth marks on them.

I was trying to protect myself, and her, and felt as if I wasn't doing a good job at either. Things kept on like that most of the month at a level so intense it was frightening.

We had a reprieve for several days around Christmas, which we were so thankful for. But on December 29, I was all alone with her and at a disadvantage from the minute she got up. I had never been afraid of her but at times I would get so tired and weary that I didn't know if I could go on.

That was such a day. At eight in the morning, she didn't want to eat her "Rice Kreepies" for breakfast and began destroying anything in her path. She threw a heavy decorative object directly at me, defecated in her room, attacked me, and trashed her room. It went on hour after hour. I had several fifteen-minute restraints that left me feeling battered and weak.

At 12:30 p.m. while she was busy smashing a toy up against the wall in her room, I closed her bedroom door. Unbeknownst to her, I quickly tied a nylon rope to the handle and stretched it across the hall to the staircase and tied it tightly to the staircase banister. Her door opened inward, and now she was securely shut in her room.

I ran to grab the telephone and dialed CHC's emergency hotline just as she discovered she was locked in. A caseworker answered my page and could barely hear me over the door kicking and profanities. I told her what I'd done and that I needed help.

She calmly said, "It sounds like you could use an emergency respite. I'm pretty sure we can have someone over to get Lilly in about an hour. Hang in there."

I was jittery and trembling from mental and physical exhaustion. Trying to collect my thoughts I hurried to get all of her medications out of my lockbox in the kitchen so they'd be ready. With a shaking hand I drank a glass of cold water, while it sounded like Lilly was smashing her wicker toy box against her door.

Would she break it open before CHC got here? What then? What if she smashed out her window? WHY hadn't she smashed out her window? I was literally a nervous wreck. I also wondered if I was in trouble for tying her door shut.

Two workers showed up, and Lilly must have heard us talking and knew she was outnumbered because the noise on the other side of her bedroom door stopped.

"Lilly," I said, "you are going to an emergency respite with these women. I'm going to open your door."

She was red-faced and sweaty, and the room was stinky and destroyed. The window blind had been pulled down almost to the floor. I wondered if she had forgotten the window was behind it. She accepted a drink of water that I'd set on the table for her.

"I hate this place. You don't love me. You hate me," she grumbled.

I picked through all the clothes on the floor that had been pulled out of her dresser, trying to find pj's, socks, and clothes for the next day.

After they left, I closed her door and wound up the nylon rope, still amazed that I'd been reduced to using it. *What about my superior foster training? What about being a therapeutic foster home?* I was exhausted, and sat down at the kitchen table and looked at the wall clock. It was only two o'clock in the afternoon.

CHAPTER THIRTY

Some medications were adjusted before Lilly returned to Eastland School after Christmas break. Whether it was that or just getting back into a structured routine, I don't know, but she went on to be named January's "Student of the Month!" (Go figure?) We still had small incidents at home in January but not much in a big way to stress us.

We continued to attend training classes, and sometimes we were envious of the other foster parents because they had things so much easier than Bruce and I. Why, from talking to some of them, they made it sound as if the kids they were fostering behaved no differently than their own children, and we believed them. We figured that there was a reason Lilly landed at our house instead of theirs, and we would be faithful to her.

One class we attended was designed to help us get through tough moments without "losing it." That sounded like a good class and I didn't want to miss it.

While we were there the instructor brought up different scenarios, and we discussed possible ways to solve problems.

The trainer asked, "How many here have ever had their hair pulled?"

A beautifully dressed woman with perfectly coiffed blonde hair raised her hand. I could not picture her hair the least bit messed up.

The instructor urged her to, "tell the class what happened."

"Well, I had two little sisters in the bathtub, and I was bending over the tub washing the one girl's back with a washcloth. She reached out and grabbed my hair with both hands."

"Oh I see," said the instructor, "and what did you do then?"

We were all on the edge of our seats waiting to hear.

The woman blinked and replied, "I pulled *her* hair!"

Our whole class burst out laughing. Not one of us had expected that response.

It so happened the very next month after one of Lilly's baths, that she was standing on the bathmat with a towel wrapped around her as I was putting lotion on her lower legs, when she grabbed my hair with both of her hands. I couldn't believe it. It was like she'd been at the class and was testing me.

I told her to let go, but she wouldn't so I held her upper arms firmly to get her to release me, but she held fast. I remembered what the blonde had admitted and grabbed Lilly's hair. She immediately let go. *Come on, Nealie, how therapeutic was that?*

The only other excitement from my little Student of the Month was damaging the break-proof goggles one day and throwing a glass dish up against the wall another time. Definitely low key incidents in a home usually filled with much livelier action. When would the storm begin again? We didn't have to wait long.

Mid-February just before her eighth birthday, Bruce and I arranged for a respite worker who had been to our house before to come for the evening so we could go out for dinner and do some birthday shopping.

As usual we didn't tell Lilly our plans because of her anxiety issues. We were excited to be going out, and she didn't need too much information. She had been doing so well, and we left with spirits high.

When we returned, water and blue glass pieces were all over the bathroom floor, and the young woman who had come to baby-sit had cuts on both of her hands.

She said Lilly "went nuts" in the bathtub and sloshed tons of water out of the tub before jumping out and squirting shampoo and cream rinse all over the four walls. Then a dripping and naked girl slipped and slid across the floor as she headed towards the bathroom window and tried to break it out with the shampoo bottle.

The young worker, who was soaking wet from the melee, said she tried to stop the window-bashing, and her hands were cut when Lilly knocked a set of five blue glass jars off the windowsill and they shattered.

From there, Lilly ran from the bathroom and grabbed two pictures off the walls and threw them into the hallway. Both of the glass picture fronts were broken and glass went everywhere on the hall floor. It looked like we had a couple hours of cleanup work ahead of us.

Bruce and I worked for forty-five minutes picking up the biggest pieces of glass and soaked the water up off the bathroom floor before we decided to leave the rest for the next day and went to bed. We were exhausted. Sometimes it didn't seem worth trying to get out for an evening.

In the morning I told Lilly her consequences: she would not be allowed to have guests for a birthday party. "I will still make you a very special cake and you will still have presents to open, but after last night's destruction, there will be no party."

She glared at me.

There remained a lot of cleaning up to do from the night before, and I told her she was going to wipe down the walls in the bathroom after I swept up the glass pieces and carried wet towels down to the basement.

When her turn came to wipe shampoo and crème rinse off the bathroom walls, she would have none of it. She was in a conquering mode and it was me she planned to conquer. Bruce was at work and she knew it. She started throwing things, moved her dresser, ripped up a wall hanging, and (along with hundreds of foul words) said, "No, you devil; I will get you, Henry Higgins, JUST YOU WAIT!"

Well, I decided that I wasn't going to wait. Things needed cleaned up and I was alone. I couldn't call CHC every time I felt overwhelmed, so I had an idea. I tied a piece of finger-thickness fuzzy blue yarn to a buttonhole in her blue jean vest.

She was curious and stopped being crazy long enough to let me put it on her. I buttoned it on backwards with the yarn trailing and fastened the end to a doorknob on the far side of her room. I told her that since she didn't want to help me, but only wanted to cause more trouble that she'd have to be in the vest until I was done.

Nealie Rose

The critical incident report I submitted to CHC stated, "I put a little blue jean vest on her backwards and tied heavy blue yarn to the bottom buttonhole. Then I took the 13 foot-long piece of yarn and tied it to a doorknob in the far corner of her bedroom. This gave her full use and mobility of hands and feet and anything she wanted to play with in her room, but secured her until I could clean up last night's glass without her being more destructive and violent, running throughout the house while I cleaned up. This was far less restrictive than her school bus harness, and she was able to do anything she wished mobility-wise except leave her room. I would not have done this unless absolutely necessary for safety."

The vest idea worked, but I felt uneasy about it. It was one thing to try something out of what seemed like necessity. It was an entirely different matter to explain it if someone had come into my house unexpectedly. In short, I did not ever plan on using that method again and saved the vest and yarn so it could be shown to the current caseworker.

My report was received without any backlash by CHC and the county people, probably because we were respected and trusted by all concerned. The entire team was often grabbing at straws, trying to figure out how to keep her safe while effectively helping her at the same time.

I think there was so much uncharted territory with Lilly's case that no one knew exactly what to do (or not do). Her team of people didn't always agree on what was best but we had to figure a way to work together. They were often as stymied as we were. In fact, sometimes we felt like they were looking at us to come up with ideas. If that day were to ever be repeated, I would swallow my pride and call for emergency help from them, hoping it would be available.

I think that there has been more research and study about Reactive Attachment Disorder in the years since Lilly was small, and that's a good thing because there is more awareness about the dangers that undiagnosed and untreated children pose to society.

Professionals are learning that children with RAD are able to heal and progress, provided they have early therapeutic treatment interventions, and people willing to attach to them and love them.

CHAPTER THIRTY-ONE

Lilly's second anniversary in our home came in March. She was eight then, and the winter weather had started breaking. We actually had some sunny days where she could play outside and hunt for bugs. One day I heard glass breaking outside and ran out to find her bashing out the garage windowpanes with a large stick.

"What are you doing, Lilly!?"

Lilly dropped the stick to her side. She was wearing a blue jean jacket, red sweats, and muddy white tennis shoes. She pointed to the window. "I was letting the ladybugs out. They were stuck in the garage."

I guess that was one way to free them. *What was it with her and windows, anyway?*

She didn't seem to fear shattering glass (that was obvious), but why hadn't she made any attempt at breaking the big window in her room? That nagged at the back of my mind. At some time in the future, would that large window become a casualty as well?

Not long after the ladybug incident, Lilly began to self-harm with broken pieces of china from a miniature tea set that was given to her for her birthday. It took us a while to figure out that she had stomped on a tiny cup with her shoe to break it and hid the sharp pieces. When alone for any period of time, she'd use the sharp edges to cut her gums or lips. She had innocently admitted the cause of her wounds, but was secretive as to the whereabouts of the broken pieces of china.

It never occurred to her that anything besides porcelain or china could be used to cut herself. She rarely touched any of the decorative glassware that I had in most windows, but when my mother gave her a doll with a porcelain face and hands, she broke it so she could cut.

We felt that the cutting was a spin-off of the self-harming that she did at two-and-a-half when she had the head banging issues. (I think that feeling pain reminds children with RAD that they can still feel something, because they have experienced so much pain that they can be numb.)

Spring also brought with it the usual no-holds-barred school behavior. We'd seen it the year before when she was seven. In March, to everyone's shock and concern, she mastered removing her bus harness. The day she did that was a long one. She got out of the four-point harness on the bus and removed it, as well as her shoes, socks, and pants.

She climbed over the seats, jumping from one to the other while a worn-out bus aide tried to catch and keep her away from the other four disabled children on the bus.

The driver was upset. Bruce and I knew that if she couldn't be safely transported to and from school, we were all in deep doo-doo.

After hearing the driver's report, I was so angry and ordered her to go straight to her room, which she reduced to a ghastly scene within fifteen minutes. That tiny girl took the mattress off her bed, pushed the bed frame across the room, cracked the hinges off her door, and started to beat on Bruce as he tried to stop her from flipping over her four-drawer dresser.

Bruce at one hundred eighty pounds was not afraid of her, but he was always afraid he might hurt her if he ever became unglued. Lucky for all of us he has a great deal of self-control.

If we had been a reality show the whole world would have been riveted to the screen. I watched as he single-handedly hauled her mattress, dresser, and the bed frame out of her room all the while fending off kicks, punches, and flying objects.

I put in an emergency call to CHC and told them that someone had to come quickly. Then I frantically searched for the discarded blue jean vest that had been put with a pile of junk to go out with the trash.

Bruce had just emptied Lilly's room when a tiny lady from CHC arrived "to help." I explained to Tiny Lady that I felt we needed to secure Lilly again until she calmed down or we'd ALL get hurt.

She seemed to agree because she made no objection to putting the backward vest on Lilly again. Lilly was on her "safety leash" in the emptied room with our collective surveillance for close to an hour before she regained her senses and gave up the overwhelming fierceness.

At that point we took off the vest and gave her a trial chance to play peacefully with a few toys in her empty room with the baby gate up.

Unfortunately for Bruce, her room would have to be entirely re-assembled for bedtime.

Tiny Lady stayed until she felt it was safe to leave, and after she left, I threw the vest with the yarn still attached in the kitchen wastebasket. If it ever got to that point again, Lilly would have to be taken out of our home until she was safer because the whole thing was getting scarier and scarier. We did not want to be in the newspaper because she had boxed us into yet another "extreme measures" corner.

Sometimes a picture of the potential nightmare went across the screen of my mind:

"Illinois couple ties tiny girl to door," or "Foster mother ropes child's door tightly shut."

First and foremost was our marriage and integrity. If either of those unraveled or came into question, it would ruin us and her chances as well. We came to the conclusion that we must tread very carefully because one misstep could potentially destroy everything in our lives. My mind went back to her angelic face and peaceful demeanor the day Mr. and Mrs. Garth came for dinner. They might not have believed the real story.

What average American would?

CHAPTER THIRTY-TWO

Though our world swirled chaotically around us as we continued to work with Lilly, we did have some times that were comparable with that of any other family with an eight-year-old. We were driving to visit my parents one Saturday, and she had to be reminded several times not to interrupt Bruce and me as we talked to each other in the car. Each time she complied and waited her turn. On the way home she began to engage Bruce in a little game they usually played when it was just the two of them in the car.

She said, "Ring! Ring!"

He answered, "Hello? Jasmine?"

Back and forth the play-banter went until I had listened to enough and interjected, "Hey, I thought you two agreed not to play that game when I was in the car?"

Lilly became indignant and chastised me saying, "Mom, you are 'rupting me. I hate to tell you this, (and she lowered her voice) but you are so, so rude."

In her own little way, she had a point.

We tried to keep her life as balanced as she would allow, considering her conduct. She tried a couple dance lessons and loved it. Actually, the appeal was wearing the ballerina outfit and carrying the pretty shoe tote that went with it.

The night before her second lesson she made poopy "skid marks" in her panties. Standard procedure was that she had to scrub them in the basement laundry sink. That night she kicked them across the room and said, "I won't, and you can't make me!"

I left them where they landed and didn't respond.

The next morning she put on her pink outfit and had her tote on her arm. "Mom, let's go! I can't be late!"

I was sitting in the kitchen and slowly looked up at her and calmly said, "I won't, and you can't make me."

Understanding immediately dawned on her, and she dropped the tote and raced to find the panties that she'd kicked aside the night before. Grabbing them up, she rushed down to the basement to clean them, then scrambled back up the steps and scooped up her shoe bag as I stood ready to go with my purse and keys in hand. I smiled at her, and we left.

I waited in the little waiting room during her class, and afterward a brooding and angry Lilly came out with the teacher. Evidently she had gotten into someone's purse and taken a chocolate bar when she should have been dancing. The teacher said it was the second time in two lessons that she had been doing things other than dancing.

It became clear to me that wearing the outfit wasn't the only thing that drew Lilly to dance class. We decided the lessons had to end because we could not risk a major explosion and possible harm to the other little girls. I was sad for her but could see no way around it, and thought maybe we could try again when she was a little older.

Not long after we arrived home from dance, a CHC woman picked up Lilly for a day-respite which included going to a movie theater. During the movie, she did one better than just a candy bar out of a purse. She took a man's coat, wallet, and keys while the movie was playing.

I wondered where our journey with her would end. She had been with us two years, and when we saw improvement in little areas, we were joyous. But she was growing some in size and at eight, was fast becoming a much bigger challenge for us physically when she "went off." Our conglomerate team of teachers and CHC workers had started using descriptive terms such as "mania mode" and "massive meltdown."

The respites with the Pancer family were still not going well. They (of all people) had to cut short a respite in April and send Lilly to an emergency CHC group home. They said they "feared for the safety" of everyone in their home. Mrs. Pancer advised that we seriously look into residential treatment.

There it was again, that word "residential." Residential facilities are where kids live and go to school year-round when they can't be safely kept in a family. Security is tight and there are visiting hours. It meant only one thing to me at the time. It meant we had failed Lilly and there was no hope for her. I did not want to consider "residential."

When she returned to Eastland after the disrupted weekend respite with the Pancer's, she had three awful days in row. Her teacher wrote, "Spent 9:15 to 2:00 with the HELP team, (all day long). Hitting, biting, throwing toys, chairs, knocking over divider walls, spitting in faces . . . physical and verbal aggression all day."

I felt hope dwindling and called my mom and best friend and asked them to pray. That was something I'd asked them to do many times before, but this time I told them they had better step it up. From day one, my friend was always worried for my safety with Lilly, so I think that is what motivated her prayers more than anything. I knew there were many others who would pray for her, but it could be wearying because unlike cancer where you either die or go into remission, this "condition" seemed never-ending.

Interestingly though, when sincere corporate prayers were being said for her, we'd receive a glimmer of light, a spark of hope, a new direction, a helpful medicine change, or maybe just a day or two of household peace. That alone would often be enough for us to recharge and keep going.

On the lighter side, that April I decided to get some spring cleaning done before school was out and it would be impossible. I started in the den first, and washed the two windows, took down and washed curtains and blinds, cleaned baseboards, and even got a ladder to take down the glass ceiling globe from the light fixture. I re-hung the clean blinds and curtains, and when Lilly got home from school, I got up on the ladder to return the glass globe to the light fixture.

She noticed how nice everything looked and her eyebrows shot up as she excitedly asked, "Will you pay me a quarter if I sweep the rug?"

She had used the upright vacuum cleaner before, so I agreed. She ran to the coat closet down the hall and wheeled it into the den, shutting the door behind her.

I soon heard the vacuum roar to life, followed by immediate screaming and coughing. I burst into the room to see what had happened and could hardly see for the dust in the air.

She had unzipped the outer jacket casing and torn the sweeper bag inside it before turning on the vacuum. Lilly had unwittingly managed to get dirty gray dust on every square inch of the room.

Concerned that she'd breathe in what hadn't settled yet, I pulled her out of the room and shut the door before I started crying. In the back of my mind, I knew it was a story that could be told to the family in the years to come, only I wasn't sure how many years I had left if I continued to be Lilly Angel's mother.

As long as we had been married, Bruce had worked at least fifty hours a week. That didn't change when Lilly joined our family. He was always helpful and tried to ease my load at home. I had an entry in my diary dated about the time of this particular chapter that read:

"Bruce worked about sixty hours this week and I felt the strain of managing the house, Lilly, and Torie. I also missed my companion. Today he is home and I am so happy about it. Evidently I didn't know how happy, until I asked him if he'd watch Lilly while I went upstairs to iron a few of my clothes. He said, "Sure."

I smiled and sang out in a very deep manly voice, "I'm on my way, I'm on my way, I'm on my way upstairs!" Surprised, I caught myself.

He had been reading something, but stopped and looked intently at me.

Using the same deep voice, I asked him, *"Are you afraid?"*

Sometimes all it took for me to be recharged was to be around Bruce. He gave me immeasurable support and always had my back. When he was home I could count on him to handle things with Lilly and do it well.

One time before school ended and summer break started, she cut her arm with a steak knife that had accidentally been left out. She had never touched a knife before at our home even though she would threaten verbally about using knives at times. When Bruce took the knife from her and asked her why she cut her arm, her lower lip trembled and she started crying.

She said, "I want to see Jesus!"

Bruce sighed and said, "Well, you'll just have to WAIT to see Jesus, and we're not leaving knives where you can get them."

A week later she ran out into the street outside my kitchen window and flagged down an approaching motorist. Between that alarming incident and the knife cut, we once again wondered where things were headed. Summer vacation hadn't yet started, and I feared it might be a very long summer.

CHC had found a new respite family for Lilly. Bob and Lorna were in their early thirties, and they lived in a big house that sat back from the road on ten acres, and they had an in-ground swimming pool. Bob was as big as a bear and had a deep voice, and we thought he would be perfect for keeping Lilly in line. The first weekend respite was in June at their home.

Whenever I went to pick up my girl to bring her home after a respite, I would check in her suitcase for stolen items. This time I found nothing of Bob and Lorna's and was thrilled. She hadn't even been tempted, and Lorna said everything had gone wonderfully.

The next day while she was at Eastland for the last week of school, the teacher called me to tell me she had come to school with a "pants-full," only it was not of the sort the term usually meant. She had in her underwear nail polish, lipstick, eye shadow, and a digital thermometer. Needless to say, Lorna didn't want any of them returned when I called to tell her about it.

The subsequent visit to Bob and Lorna's was two weeks later. Nothing much happened that time except Lilly had gotten up on a top bunk bed and kicked out the window screen near it, and then climbed onto the roof of their house.

They took everything in stride though, even when the third visit got a little hairier. Lilly threw and shattered a drinking glass in the kitchen, fed the fish in their big aquarium a whole quart of fish food, and when Bob asked her why she had taken a crayon and scribbled all over one of their walls, her response was, "Don't you know I have problems?"

All summer long she went to their house every other weekend, and in between there was a CHC "Summer Group" that was an all-day field trip once a week. A van would transport the foster kids to various activities as a group. After I dropped Lilly off at a nearby CHC group home, their white van would take off for the outing.

Once they went an hour away to a big zoo. Lilly did reasonably well there, but on the way home she started swinging a water thermos on a strap in the van, and it hit several kids. This forced the driver to stop as six kids and three adults endured a long thirty minutes of screaming and restraints in a hot sweaty van in July.

I knew how they must've felt because I'd taken Lilly to swim in my parents' pool and on the way home I had to pull over four times because of unbuckling, kicking seats, and trying to get out of my moving car. She certainly knew how to ruin a perfect summer day.

When Ingrid from across the street wasn't busy, the highly educated professional would come over to our porch and play "Pet Store." Ingrid knew there were some health risks from being around Lilly but she cautiously kept up on the relationship. After a while she wondered if maybe she'd able to walk her to the nearby park for fifteen minutes at a time.

On one of their short outings, Lilly saw a cat down the street and took off running after it, leaving Ingrid standing panic-stricken. She started running after Lilly, hollering desperately in her German English, "Lilly, no! Come back! Don't chase the kitty-cat!"

Lilly could have cared less that the slim, long legged, and dignified Ingrid was being forced to scream and run knee-to-chest after her.

After the incident was over, and Ingrid was telling me about it, she said, "Lilly just kept running and running. I didn't know where the kitty-cat went, but she ran around a corner. I went around the corner, too, and saw her run up some steps and right into a duplex!"

I looked at her and said, "You're kidding?" I tried to picture the scene and asked, "Then what did you do?"

Ingrid put her hand over her heart and replied, "Well, I ran in too!"

"What?!" I blinked, trying again to envision it as she continued,

"And there, standing by his stove in his kitchen, was a man in his UNDERPANTS!"

We both started giggling and laughing. "What happened then?"

"Lilly ran back out, and I ran out, too!"

She was still shaken from the escapade. She went on to tell me that after catching up with the runaway, Lilly bit her on the hand.

After that she never took Lilly anywhere unless I was there, too.

Both she and the Smiths who lived below her had a good many windows looking out over our property. They'd see Lilly outside during the summer catching bugs while wearing old dress-up formals that I purchased at the Goodwill for her. They might also catch a glimpse of her peeing beside the garage or picket fence and call me on the phone, and I'd call Lilly indoors.

"How do you always know?" she'd demand.

"I always know EVERYTHING," was usually my solemn reply. She never figured it out, and there were other things she did that showed that this swearing-like-a-sailor, bird-flipping, death threatening eight-and-a half-year-old was an innocent at heart. There was so much that went over her head.

There were certain tunes to popular songs that she knew were meant to be loudly sung, and she sang the lyrics however she thought they went. She would ride her bike out on the sidewalk and sing with gusto any song that was her favorite at the time. The words were all wrong, but she had the tune down perfectly on a song that used the word 'complicated.' The only problem was Lilly's loud and joyful version was, *"CONSTIPATED . . ."*

CHAPTER THIRTY-THREE

CHC wanted Lilly to go to Camp Hope, which was a week-long special-needs camp. Developmentally, she was much younger than her age and I had sincere doubts about her making it through even one day of camp, but CHC thought we should give it a try.

Bruce and I attended a pre-camp meeting where a group of camp reps came to answer foster parents' questions and register the kids. The event was set up outside on the lawn at CHC.

While we were there I asked a camp rep, "Has there ever been a time when a child was not welcome at camp?"

"Only once in eighteen years. There was this violent boy who was huge, and he wasn't allowed to return because of all the trouble he caused. Don't worry about anything."

I've heard that before.

While we were there I noticed a skinny, dark-haired girl going from one person to the next throwing grass from the ground on their heads. She tried to grind it in with her hand and would laugh. We were told her name was Gertie. She was around Lilly's age and new to the agency. Her foster mother told me Gertie's birth parents had often kept her in a dog cage. What a sheltered world I'd lived in before fostering. Gertie would also be at Camp Hope in August.

Even though we thought camp would be a fiasco we hoped that the wonderful opportunity would somehow be successful. Everyone told us, "Don't worry. Just enjoy your week while she is at camp."

Bruce and I thought maybe we could take a trip to Put-in-Bay, which is on Lake Erie, while she was gone that week. Maybe it would work out. Was I the only camp-worrier in the equation?

It was still on my mind as I counted out six quarters for her allowance and placed them out of her reach up on the kitchen windowsill. She loved to get those quarters each Friday.

I went to look for her and found her with three plastic horses lined up on the living room floor. There was a Barbie doll in her hands, as she play-acted and talked to one of the horses who was being much too wild to ride. "Thunder, whoa, boy!"

I sat down on the floor beside her and watched. Her hair had grown to her waist and it was pulled back. Her left thumb was in her mouth when she wasn't speaking to the horse. There were usually thoughtful pauses in her play-acting where she'd suck on her thumb and think, then take it out of her mouth and continue the play dialogue. She placed the Barbie on the floor and picked up the horse she called Thunder. She had him buck and kick while his hooves clattered on the wood floor.

I picked up the Barbie and stood her up near Thunder. I said, "Thunder, you'll scare these other horses. Shhh . . . Settle down Thunder, whoa . . . I won't hurt you. I just wanted to pet you. Whoa, boy."

Lilly didn't mind me entering her play. She had Thunder immediately settle down and come near Barbie. The doll's plastic hand stroked Thunder's hard, shiny, black back.

It seemed like a good time to tell her why I came to find her.

"Hey, Lilly there are some things in your room that need to be picked up and put away. It will only take you a few minutes."

Abruptly, she stood up and pointed down at me. "No! I won't!"

I looked quietly up at her and wondered what a camp counselor would do if she refused to obey requests. I broke eye contact and looked at the Barbie still in my hand. "Well, you have six quarters. You could pay me with two of those to do it. I like money."

She put her hands on her hips and replied, "Fine. Go for it!"

I spent about five or six minutes picking up and putting things in order. I called her to the kitchen when I was done so she could pay me. I took down two quarters from her stack as she watched, and I pocketed them.

Later that evening she stole mints from Bruce's dresser. I caught her before she could eat any, and when he came home from work she had to pay him a quarter and return his mints.

The next morning she took a box of granola bars and hid them under her bed. She had eaten one bar when I discovered the theft, and I told her she would have to pay a quarter for the one she'd eaten, and to put the box back. She did, and as I paid myself another quarter from her dwindling stack, she blurted out, "I only have TWO LEFT!"

I nodded and commented, "Yes, you are lucky."

Lilly looked at me sadly and replied, "No, I was lucky when I had SIX."

It took what seemed like forever for me to get her packed with every requirement on her camp list, as well as pack for myself and Bruce for our Put-in-Bay trip.

After two hours of endless wilderness driving, we pulled our car into the camp's crunchy gravel parking lot. Bruce couldn't find a place to park because people had jammed the lot every which way with cars and trucks. He had to pull around and park along the entrance drive near a muddy ditch.

As soon as the car was stopped, Lilly unbuckled quickly and asked, "Can I get out?"

I turned around a little and asked, "Ready to check out this place?"

Her door flew open and Bruce said, "Wait until we get all your stuff out of the trunk!"

We three maneuvered the mud and little stones as we headed toward the woodsy check-in area building where people were milling about.

I could tell Lilly was anxious and excited at the same time, because her thumb would be in her mouth one minute, and then she would take it out and jerk her head around to look at the other kids or the cabins covering the grounds.

We saw lots of people and young campers that we knew, including little Gertie. I wondered if Lilly would want to hang around her because they both had such huge issues.

I watched Lilly closely to make sure she didn't wander off before we had her checked in. She was wearing navy shorts and a blue and yellow striped T-shirt, old tennis shoes and her gold rimmed glasses. I had pulled her hair up into a bun on top of her head and she looked pretty cute. We had been told not to pack any nice clothes because they might get mud on them. I had to smile at that because she always had magic marker, jelly, chocolate, or lunch all over her shirts, as well as holes chewed in them. (I had to hide any good outfits from her to save for going shopping or to appointments. Sometimes they didn't even last a day.)

Our girl seemed to be happy to be at the camp and didn't seem to care that we were leaving, which made it so much easier for us, but I was a little sad about that.

We spent the next four days in the Sandusky, Ohio area and had a blast. Torie and Hannah took care of Baler and Peek at the house while we were gone, and the cats were probably kicking up their paws at their own little vacation.

We arrived home one day before we needed to return to Camp Hope to pick up Lilly. Since I wasn't at camp with her, I did not have firsthand information at what had transpired while we were speeding around the island in a golf cart. It seemed to me that some counselors were looking at us when we arrived as if to say, "*You are the ones who brought that kid here.*" Paranoia was setting in.

My diary, dated 8-1-02 best summed up the camp experience: "Lilly had a horrrrendous week at camp. She bit her counselor repeatedly, tried to hit her with a burning stick from the fire, peed on her as she was being held on her lap, stayed up ALL night, tried to escape, crunched her eyeglasses into a ball, and on and on. She has been home forty-eight hours and the behavior has continued. We've had to take all privileges from her and we decided she's got to earn each one back slowly. Tomorrow we go to our first appointment with a new counselor, Bridget Sommerly. She is a severe behavior and attachment disorder therapist."

CHAPTER THIRTY-FOUR

Bridget Sommerly was a respected lady who counseled desperate families with difficult children. Indeed, we were desperate and had a child who gave new meaning to the word "difficult." How about adding some other "d" words such as defiant, deliberate, defecating, destructive, devious, and developmentally disabled?

We found out at our first session that Bridget was kind, all business, and her method of working with Lilly would be most unusual. She had Bruce and I sit on a small couch with Lilly lying across our laps with her head (and teeth!) on a pillow by Bruce's right arm. Her legs and feet were across my lap. We felt very much in the hot seat, and she was the reclining offering. Bridget would angle her chair so she would have an easy view of Lilly's face just six feet away. The little kid on our laps liked the closeness of us, but disliked being in Bridget's office.

This wasn't the interesting play therapy she had been used to with Kathi Beadle over the previous few years. Kathi had recommended Bridget though, because she'd reached a point where she felt play therapy wasn't helping, and Lilly was headed toward residential if there weren't some definite changes soon. So began our weekly trip to see Bridget.

Those visits were welcomed by Bruce and me but Lilly did not always like to go. The week would be reviewed as she reclined across our laps on each visit. She would sometimes be very cute and sweet, and other times she'd glare at Bridget with her arms crossed or turn her face away.

It was usually rather unpleasant for all of us but we still felt we needed to go to help her make some progress. If she cooperated with the dialogue she'd be rewarded with candy, and we would take her to Bob Evans for dinner afterwards. We didn't need to worry about breaking the bank because that didn't happen very often. As a matter of fact, I wondered what Bridget would do if Lilly went into a full-blown rampage in her office?

Besides Bridget being a new addition to the team, CHC added Sasha as well. Sasha wasn't a social worker but she was the mother of four who had been trained to help with the foster kids. Lilly loved to hear that Sasha was coming but didn't always treat her well.

Sasha was fun but firm, and I learned some things from her. If Lilly would start screaming, shouting, crying, etc., Sasha would say, "Scream and cry as much as you want to feel better." That somehow comforted Lilly as well as made her want to stop.

We started doing a similar version of that when she would call us every foul name in her huge repertoire trying to get a reaction out of us. I'd say very calmly, "How many bad words do you know?" or "Do you think you could keep swearing for five whole minutes?" I'd look at her expectantly. If she wasn't in MM (mania mode), she would get mad and quit because nobody was going to make her do anything she didn't want to, and that included swearing. We tried it with the spitting as well, (without making fun of her), and curiously asked if she could spit fifty times without stopping.

There was nothing that worked every time, but we were always looking for new ways to help her (and us). One trick I had tried a couple times helped her to snap out of some terrible behavior. Actually, the first time was an accident. She had me so worn out and shaken that I dropped a bowl of food and it landed with a crash on the floor.

She instantly forgot all about her bad mood and violence and helped me clean up and consoled me about the mess it made.

I remembered that, and occasionally tried to make something "happen" that would reverse what was in progress, and sometimes it worked.

I remember "spraining" my ankle one day and she had an instant heart change toward me. She turned into the best little nurse in the world and said, "Mom, Mom, sit down on the floor and I will fix you up." She ran to the cupboard for the Ace roll and hurried back with it, sliding to a stop beside me on the smooth floor. She very gently bent over me while sitting on both of her knees, and with her little hands she carefully wrapped my ankle with the bandage.

"I'm sorry I give you a hard time. You are a good mom. There, is that better?"

I would be sure to talk about that at our next session with Bridget, because Lilly needed to hear good things said about her. I knew she had heard very little positive feedback in her short lifetime.

In the fall of 2002 Lilly had lived with us for over two and half years. Joy was married and her son Pete was walking. Torie was beginning her final year of high school. Hannah left us that August to get married. Tina Wells was seven and had formed strong bonds with Ann, Marty, and Sarah. (Tina was thriving at school and in the community as well.) The sisters still got together regularly unless Lilly was too unstable or unpredictable in dangerous ways.

Speaking of that, she was without a dresser then and was using cardboard boxes for her clothes because she had smashed her four-drawer dresser to pieces, and it was out by the curb for pickup.

When the bus screeched to a halt right beside the destroyed dresser, it wasn't a good sign.

Lilly walked past it and up the steps and sat in a seat.

I stood on the sidewalk wondering with some trepidation how the school year would begin. Through the bus windows, I could see her aide walk over and redirect her to a seat that had been prepared with the harness.

Lilly saw it and let loose with kicking and screaming, so I ran up onto the bus to help, and she kicked and slapped me and the aide before we finally got her buckled in. Once she was fully immobilized I stepped down off the bus and turned to wave goodbye.

She had her hand by the window and her middle finger was up.

"Have a great day," I mouthed as I walked past the dresser parts and back into the house. I guess I was getting used to that kind of a life, because it wasn't hard to get on with my day when the bus pulled away in the mornings. What good did it do me or Lilly to worry all day anyway?

It was still early September and there were days after she went to school when I'd weed around our many perennials. The flowers still looked colorful and I liked to pick bouquets of dahlias and blue bell-flowers to put on the table. There was one bush with white flowers next to the bell-flowers that seemed to attract little beetles that seemed to attract Lilly.

Ten days into the school year she ran outside to catch bugs after school. I watched her out of the kitchen window as I prepared dinner. She had on jean shorts and a little green checked top, and her hair was still up in the ponytail that I'd fixed that morning. *It must have been a good day at school.* She was all over that white flower bush, and I assumed she was probably catching dozens of those little beetles.

After a while she came through the back door into the kitchen and headed to the bathroom. I stopped her to make sure she hadn't brought in any contraband bugs, but she hadn't.

On the way back from the bathroom she stopped in front of me and said, "Mom, I put a beetle in my ear, and he won't come out."

I frowned incredulously at her. "What? You put a beetle in your ear?" I felt sick. I'd seen a movie once where a scarab beetle crawled in a sleeping man's ear and into his brain and he had gone mad. I wanted to throw up, and fought to stay calm. "Lilly, get in the car right now! We're going to the emergency room and they'll get it out."

She looked at me and smacked her ear a few times. "I can hear him. He is very angry."

Sure enough, I could hear him, too. He was making a clicking sound, and I thought I'd faint before we got in the car.

The hospital wasn't busy, and Lilly was put in a patient room almost as soon as we got there. A young female nurse sat Lilly up on an exam table and I sat down on a stool nearby. Then the doctor came in to examine her and checked both ears by peering through a black otoscope.

He nodded his head and said, "Yes, there's a beetle in the left ear. We'll just flush it out." He put his instrument in a pocket and left.

Lilly was still smacking her ear, and I could still hear the beetle inside it clicking. I had to force myself to think of something else –anything else -while we waited with the young nurse.

Soon a woman breezed in and while Lilly sat up on the exam table, the nurse placed a pink basin under Lilly's ear, and sprayed water into it from a syringe. On the second plunge of water, the beetle was flushed out and actually went flying across the room. The younger nurse hurried after it, probably to catch it and do away with it, but Lilly shouted, "That's MY beetle!"

I was so relieved they got the bug out of her ear, but I was angry at the same time because they put that stupid beetle in a lidded container for her to take home.

A few days later as I was putting her to bed, she was especially quiet and seemed thoughtful. All covered up, her head rested peacefully on the pillow.

I crouched beside her bed at eye level and smiled.

She started her prayers: "Dear God, thank you for Mommy and Daddy. Thank you for Tina and Baler and Peek. Thank you for me. Amen."

I gave her a kiss on the forehead and rose to leave. I was about to pass through her doorway when she said, "Mom."

I stopped and turned to look at her.

"I didn't want to tell you this, but I put another beetle in my ear."

CHAPTER THIRTY-FIVE

Still shuddering over the beetle misadventures, I packed Lilly for a respite at Bob and Lorna's. Lorna was a beautiful petite brunette, and as I had mentioned earlier, Bob was a big guy. His rather large mid-section was the only thing that kept him from looking like a serious body builder.

We had a contented little girl in the back seat as we drove along the country roads to their house. It was too cool outside for Lilly to swim in their pool so Bruce had packed her little blue bicycle into the back of our Jeep, beside her gray suitcase. We dropped a happy girl and the bike off and forgot all about our troubles, which is exactly what foster parents are instructed to do when their child is at a respite. We were told later about the events of the weekend.

Friday evening had been non-eventful.

Saturday was cool and sunny, and Lorna had invited her little niece over to ride bicycles with Lilly on their expansive cement drive. She had gotten the girls situated with their bikes, saw that they were having fun, and went indoors.

Bob was also outside behind the house, wearing only swim trunks and tall wading boots while he worked on the end-of-season pool chores.

After a time of riding, Lilly asked the other girl if they could switch bikes. (Lilly's bike was quite functional but had been wrecked many times and looked pretty battered. The other little girl's bike was shiny and new and was a recent birthday present.) She had refused to trade, so Lilly began brooding while she rode her old blue bike.

It wasn't long before she stopped her bike abruptly, got off, and threw it down. She then said, "Then forget it! I'm not riding bikes with you anymore!"

She began to run across the large front acreage towards a woods not far away.

Startled, the little girl ran around to the back for Uncle Bob, who was still working on the pool, to tell him Lilly was running away.

He dropped what he was doing and immediately made fast tracks around the house just in time to see her enter the woods. He started running after her as fast as his big boots would let him, but she had a good head-start and had already disappeared into the trees. Bob awkwardly crashed through the trees and brush while he yelled desperately for her to come back.

He was very alarmed not only because she was in his care but because there was a highway on the other side of the woods, and he couldn't risk her getting that far.

Of course Lilly ignored him, and she had a good lead. She broke through to the edge of the highway before he could get to her, darted across it and ran up to a house on the other side. Then she frantically pounded her fists on the front door and screamed, "Help! Help! That man is chasing me!"

Someone opened the door to a small "very frightened" little girl, and must have seen a huge man in swim trunks and wading boots clomping across the highway straight toward them.

Needless to say, Lilly was immediately rescued and the police were called.

It took a couple hours to straighten things out once the police arrived, but Bob told his side of the story and CHC was contacted to verify it. A social worker had to drive clear out to that location before things could be wrapped up.

Bob's humiliation had been great, and it was sad because he was such an awesome and kind man.

There wasn't a single person at CHC who could tell the story without being in stitches. I think it made them feel better about themselves in their own misfortunes with Lilly Angel.

The group of us was growing.

Back on the school scene, the second year at Eastland wasn't going so well. School personnel were having a difficult time just keeping Lilly where she was supposed to be. The first week of school she had managed to hide in the Phys Ed teacher's office, and while everyone was searching for her, she loaded up her pockets with items from the teacher's desk. Then she discovered a big pair of shears and cut up her waist length hair.

That evening at home I did what I could to even up her long locks, wondering if I should just cut it much shorter. Her hair tangled so easily and she chewed on the ends, which was gross.

I didn't shorten it then, but I did in October because the hair problem was becoming a huge morning conflict. I cut about five inches off the length and she cried after seeing the hair on the floor. I found out it was fine for *her* to chop it up any time she found scissors, but not for me to cut the actual length off. I felt so bad about her genuine sadness that I gave her a five dollar-bill as a form of apology.

The shorter hair did help the mornings go better. Instead of ten things making her very angry before school, there were only nine. If she was in a snit before she boarded her bus, then the ride would be miserable for everyone else on board. That time period was filled with reports such as:

"Bus driver said today was the worst day ever on bus. Throwing shoes, getting out of harness, jumping over seats, violent actions . . ."

"Bus driver stated that Lilly got out of her harness this afternoon and caused havoc. She threw her shoes at other riders and was spitting across aisles."

One morning only minutes after Bruce had put her on the school bus, it circled around the block and screeched to a halt back at our curb. Bruce heard it and said, "Just great."

He went out and the bus door opened for him to board. Lilly was loose and was swearing, spitting, and kicking at the female aide. Bruce quickly overpowered her and securely refastened the harness. The aide sat behind the seat to hold onto the back of the harness so she couldn't squirm out.

It was too bad if any of the other children with disabilities needed any assistance because Lilly's care was all-consuming.

A week later her teacher said, "Lilly had a complete meltdown. She emptied and threw several boxes of toys, pencils, etc. all over the classroom. She tried to bite me when I restrained her. The HELP team was called."

After school that day the bus attempted to bring her home *twice*, but both times the driver had to turn around and return to the school. After the second time, the HELP team went up into the bus and captured her. Using teamwork, they took her back to the school's safe room until we could get there.

Thank goodness Bruce was not at work and was able to go with me. He sat in the backseat with her while I drove home because she started up as soon as she was buckled in.

Earlier, she had bitten through a mesh glove on the hand of a HELP team member and into the soft tissue. Both she and the woman would have to get blood tests for HIV and Hepatitis B. Lilly was required to go to our family doctor to be tested, which was one more appointment I had to schedule and take her to.

At that point the principal and assistant principal both expressed "serious doubts" about their ability to continue to keep Lilly and others safe.

I was beginning to feel like we were quickly running out of options for her. Where did this train stop? We were also seeing increased anger and aggression at our counseling sessions with Bridget Sommerly.

Lilly Angel was more work than we could have imagined in our wildest dreams. Could anyone ever have thought up all the possible scenarios that had actually occurred? Even CHC was wondering how much longer they could help us maintain her in our home. Everything was once again pointing to residential treatment.

Then a strange thing happened. December first rolled around, and for the next six weeks, she was a reasonably well-behaved child. Not one incident report in all that time. Not one act of violence at home or at school. She was wonderful in the classroom and helpful at home.

During that time, Joy and Pete's father divorced (*sigh*), Torie turned 18, and I once again started ever so slightly considering adoption. Bruce was not remotely convinced that it was a good idea and said six good weeks was not enough to sway him because he'd seen too much.

When it came to Lilly, I was such a hopeful person that I often refused to consider the negative. I figured if we could get a safe adoption contract set up with the county, maybe everything would be okay.

Safe contracts were called that because they had every base covered for the foster parents to feel good about going ahead on a special-needs adoption. Medical insurance, counseling services, a monthly stipend for expenses, (and maybe if you were lucky) perks like braces and summer camp.

I eventually came to see that even if we could get a contract that was "safe," we'd really be on our own with no CHC emergency hotline and respite, no agency babysitters to come to the house, no training classes . . . Our whole support network as we knew it would evaporate.

Bruce and I needed to have that support network because of the severity of Lilly's issues. The necessity of these things wouldn't have been so concerning if Lilly hadn't required a huge network, and once again, she wouldn't have been a typical adoption.

I wanted to adopt because I did not want her to have to leave and readjust to another home and to another set of people. I felt sincerely committed (and somewhat obligated) to her. But the truth was that had any other family come to take and adopt her, she would most assuredly have landed back in our home sooner or later anyway. How would they have handled her? Lilly truly was a child who needed to have a community raise her.

The six weeks of unusual reprieve ended around mid-January when Joy and my cute little grandson moved in following the divorce. Joy and Pete, who was then fifteen months, had two of the upstairs bedrooms, while Torie still had her same old room.

Lilly was protective of Pete but not overly obsessed with his whereabouts in the house. She always seemed to have her own little agenda going on, and it didn't necessarily include him. Her plans were about what she'd be playing, eating for dinner, or getting by me. Always up to something.

CHAPTER THIRTY-SIX

We went to Bridget's for therapy on a Monday after school, toward the end of January. The session started poorly because Lilly did not want to follow the rules of eye contact and lying on her back across our laps. She wanted to fidget with her little pillow and chew on the neckline of her shirt. She refused to look at Bridget, turned her head away, would not answer, and sucked her thumb.

All of those things were not allowed during the therapy time that Bridget always tried to keep pleasant. She was neither loud nor overbearing, and therapy was just talking about the week's ups and downs and helping Lilly troubleshoot for herself to some degree.

That particular time she tried to bite Bruce's arm, pinched him, and hit him as we kept trying to keep her on our laps. She had become enraged at Bridget and it seemed she was trying to get loose to go after her.

I wondered if Bridget was scared, but she didn't act like it. Bruce and I did our best to keep Lilly where she was.

Finally the session ended, and as we were leaving the inner office to exit through a waiting room, Lilly tried to bolt out the exit. I grabbed her leopard-print coat sleeve just in time or she would have run out of the building.

She flung herself onto the waiting room floor and kicked at us while on her back. Horrible words were spewed through the offices, and people rushed to see what in the world was going on. Bridget instructed us to take her around the corner behind a reception desk to keep the drama to a minimum because we all knew that drama would feed the problem.

Bruce and I got her arms and legs and carried her around behind the desk, but as soon as we put her down, she jumped up and picked up a large office roller chair and flipped it over. At that point Bridget suggested a call to the police, and we agreed.

They arrived quickly, and soon two uniformed men stood over the little girl in the leopard-trimmed coat.

Lilly snarled as she got up from the floor. "Take me to jail! Right now! I hate deez damn people!"

The officers looked at each other, then at Bridget and us. Lilly was almost nine, but looked about seven and didn't even have all of her front teeth. The senior officer cleared his throat and looked sternly down at the little girl. "No, you aren't going to jail. But I warn you, you had better start behaving."

She raised her arm and hit the base of the upturned chair. "I want to go to JAIL! I don't want to listen to these damn bitches!"

We all knew she had us over a barrel. The policemen could only authoritatively buckle her into the car-seat in our car, and give the little darling a lecture. She seemed to enjoy their attention and getting buckled, and settled down accordingly; so we got in and started the drive home.

I sat tensely in the front seat almost afraid to breathe. *This can't be over. I can feel it.*

About two minutes into the drive, I heard what I had been dreading: the un-clicking of her seatbelt. It is a unique sound that my ears had been trained to catch.

She stood up on the backseat and used her foot to kick at Bruce as he drove.

He pulled into a parking lot and went around to the back to grab her.

"Call the police," he barked.

I did, and paramedics were sent. I wasn't needed and there was nothing to do but sit in our car during all the excitement. Somehow I was trying to disentangle my emotions from what was happening.

Then Bruce opened my car door and said, "They are strapping her to a gurney now, and they'll take her to Columbia Children's to be admitted. I'm going to ride along. Please call CHC and let them know what's going on. We'll meet in the ER."

That woke me out of my "everything's normal" fantasy. I hadn't thought of CHC. My hands mechanically pressed the phone buttons. A caseworker would meet us at the hospital.

I drove carefully to the hospital while ambivalent thoughts raced through my mind. *Lilly just had a great six weeks. She has been with us almost three years. I don't want her in the psychiatric ward. Will she bounce back? Will she be in long? Will she have to go to a residential facility now? What is happening?*

Once inside Columbia, I found Bruce conversing with a male nurse in a small waiting area of the emergency wing. I could hear Lilly's shouts and cursing coming from one of the patient rooms down the hall. Bruce was explaining how she had come to be there, as well as answering questions about her medications.

The person from the agency arrived a little while later, and we three sat in the waiting area and talked. Bruce told us Lilly was still tied down securely while in ER because she was combative. He also said the paramedics had covered her face with a cloth during transport to keep her from spitting on them. It sounded crazy that a little girl would be handled like that. I knew they hadn't had a choice, but I was having difficulty thinking about them actually tying her arms and legs down.

The strength in numbers helped tremendously. Besides myself and Bruce in the hospital emergency room, there was a social worker, two nurses, the ER doctor, and a children's psychiatric doctor on call. We were all holding a paddle in the boat, consequently Bruce and I were able to relax some while the details were being ironed out.

After several hours in the ER, Lilly was almost ready to be moved to her room "upstairs." She was still mad at us (imagine that), but had settled down because of a combination of evening meds and exhaustion. They had released her from the constraining ties that had been on her wrists and legs, and she was watching a little TV in her ER room and eating a sandwich while final preparations were made to wheel her out of ER. The CHC worker would go along, while Bruce and I were advised to go home and get some sleep, as it would be about 11 p.m. by the time we pulled into our driveway.

We went to see her the next evening during visiting hours and she was genuinely glad to see us. The day after, we brought her home.

She seemed glad to be back in her environment with all of us. She said little about the episode that had started in Bridget's office. What was there to say? The facts were obvious and we were all a little frightened that it'd happened at all, including Lilly.

I don't necessarily think the session at Bridget's is what put her over the edge. I think that it had something to do with Joy and Pete moving back in and the household dynamics changing, as well as the fact that she had never been able to keep things together for more than a couple months at most. She always seemed to be in some sort of a cyclical existence that just could *not* be tracked or figured out.

We could say that she was usually great in December, and then one December she would be awful and prove that theory wrong. Was it the full moon? Was it the weather, or was it the food she ate? Just when we began to think we had a pattern of moods figured out, our theory would go caput.

One good thing that came from the hospitalization was CHC found another children's psychiatrist. We needed to get another opinion, and Dr. Lisa would be it. Dr. Lisa asked me about Lilly's diet and if she slept through the night. She actually observed her play in the office, and said she wanted to have a strand of Lilly's hair analyzed for heavy metals and toxins. (None were found.)

The doctor began gradually changing medications by slowly tapering off one and slowly adding another. I felt very happy about Dr. Lisa's approach and reputation, and hopeful that she might be a vital piece of the puzzle.

CHAPTER THIRTY-SEVEN

February was approaching and Lilly would be turning nine. Her behavior at home following the hospital trip had improved, and we were also noticing progress coming from school speech therapy. Her diction was not so baby-like, although I doubted she'd ever be in danger of sounding overly mature at any age.

The home-front was good enough that I quickly started to plan a dress-up party for her birthday before the harmony evaporated. I knew it would, because we had received a report from school stating that in the previous thirty days she had begun exposing her privates at school and had stripped naked in the safe room. The gloomy report read:

• fourteen chair timeouts,

• ten restraints,

• thirty-eight HELP team interventions

Really? Thirty-eight interventions in 20 days of school?

Many of those were post-hospital, indicating something was simmering under the much calmer home waters.

The ninth birthday party was a great success, and it was the first one we'd been able to have for her with real children as guests. The birthday girl wore a peach satin dress that went to her ankles, and I had tied the ponytail on the top of her head with a length of peach boa feathers. She kept her gold rimmed glasses on her face for the entire party, and the blue eyes behind them danced with happiness.

My sister Tibby brought her three elegantly dressed children, ages three, five, and seven. She stayed to help, just in case. We'd come a long way since the brief falling-out over her daughter's party.

Ann Wells came with Tina, who was dressed in a 1920's flapper outfit, and three-year-old Sarah was dressed as a bride. Tina may have been a year younger but she was definitely the confident leader of the group of children. Ann kept me abreast of their lives whenever we got the two sisters together. Tina was excelling at school and in athletics but had repeated issues with honesty that kept them on their toes.

About that time we were assigned a new caseworker from CHC -Delsie Whiteleather. She would end up being our caseworker from then on. We still had our county worker, guardian ad litem, psychiatrist, nurse, Bridget Sommerly, and Sasha would come one evening a week so we could escape for four hours.

On April Fools' Day, Sasha came to watch Lilly for us from five to nine p.m. The day after, she wrote an *eight page* critical incident report. Printing it exactly as she wrote it gives the reader great insight into caring for Lilly. Of course, names were changed, and this is the *speed read* version:

"At seven p.m. I (Sasha) informed Lilly it was time to go to bed. Bed time meds had been given at six. Once upstairs she spotted Baler. She chased him trying to catch him. I asked her not to . . . She did not listen . . . and caught him. She was being easy with him so I told her to give him love and good night. Then I told her to let him go so she could get ready for bed. She said she wanted to put him down stairs in the basement. I allowed her to do so and instructed her to get pajamas on . . . She ran into her room, laid down on her bed, and began kicking the wall. She stopped kicking. I sat on the bed beside her. We talked about why she did not want to go to bed, and she explained she wasn't tired and didn't like going to bed. I offered to read to her until she got sleepy. She flat out said, "NO!" She became agitated once more and left her room. She ran down in the basement trying to get the cats that were hiding in the rafters. I tried to calm her by making a deal. I offered to get Baler if she got her pajamas on but she refused . . . Slowly edging away . . . Yelling she did not want to go to bed. She acted like she was going to climb on a table and try to get the cats. I got closer . . . She hopped off the table and ran yelling, "Ha, ha, ha! I fooled you!" She ran up steps and I followed . . . The door was slammed in my face and hit my head. I lost my balance but did not fall. As I entered the kitchen I noticed the blinds on the back door were swaying. I went outside and called . . . I did not see any sign of her. I searched the house screaming her name. I called Peoria police at 7:17 PM to report a runaway. Called CHC on call . . . I took cell outside to continue looking for Lilly. At 7:40 PM a blond-haired woman came walking up the sidewalk holding Lilly's hand. She said Lilly had been eight blocks away chasing cats. She had noticed that she didn't have a coat or shoes on and the man that owned the cats was yelling at her to leave them alone . . . She refused to go in the house . . . We sat on the steps outside . . . I tried to coax her into the house and she agreed to go in . . . we got up to go in the house and she pushed me and yelled, "Fooled you!" Ran out of the room, slammed the door, ran downstairs and out the back door. She ran past the neighbor's and ran into a park. The neighbor yelled to her that she had ice cream. It worked. We went inside the neighbor's house and she gave Lilly a small scoop of ice cream to take home. We walked across the street to go home about 8 PM or a little after. The police finally pulled up. I explained the situation . . . He asked what I needed him for and I assured him I no longer needed his assistance. He laughed and I took Lilly home. She finished her ice cream and wanted to take the bowl back to the neighbor. I told her we had to wash it first . . . She tried to leave . . . Took off again upstairs . . . Ran into Joy's room . . . Grabbed a bag of candy and dumped it on the floor. I took the bag . . . Lilly shoved as many as she could in her mouth and tried to grab more goodies off the dresser. She went into the upstairs bathroom and I followed her in and closed the door and blocked it. Lilly lay on the floor kicking and squirming . . . We heard a knock at the door. It was the

CHC on-call person. She came in and began talking to Lilly who ran into the living room to hide for the next half hour . . . and continued to run all over the house. In Joy's room got cookies and candy, dumped it out on the floor in the room, hallway, and down the steps. We were able to convince her to take some medicine so she would not get a tummy ache. After Benadryl she calmed down . . . Bruce and Nealie arrived. PS: While in basement Lilly threw some 2 liter bottles out of the refrigerator and smashed a ceramic cat food bowl . . ."

If you got tired of reading that shortened version, think how tired you would be if you had lived it.

Sasha had done everything "by the book." We were not allowed to spank foster children, and had signed a form agreeing not to. I understood Lilly had been abused, and up until then hadn't "lost it" to the point of breaking that rule. But one morning not long after her ninth birthday, she started the same games with me from the *minute* she got up that morning. I never had a chance to eat, dress, put my makeup on, or brush my hair.

After doing everything by the book for hours (only to have her yell continual threats and profanities as she ran from room to room snarling and throwing things), I grabbed her and quickly flipped her over and gave her a good spanking.

She immediately stopped everything. I think she and I were both startled that I had done it. What resulted was interesting:

• Lilly calmed down for half an hour, then started up all over again. I realized I had made myself more work because I had to do a critical incident report.

• CHC decided I needed to attend an anger management class. When I told Bruce my consequences he literally shouted, "Tell them to sign me up, too!"

• Kathi Beadle brought the "class" to our house one day while Lilly was at school, and we three just talked. It was nice.

• We learned that in Lilly's case, spanking did not work.

• And last but not least, the desperate feelings that we had tried to suppress became more real, because my halo had C-R-A-C-K-E-D.

CHAPTER THIRTY-EIGHT

Not long after Lilly's ninth birthday, it became a struggle for us to see the good in her. Was she incorrigible? She had been with us for three years and we tried to keep at bay thoughts that things were hopeless and that we'd have to admit defeat at some point.

She also sensed that she was losing ground and hated herself for it. Her conclusions about herself were that she was bad, mad, and sad -three words she often used to describe herself, as well as saying that she wanted to die.

She didn't seem to be able to control her reactions when things didn't go the way she wanted, and her increased size and knowledge made her quite an adversary when she was on the warpath.

Respites became even more necessary but less available, because at that time there weren't any respite families who could handle her. Ordinary respite families were available, but nobody equipped with what it took to care for Lilly: an understanding of Reactive Attachment Disorder, stamina, ingenuity, a safe environment, and no pets.

CHC had purchased an older house that was being renovated for use as a temporary home for just such respite situations. Roger Stevens (the older man who with his wife Mary, had once done day-respites for us), had been assisting CHC in painting, repairing, and getting the big house ready for the kids. When it was deemed livable, Lilly went there to spend a weekend for respite.

During her first evening she turned the place upside down with her antics. She threw laundry detergent and bleach at caseworker Delsie Whiteleather, but only on Delsie's lower body. (Lilly never intentionally tried to harm anyone's face.) Later that evening the havoc continued until she broke out a bedroom window on the second floor. Then the police were called, and they took her to Columbia Children's for a ten day stay.

When we weren't going to visit her or talking to team members, I worked on repainting her bedroom a pretty pink and changed the floor color to light yellow. I painted colorful large flowers growing up the walls from the floor and repainted all the trim white. It was done to help her feel as if she had a fresh start when she came home from the hospital. The room looked vibrant, but it did not help because four days after discharge she was readmitted for another nine days.

The medications were changed during both stays. We visited her and so did Delsie and Kathi. Kathi made it a point to take the doctor there to task over medication changes that she did not agree with.

The doctor was not at all happy to have Lilly return to his floor just four days after the first release and kept insisting that she needed a respite, and *not* hospitalization.

A respite? Who? We were all astounded at his response. Just what was available for a child like Lilly? A respite was a ludicrous recommendation, but I will say in his defense that his motivations may have been caused by insurance guidelines.

We understood a hospitalization was far from ideal, but they had a secure area, medications, and trained professionals. A respite was just a family from the community of foster parents.

All in all, she was gone nineteen days in May and June. The way home from the second admission was filled with hitting, spitting, kicking and unbuckling. Bruce was working, so Torie had gone with me and drove while I held Lilly down for forty minutes in the back seat during the drive home, which is one crazy way to travel.

It was ten p.m. when we go home, and she threw herself down on the driveway and began to scream loudly, "I'm going to kill you! I hate you

M-F-ers! I want to go back to the hospital!" (Welcome home, Lilly Angel!) Torie and I worked together to carry her into the house while she fought.

Soon after the tumultuous homecoming, I set to work on designing and making a vinyl harness-vest for her to wear in my car. The vehicle situation was getting worse by the day. I wrote to CHC and the county and said, "In order for Lilly to be transported safely in the future, I am making a type of vest that will go over her and hook to the floor behind her seat. The vest will not keep her from unbuckling, but hopefully she will not be able to lean forward to attack others and get loose in the car. If something like this cannot be put into working order I will no longer be able to transport her due to increased size and aggression."

Just like when we showed Lilly the blanket wrap, she was curious and wanted to try the vest on for size. I slid the black vinyl contraption over her front and the straps hung from behind.

She was excited and smiled. "Mom, hold the reins and say mush!"

I caught on and figured out she was pretending to be a sled dog. I held the "reins" and hollered "Mush!" while I trotted after her as she galloped around like a sled dog in a harness. She really got into it and pranced and "woofed" and very much enjoyed the new vest.

Who would've believed it? I was glad we were in the house where nobody could see us.

Not long after my letter went out, we received the go-ahead from our people of authority without any hesitation, so if she was in my car, the vest was on with no exceptions.

For a while Lilly seemed fine with wearing her harness. I think she felt special when it was new, and I kept my fingers crossed hoping it wouldn't have to be tested anytime soon.

It was about the fourth trip in the car when she tried hard to get out but couldn't, although she was still able to kick the back of the front passenger's seat and throw her glasses and anything within reach. Her little white face became all sweaty and red with exertion trying to get out of that vest. My car was filled with ear-biting curses but we were both safe and the wheels were taking us down the road.

When I finally pulled to a stop and turned off the car, she kept up her antics while I just sat and waited.

"Get me out of this stupid thing! I hate this damn vest!"

I replied, "As soon as you settle down and stay calm for two minutes."

There was more fruitless struggling for another minute before the sweaty girl stopped and inhaled deeply. I thought a new round of nasty words was going to come out, but she just let out a sigh and put her thumb in her mouth.

I looked at the perspiration on her cheeks and felt kind of sorry for her before I went around to the back of the vehicle and lifted the tailgate to unhook the harness from its anchor.

She sat up in her seat and turned around to see exactly how that thing had held her.

I knew she would eventually figure out how to get free of it, but I had read where Jesus said, "Don't worry about tomorrow for tomorrow will worry about itself. Each day has enough trouble of its own."

He sure knew what he was talking about.

Nealie Rose

CHAPTER THIRTY-NINE

July was a weird month. Lilly had terrible tremors in her hands and feet that alarmed us, but because her medications had been switched around during the hospitalizations, Dr. Lisa couldn't just switch them again. It was an awkward time of feeling scared and out of control.

Her prescriptions numbered nine that month, at age nine-and-a-half. *Six* were mental health related, two were prescriptions for a rash on her bum, and one was for prescription eye drops. Each dose had to be documented with date, time, and amount, then locked away safely (only to repeat the process for the next dose).

Lilly managed to find a bottle of rubbing alcohol that either Torie or Joy had left out. She knew her mother's inability to care for her had been due to drugs and alcohol so she drank some, "So I can die! I know my mother drank alcohol."

I took her to ER and the doctor determined she was okay, and when we got home I filled out an incident report.

Within a week she somehow discovered something the previous owners of our home had left behind -an old box of rat poison. Do you believe it? Lilly said she found it in a back corner of a dark basement closet and ate some, as well as mixed it in with the cats' food. I really freaked out over that, and Bruce put the cats' food away while I buckled Lilly into her booster seat so we could hurry to the ER again.

Once we got there, she was examined, and Bruce and I were told the poison wasn't very poisonous, we could take her home because she was okay. Either it had lost potency because it was so old, or she hadn't ingested enough to matter, or both.

When we got home, Bruce checked out all of the cat food, but didn't see a single poison granule. *Why did she say she had done that?* Regardless, I was very embarrassed that yet again we had not kept her safe and had to do another report.

After the implied threat to our beloved pets, she almost never got to see them because they were off-limits.

CHC was always trying to help us. In mid-July they had us taking her to the big old group home for activities similar to the previous summer's activities involving the van trips.

On one day while she was there, she broke Sasha's glasses in a tussle and ran from the group home twice. Each time she took off, they had every available adult looking for her until she was found.

Once we got home, I had to put her in a basket-hold because she just wouldn't quit. My arms were tiring and I wanted to release her so I said, "Lilly, if I let you go will you stop kicking down the baby gate?"

She screamed, "No! You devil, I will get you Henry Higgins -just you wait!!!"

I had heard that many times before and knew I had to keep holding on. After another five minutes I asked again. Her response that time was far worse than the Henry Higgins one.

And so it went. At some point Joy and Pete came home. He was about two, and he always seemed to be totally unfazed when Lilly was causing a commotion.

Joy helped me get my little kid off the floor and tortilla'd. Once secured, I was able to let my aching limbs rest a bit while Lilly screamed, spit, and blew snot out her nose.

Pete walked into the bedroom while this was going on and went up to the head of the bed. He stood there and watched her for about thirty seconds, and then he pulled himself up onto the twin bed beside her pillow. He sat Indian-style and bent over her red, snotty, sweaty face with his own face almost touching hers and asked, "Lilly, hey Lilly. You gonna be all right, Lilly?"

She stopped yelling and blinked. She turned her head and looked into his little face and sighed, "Yeah, I'm okay."

No more fighting, screaming, or struggling. She totally calmed down, just like that.

I immediately freed her from the wrap and she hugged him. Then he got down and went off to play while I put her in the bathtub.

That ended the strange month of July.

CHAPTER FORTY

We knew we had about a month to go before Lilly could return to Eastland School for another year, I wondered if we could make it. She was becoming even bolder in her aggression toward me in particular. The first week of August brought threats of "killing you with a knife." First of all, I had knives put up, and secondly I was sure she was all talk. Scary talk to be sure, but just talk.

I knew I had connected with her on a deeper level after caring for her for three and a half years. I was certain that although she would wrestle with me and put up a fight, she would never hurt me on purpose in a life-threatening way. Still, she was readmitted to Columbia for five days in August because of threats of harm and being very unstable and aggressive.

The hospital doctor almost needed psychiatric care himself when Lilly showed up again in his ward. We pleaded with him to continue monitoring her meds and progress for a little while after the upcoming discharge. But he adamantly said he did not see any outpatients, so consequently he couldn't treat her outside of the hospital.

On the other hand, Dr. Lisa had no inpatients and couldn't treat Lilly *in* the hospital. The doctors had two very different opinions on medications. I can't say either doctor was right or wrong, but we would be in a quandary once she was released.

Kathi Beadle met with the hospital doctor while Lilly was there and backed him into a corner in a heated argument on the treatment plan and lack of follow-up care.

He finally very reluctantly said he would treat her as an outpatient after discharge under his direct care for one month, but only to get her medication stabilized. He held to his word, and it worked.

(Thank you, thank you, Kathi!) Lilly was by no means cured but the vicious edge had dulled and we were back to having just a very, very, very difficult child. We could live with that.

We hadn't seen Dr. Lisa much during all of this so she kind of went by the wayside, and we started taking Lilly to a psychiatrist much closer to home, after the hospital doctor was done with his commitment. (We were thankful to him as well.)

When the third year at Eastland finally started, her hair had grown again just past her shoulders, and she was slim and still short for her age. When she was happy and dressed nicely, she was absolutely beautiful.

On the home front, Joy and Pete had moved out but I still watched him two days a week. Lilly would put a helmet on him and have him sit in a Big Wheel and prop his feet up on it. She'd get behind and push him as fast as she could around the big basement floor. They would both laugh and laugh. She was always very careful with him, and they were quite an odd couple: Pete was small and wise while Lilly was taller and troubled.

Torie had a serious boyfriend but she was still around at times to help with "the punk," as she referred to Lilly. They also had an interesting relationship. Each respected the other's ability to be tough. There was definitely a good bond between them even if they didn't sing each other's praises.

It didn't take long for the school scene to get bad again. CHC knew Eastland was struggling to keep Lilly as one of their students so it was decided to double-up on counseling. She would continue with Bridget Sommerly, and she would also go to a play-therapist at Job and Family Services. (Thank goodness for the harness in my car.) The new play-therapy sessions began just before Halloween.

Lilly wanted to be a cowgirl for the school Halloween party. She loved Shania Twain's song, "Man! I Feel Like a Woman!" Whenever she felt like singing it, she'd don a beat-up red felt cowboy hat that belonged to Pete, and her "horse" was her blue bike. There would be a little hip-sway in her walk as she sang a pretty good alto. The whole neighborhood could hear her whizzing by, belting out a sassy, "Man! I Feel Like a Woman!"

We got her cowboy boots and a fringed cowgirl dress to wear to the school party. All the kids collected candy from room to room in Eastland's halls. I doubt many parents were able to take them door to door in their neighborhoods, so it was nice for the many children in wheelchairs. I loved that school.

Lilly was down to three mental health medications. School was very up and down but home was bearable, and some days were actually good. We were all starting to be encouraged, including Lilly. She smiled more and seemed to understand that we loved her.

Because of the poor school behavior though, CHC began to look into her spending a year at a place called Mayfair, which was about ninety minutes from where we lived. A year was the usual therapeutic admission plan, and although nobody was saying she would have to go live there, that Plan B had to be in place if we and/or Eastland couldn't safely contain her.

I didn't dwell much on all that because I was hopeful once again that things were turning around.

I looked back one day at Lilly's class picture for the 2003 –2004 school year. There were only six children pictured and she was not among them . . . must have been another bad day with the HELP team.

She did well the month of December and shocked everyone with a beautiful, spontaneous solo dance performance in front of a gymnasium full of people at school. She also did well at CHC's annual Christmas party. I have pictures of her posing happily with Kathi Beadle and Delsie Whiteleather. John and Doris Champion, Roger and Mary Stevens, little Gertie and her foster family, and many others were there as well as Santa Claus himself.

I'm so glad I didn't know then that the next Christmas would be vastly and sadly different.

CHAPTER FORTY-ONE

When Lilly went back to school in January it was as if the successful December had never happened. A school report stated: "Lilly was beyond control all day, every little thing got her going, and she just couldn't get it back together long. She was with HELP team EIGHT times."

In one day?

The next month was her birthday month and it started out well, so to celebrate her tenth birthday we decided to let her move to an upstairs bedroom. All three were empty now that Joy, Pete, Hannah, and now Torie were gone. We decided she couldn't do much harm on an empty floor. She was overjoyed with the room change and ended up having twenty-four perfect days in a row that month. On the twenty-fifth day, however, it all crumbled.

Bruce and I went to see a movie because it was Sasha's regularly scheduled day of the week to watch her. Right as the movie ended we got a page.

Sasha said Lilly had locked the downstairs bathroom door and was in there getting into my makeup, swearing, and throwing things. She called the police and they were there trying to get the door open.

Oh, the thoughts that went through my mind as we rushed home. The makeup cabinet also housed all of my jewelry, and it had a hook-lock on the door about six feet up from the floor. She must have climbed up on the sink-top to reach the lock.

Bruce told the policeman over the phone how he could unlock the bathroom door.

We arrived home to find that Sasha had called another CHC worker for backup, and the police were gone. She said Lilly was in bed but not asleep.

I checked everything that Lilly had access to in my cabinet but she had not ruined a single thing that I valued. Rather, she'd gotten into shave cream, an old lip gloss, hand cream, and broke a pretty plastic drinking cup that was her own. She had been very careful not to disturb my things.

It turned out the items Sasha had heard being thrown behind the locked bathroom door were just bathtub toys. *If Lilly had access to my things of value but avoided ruining them, then she must care about me.*

I went into her room because she was still awake, and I was sorting out my own feelings and wanted to see her. She was pretty sleepy but looked at me when I sat on the side of her bed.

"I see you've been busy tonight. You know we still love you."

There was no response from her, except that she closed her eyes and sighed.

After I'd gotten to know her, I would end her bedtime routine with an "I love you." Initially, she would look briefly at me with those blue eyes, put her thumb in her mouth, and roll away from me without saying anything. The look was a silent, *No, you don't.*

After at least a year of that, she started to "parrot it back" as soon as I said it, unless, of course, she was mad at me.

Two weeks after the police/bathroom shenanigans, I was pulling the covers up over her at bedtime, and she looked at me with those blue eyes and a tired expression, and barely audibly said, "I love you."

It took four years for that to happen, and after her bedtime prayers, I went to my room and cried.

CHAPTER FORTY-TWO

Eastland decided to expel Lilly whenever she was too much to handle because she was causing a humongous ruckus at school on a regular basis. That made it difficult to make any plans during the day, and I decided if she was kicked out of school for poor behavior, then she wasn't going to have any fun at my house.

I started "Kicked-Out-of-School Home School," which included doing chores and school work. I also read to her, and each time I would ask her questions to see if she had been paying attention. She really liked that little challenge and would try to listen well.

One day I read a story about how Abraham was so rich because he had large flocks of sheep, goats, and camels. At the end of the story, I asked her, "What made Abraham so rich?"

She smiled and very confidently answered, "His flop of cheeps."

That's how we got through the last two months of the school year. If she behaved well, she was rewarded with a swim at a small community center that had an indoor pool. The pool became a big incentive for her, and we used it even more after the school year ended.

She had never had any fear of water, and Ann had said Lilly just seemed to have a natural instinct to swim. We figured that was part of the survival instinct that she had acquired as an infant. The pool always had a lifeguard and based on what I had observed when she played in the water, I did not worry about her when she was in it.

One afternoon, my doctor's appointment was looming and my ten-year-old had not been nice that day. I would have to drag her along with me because Bruce was working. Wanting to somehow get her "on my team" so she would behave at the appointment, I called, "Lilly! I have an idea!"

She came running to me in the kitchen with a cautiously expectant look on her face.

"I have to get dressed because I'm going to a doctor's appointment, so what if we leave early and stop at the community center so you can swim for an hour first? Then we'll go to my appointment."

She lit up and shouted, "Yes!" and did a little victory dance. She ran to gather her things while I put on a dress, and soon we were out the door.

When we arrived at the locker room, I had her change into a purple one-piece swimsuit and do the required pre-shower. Then we went into the very hot and humid, chlorine-smelling pool area, and Lilly ran for the water and jumped into the shallow end.

I immediately began to roast in my dress but went ahead and took a seat on the pool-side bleachers. I started reading a book while I waited for that very hot hour to be over.

After forty-five minutes I got up and went to the side of the pool and said, "Lilly, you have fifteen minutes before your hour is up."

She didn't answer but I knew she had heard, so I went back to the bleachers and sat down. When the hour ended I went back to the edge of the pool and said, "It's time to get going now." (You know, nice middle-class mother speaking in a chipper voice to her child in the pool.)

Lilly looked at me, expressionless, and swam to the *other* side of the pool.

I walked around to that side and said firmly, "Lilly, you have been in an hour and we made a deal. Now get out of the pool."

That time when she looked at me in the chin-high water, her blue eyes darkened. Then she turned and swam to the other side.

I knew she would be watching me out of the corner of her eye so I went to the bleachers, picked up my book and purse and went into the locker room as if I was leaving her. I waited but she didn't follow.

The humidity in the place made it feel like a steam room, but at that point I think I actually had steam coming out of my ears because she knew exactly what she was doing.

I peeked out of the locker room door and there she was without a care in the world, playing in the center of the pool with some other kids. My gaze went to the lifeguard who had her skinny back to me. She looked like she was thirteen years old, and I knew she would be no help at all. In fact, Lilly could probably drown her. If not, then we'd certainly be barred from ever coming back again if she attacked a lifeguard who was trying to get her out of the pool.

By then I was boiling mad and decided I had no choice. I marched out of that locker room straight for the pool.

Lilly saw me coming, but her expression didn't change until she saw me jump in and make like a tsunami after her.

She didn't have a chance. I grabbed her and plowed through the water to the edge and heaved her out of the pool. As I swam for the ladder, she gathered her wits and ran for the locker room.

She dashed into a changing booth and slammed the booth's steel door in my face just as I got to it. I heard her slide the bolt to the lock.

She must have felt safe in there because the locker room began reverberating with shouts of, "You M-F-er! M-F-er! M-F-er!"

I was about to stroke-out; I had never in all my life been so angry. With a deep voice and through clenched teeth, I said, "Don't you think for ONE SECOND THAT THIS DOOR WILL KEEP ME OUT!"

Instantly, Lilly slid the bolt to unlock the door and stepped out. She stood there contritely in her wet purple swimsuit and said, "Sorry about your dress, Mom."

I was silent as I sat in the driver's seat, soaking wet, on the way home. I'd missed my appointment and my dress was going to need to be dry-cleaned. I just couldn't believe she had done that to me. We had made a deal. On the other hand, I couldn't believe *I had done that.*

The only thing I could think of to be thankful for was that she had saved her eyelash-curling profanity for the locker room.

I was still furious when I handed her over to Bruce when he came home from work. She was as nice as pie, but I was leaving the house for the evening –ANYWHERE, just not around Lilly Angel.

As a consequence Bruce decided she wouldn't be allowed to swim for four weeks. I wanted a life sentence, but he said, "What?!"

Then he smiled mischievously and asked, "You really did that, huh?"

CHAPTER FORTY-THREE

To keep Lilly busy that summer, the agency arranged for her to go to a Child and Adolescent Services "day camp" every other week, from 9:00 to 3:30. It was great at first, until the camp told us if she had a bad day she wouldn't be allowed to attend the following day. That sure nixed my ability to make any plans.

I also signed her and Tina up for twelve tennis lessons at a nearby outdoor recreation area. Tina was nine then and only lived about four miles away, so it wasn't a big deal arranging it. The girls enjoyed the lessons and the time together very much. I'd usually sit and watch by myself, but if Ann wasn't working, she'd join me.

One day I had Pete in a car seat between the girls on the drive to tennis. He was just three and we often babysat for Joy while she worked. Lilly still called him her "Matthew" because she still couldn't say "nephew."

The three kids were crammed into the back seat together and I adjusted my rearview mirror so I could see their faces. I drove along and Tina leaned forward to look past Pete to her sister.

"Now, who is he?" she asked.

Lilly leaned forward, too, and looked over at Tina and answered, "He's my Matthew."

There was a pause.

Tina asked, "Is his name Matthew?"

Lilly had enough of the questions and said, "No! His name is Pete, and I'm his ant!"

Pete cackled. "And I'm a big black spider!"

I laughed while he and Lilly giggled.

Tina was quiet. She leaned forward again to look at her sister and said thoughtfully, "Lilly, maybe someday your brain won't be broken."

My eyes darted over my shoulder to Lilly's face.

Lilly didn't answer, turned her face toward the window, and put her thumb in her mouth.

I tried to come to Lilly's rescue and said, "Her brain isn't broken. She has had a really rough start in life but she's coming along. You both are."

Wise little Pete started barking like a dog and the awkwardness passed.

We arrived at our destination a few minutes later, and Pete chased the balls that had left the court while I sat and watched Lilly to make sure she didn't run away if she got angry about something. She didn't, and the lessons were great sport for the sisters.

Time for Camp Hope was rolling around and CHC talked to the camp staff about Lilly possibly attending. They decided she would be allowed to attend only the last two days of the week-long camp. She had been barred from Camp Hope the previous year, so it was progress.

It was a ton of work getting her packed and all the medications prepared just for two days, and it was also a long drive there. We felt she needed the chance to go, though. The summer was not the worst on record, so why not?

Lilly's two days were "so-so," but after she got home, her attitude was definitely sour, and she began urinating in her room upstairs. We wished we hadn't sent her. As a consequence, we moved her bedroom back downstairs by the kitchen, which afforded her less privacy and opportunity.

Sasha was moving out of state, and that was the saddest part of that summer. She'd been so good to our girl and would be sorely missed. I know Lilly definitely felt the loss of a friend.

When she started back at Eastland I felt like we were on a leaking ship. On the second day of school we got a call at noon and they waited her to be removed for the rest of the day.

I had Pete with me at home and absolutely would not put him in my car with Lilly if she was going nuts, (and it sounded like it if they wanted her out). So I called CHC and they sent a social worker to the school to transport her to the renovated two-story CHC house for consequences, but she was so violent that two HELP team people had to travel in the transport car and hold her down while the CHC worker drove.

Lilly spent two hours at the home acting up instead of doing the homework she was supposed to do, and then Bruce picked her up on his way home from work.

She went to school the next day and was expelled again -and again the following day, and again the next day, and again for seven straight days. Each time she went to the group home or another safe house that CHC used. It was misery for everyone involved.

I decided to try incentives because the ship was definitely being torpedoed and going down. We told her if she stayed in school all day, then on Monday, Wednesday, and Friday I would take her to the pool to swim. (Couldn't believe I'd ever try that again, but something was desperately needed to turn things around.) On Tuesday and Thursday, the reward would be ice cream. Then we purchased a CD player and told her she could have it after two straight weeks of no expulsions. She actually earned it, and the relative cooperation lasted until she obtained the player and soon broke it.

There were other changes in our lives aside from Sasha moving. Hannah and her husband were expecting a baby girl in October, and Torie and her husband were expecting a baby girl in November. We didn't see too much of Hannah, but not so with Torie.

I don't know exactly how those things affected Lilly but we had no control over people's lives, or the fact that time was marching on. Lilly knew there was a baby inside Torie. When Joy was pregnant with Pete she was living an hour away and Lilly was much younger. She remembered with shame that she had hurt Ann Wells when she was pregnant, and she knew that incident was the cutoff point for her living there with her sister Tina.

During Torie's pregnancy those feelings of shame and loss may have fueled many of the behaviors but if there was a connection, nobody made it at the time. It didn't occur to me until I was writing the timeline of these events eleven years later. Reflective thinking doesn't come easily amidst chaos.

Early in October Lilly was expelled again and sent to the old CHC house, and she had to spend the night in an effort to get her attention. The next morning staff took her to school after breakfast, and she was expelled from school again within a couple hours. She was returned to the house with orders that she'd have to spend a second night there.

She had other plans though, and escaped and ran some distance until she came upon a medium-sized dog tethered in a front yard. She recognized "Lassie" immediately as a dog we'd seen many times at a park we had frequented. He was happy to see her and she unfastened the leash where it was hooked to a post in the yard, and ran off with him trotting behind.

A woman inside the house saw her run off with the dog. The lady remembered where we lived and dashed out of her house and drove to mine. (I felt everyone within a five mile radius knew where we lived because of Lilly.)

I had no idea Lilly was missing from the CHC house. I was putting a plant on my porch when a very large white object in my peripheral vision startled me. I quickly turned to see the woman from the park. No dog though, and she was wearing a white, floor-length, quilted satin bathrobe with a crisscross sash. Her hair frizzed out of some little pink curlers that covered her head.

She was one scary-looking lady, and she was on my porch. I guess when a dog is kidnapped, you drop what you're doing and go after it. She didn't give me a greeting. Mad as a hornet, she accusingly said, "Your little girl stole Lassie!"

I just stood and looked at her. She could have been pictured on a playing card in a scary- housewives board game, or trick-or-treating as a big marshmallow.

Her twisted-up face brought me back to reality and I tried to think. Lilly was at the group home . . . then it dawned on me –*she must have run away.*

My heart started beating fast as I got with the program and asked, "Which way did they go?"

A large quilted arm pointed east and she lumbered off my breezeway to get into her car.

I took off trotting in the general direction the car was headed, and after about five blocks I heard beautiful four-letter words echoing through a backyard area. I got closer and saw my darling daughter throwing someone's decorative patio rocks at CHC staff while blessing them with incredibly foul words.

A bewildered man was hunkered down in a protected area of his patio while he watched his expensive rocks being hurled at onlookers.

Four policemen and four paramedics arrived next.

The lady in the big bathrobe found Lassie patiently sitting near a stop sign with the end of the leash fastened to the post.

The gentleman who had his little paradise invaded by twelve people and a blaspheming rock-thrower probably considered putting up a barbed wire fence after that.

In the end, the paramedics took Lilly to Columbia Children's as it was the only safe place for her, and she stayed five days.

The morning after she came home, she got her large bedroom window open and climbed out. Police must have found her just as I discovered she was missing, because while talking to the 911 dispatcher, he said they had just picked up a little girl who looked to be about seven. She was found walking barefoot in pajamas in a shopping area about a mile from our home and had taken off running when they spotted her.

Delsie called the next day. There was sadness and resignation in her voice.

"Hi Nealie. I think you know why I'm calling. It's time for Lilly to visit Mayfair to get ready for the inevitable stay there. We've all done everything we could, but her safety is the most important thing right now. Can you guys have her there Thursday at ten?"

I held the phone to my ear and looked up at my kitchen ceiling. "Yes, we can take her, but she'll come back home with us that day, right?" We had talked about it before but I needed some reassurance.

Delsie answered, "Yes, but it looks like she'll have to return at some point soon to be admitted."

So there it was, big and real and coming in the very near future. I couldn't keep my mind off of it.

Bruce, Lilly, and I visited Mayfair soon after that conversation. It was sixty-one miles one way, and it was in a middle-class suburb off a four-lane highway. The only thing visible from the road was the sign.

Lilly knew we were going to visit a place she might have to stay for a while. I could feel her "caution antennas" go up as she processed what we were trying to convey: that we loved her; that she might have to stay at this place a while to help her be safe; that we would come on a regular basis and still be her Mommy and Daddy; and that she would come back to our house after a while.

We turned onto the entrance road and followed it in and around several curves. There was a little orange sign with an arrow that told us we were driving in the right direction.

Lilly had her thumb in its usual place and her eyes glued to the window.

All around us were expansive green acres with many trees. Red brick century buildings dotted the pretty landscape.

We followed our instructions to go to a small ranch house on the property where we would get a tour of one of the cottages. It was empty at the time because our tour had been scheduled around the resident children being out of the building.

A woman on staff was kind to us and spoke nicely to Lilly. She explained how all eight children ate meals together at the dining room table and how each child had their own bedroom.

From where we stood, the bedrooms were more like closets, but it was enough.

She described the routine of a typical day and briefly mentioned chores as well.

We left then because that was all we were there to see and do. Lilly seemed to be okay as we walked back to the car. Mayfair wasn't as bad as I had imagined it to be. Was she thinking the same thing? We had no way of really knowing, but tried to cut her some slack when she became out of control that evening.

CHAPTER FORTY-FOUR

Before the visit to Mayfair, Bruce and I had planned to go to Oklahoma that fall to see my grandmother. We knew that in the near future, Lilly would be going to Mayfair, but because no date had been set, we continued with our plans.

We lined up the Jones family to watch Lilly while we were gone. They were little Gertie's foster parents. Gertie and Lilly had a history from Camp Hope so they were familiar with each other. We all thought that was a plus, but she did not have anything good to say about Gertie. Lilly's social skills weren't the greatest, and Gertie had spent part of her time in a dog cage, so her social interactions were awkward to say the least. But the foster parents were capable and nice and made it work for both girls during the respites.

After the tour of Mayfair, Bruce and I nervously watched the approaching date for our trip and Lilly's behavior, wondering how things would unfold. The weeks following the Mayfair tour were good at school, and she showed almost no anger at home. We wondered if visiting there had made her want to do better.

Ten days later I went to get her up in the morning and she was gone again. It was a total shock to me because nothing had precipitated it. Bruce had rigged the window shut, or so he thought. She had gotten it open anyway and left with her backpack, which was missing, along with her broken CD player and CDs.

The hours ticked by and nobody could find her. Bruce was out looking. So were Ingrid, the Smiths below her, the police, Kathi Beadle, and even our *mailman* was scouring the part of town we lived in.

Ann Wells drove all over creation when she got home from work, and finally spotted Lilly on a bicycle, then lost her.

Police had several cars out looking for most of the day. After about four hours, someone had a brief sighting of a little girl on a bike with a backpack, but police couldn't find her.

After eight long hours missing, we got word that she had been corralled at a McDonald's on a busy four-lane road a mile and a half from our house.

Ann spotted her at the same time that the police did. Lilly was in the restaurant eating an ice-cream treat that she had obtained from a group of ten- or eleven-year-old boys in return for her backpack. The boys took off running and she was nabbed. The report was that she was a beast and threw her ice cream all over the inside of the police car.

When they pulled up in front of my house with "Taz," we surrounded the sticky, dirty, kicking, cussing Lilly and escorted her into the house until an ambulance could get there and take her once again to Columbia Children's Hospital. The hospital was the only safe option available quickly.

One of the policemen went to the front of his car to remove a pink bicycle that was strapped to his front grill.

"Wait," I said. "That's not her bike."

The weary officer replied, "Whose is it? You mean she stole it?"

I nodded, "Yep."

Kathi Beadle pulled in right after the ambulance left with Lilly. She gave me a sad smile and asked if I'd like to ride with her to the hospital.

I gratefully accepted. Caseworkers never went places with foster parents in the same vehicle. It was weird sitting there with the professional barriers gone. They were blasted away by a tiny ten-year-old girl. We were just two worn out, scraggly-haired women.

Lilly was put in the emergency room area until a room could be cleared for her admission. Kathi and I waited with her and took turns walking around and making phone calls.

After waiting three hours, a doctor said that the psych ward was full and Lilly would have to go elsewhere. She mentioned another hospital approximately thirty miles away.

Lilly was reloaded into another ambulance and taken to General Hospital. Once again, Kathi and I got in her car and traveled to the next hospital. We both wondered if maybe her admission had been blocked at Columbia by the doctor who had previously said she needed to go to respite, not a hospital.

She spent nine days in the psychiatric unit of General Hospital. They had a small section for patients who were minors. Bruce and I went to see her the first three days, and then arranged for Delsie and Kathi to take turns visiting her while we went on our trip to Oklahoma.

You might ask how we could leave her in the hospital and go on a trip. Well, we knew she was in good hands and her social workers would be visiting. We also knew we would have had her staying with the Joneses if she hadn't run away, and we really needed a break. Lilly always had a crisis of some proportion going on, but my grandmother was eighty-eight and might not be there for our next trip. That's how we arrived at the decision to stay on course and go see Grandma.

The day after we arrived back in Peoria we spent eight long hours getting Lilly out of the hospital and admitted to Mayfair. It was time. There it was -residential. It was a long and draining day when we left her in cottage number twenty-seven. Lilly and I cried upon parting that evening. Bruce was calm and thoughtful.

We were instructed to wait to hear from Mayfair concerning what to do next as far as visiting and communications. It turned out that my phone rang the next evening.

A man asked, "Is this Nealie Rose? I'm a staff member in cottage twenty-seven, and I called to let her talk to you because she's been very scared. We thought it might help."

"Oh, yes! I want to talk to her," I said as my hand clenched the phone tightly.

They put her on the phone and in between sobs, she said, "This place is evil! Even my friends are strict! I wish I never crawled out the window.

Tears rolled down my face as she talked. I said, "Lilly, we'll be down to see you as soon as we can. It's okay. We love you."

Her time to talk ended and we say goodbye. I had a hard time sleeping.

Doris Champion called the next evening. She had brought Lilly into our lives and now she wanted to know where we stood. She said Lilly would probably only be at Mayfair three months. That was interesting news.

I told her we were committed to Lilly no matter what.

Doris then asked us if we could take in a seventeen-year-old girl who was in a leg cast for a couple months until the cast came off.

I said sure, and then pressed her about how to get information about Lilly and go see her. She said Delsie was working on it and we'd get a call from her later in the day.

Delsie did call and told us we would be able to take some of Lilly's belongings to Mayfair the following morning if we were available. She had also arranged for us to meet a staff member who would be the therapist at Mayfair. Bruce was working afternoons so the next morning would be perfect.

Bruce always goes out in the mornings to get coffee. (I figured out years ago it must be because mine was terrible.) While he was gone that morning, I packed up the items Delsie suggested we take to Lilly.

I like paper bags with the twisted paper handles, and I happened to have a big white one that was snagged somewhere along the line. The first thing in the bag was a pair of tennis shoes and beside them a purple hairbrush. Then I put in three pair of pants, five shirts, undies, socks, and two pairs of pajamas. All of those things almost filled the bag. Resting on top between the handles was Polly. I slid the glasses Lilly needed for school into their brown case and placed it beside the parrot.

I wondered if she was giving her caretakers at Mayfair a hard time, and if she thought we really had abandoned her. Was she still scared? It was extremely difficult not worrying and I couldn't wait to reassure her that she hadn't lost us.

After over four years as her parents, we were definitely battle-scarred and weary. During that time we had tried and done everything that was available to us to help her. Did I feel she was hopeless? Never. Did I feel we had let her down? A little. Though everyone tried to convince us otherwise, I felt we had. Maybe if we had done this or that, or tried something
else . . .

We drove the miles under a cold, dreary November sky. The white bag sat on the floor behind Bruce's seat. Polly was on her back with her eyes and beak ever-open, and fuzzy yellow claws ready to be perched on Lilly's forearm. (There was wire in the claws and they held onto her arm fairly well.) Polly had been through a lot but was always ready to spring to life with the right handling. I prayed Lilly would be able to rebound as well, and that she would have caring people to ease her fears.

We arrived and followed our instructions to go to the big main building where we would ask for a Dan Wheatley, who was going to be her therapist.

After Bruce parked the car he looked over at me with raised eyebrows. "Ready to go in?"

I could tell from his expression he was concerned about me.

I nodded. "Yes, I can't wait to see her. Don't forget the bag."

We got out and climbed the steps of a stately building and went into a huge reception area wall-papered in antique roses. We gave our names to the receptionist, and she said she would let Dan Wheatley know we were waiting and to please have a seat.

The bag rustled as we sat in some stuffed chairs. Somewhere in that campus of many buildings was Lilly. Maybe she was in school, in gym class playing, or having a snack. Or maybe crying?

After a short wait, we heard footsteps coming our way and saw a man of about forty heading toward us. He had brown hair that was flat-topped and reading glasses on his nose. He placed them on top of his head with his left hand as he smiled and held out his right hand.

"Hi. I'm Dan. You must be Bruce and Nealie Rose."

We shook hands.

"My office is a short walk across the grounds. I'll take you there and we can get to know each other." He led the way out the entrance and held the door first for me, then Bruce.

I had hoped we would head in the direction of the little cottages but we didn't. Once outside we followed him down the sidewalk.

I leaned into Bruce and whispered, "I thought we would be going to her building?" His expression told me to be patient as he raised the white bag a bit to remind me that we did have stuff to give to her.

Dan walked casually along chatting us up a bit and Bruce stepped in beside him. The sidewalk was too narrow to go three abreast so I was relieved to walk a few steps behind. As we walked I noticed Bruce and Dan were the same height and build, and they both wore black leather bomber jackets and light khaki pants. The quirk of that got my mind off Lilly for a moment.

I looked down the walk to see we were headed to another big brick building about five stories tall. When we got to it Dan opened the heavy old oak door, and we stepped into a building that silently said, "It would be too expensive to renovate me."

He kept up the cheerful banter as he led the way to his office and put the key into yet another door. "Cup of coffee? Tea?"

We declined, not wanting to extend our little trip to his office any longer than we had to. He left to get another chair as there were only two in the small cluttered office. I saw a real old-fashioned radiator against a wall by a tall window and a very sad looking spider plant hanging from the ceiling above it. There was a box of crackers and a sleeping bag on top of the tall bookcase.

"Good Lord, does he sleep here?" I whispered to Bruce.

We settled into the offered chairs, and as Bruce and Dan each crossed their legs I noticed they were both wearing black leather clogs. I blinked. How weird was that? I glanced up at Bruce's face and it had not changed to match Dan Wheatley's. I was so relieved.

Bruce smiled at me reassuringly and put his hand over mine. I loved him, plain and simple.

I knew we had an hour with this man because Delsie had told me that was our time slot. He began his "getting to know us" by talking about Reactive Attachment Disorder (RAD). He spoke in an even, methodical voice. At one point he reached across a tiny table beside us and picked up a plastic model of a brain. He began to explain at length how the different parts worked.

I thought I would scream. We had learned all about RAD in the many training classes we had attended, for Pete's sake, and after sitting and listening for about a half hour, I wanted to grab the plastic model from his hands and brain him with it. I wanted to see my little girl and I couldn't wait politely any longer.

"Excuse me," I interrupted, "but are you allowing time for us to see Lilly?"

That caught him up short in the talking department, and he placed the brain back on the table. He glanced at me, then at some papers, and then he picked up the pencil that had been resting on his ear. He began tapping it on his other hand. "Oh, I didn't realize that you thought you would see her today. She is still adjusting to Mayfair, and while I'll be working with her, I will also be working with you. You'll be able to see her during family therapy."

I'm sure my face was frozen into a stare as I tried to digest that.

Bruce came to my aid. "But we'll see her on subsequent visits when we come here?"

"Oh yes, I'll meet together with you first, and then someone will bring her here from the cottage for therapy as a family."

He discussed more brainy things and we left. I was so frustrated.

We left the white bag in his office, and I told Bruce, "Poor Polly."

CHAPTER FORTY-FIVE

We were scheduled to go back to Mayfair twice a week for the family therapy. Although it was ninety minutes away, we tried to make an occasion for ourselves out of each trip. We'd had so little time and freedom the previous four years. We would talk and talk, and on the way home, stop to eat somewhere.

The first forty minutes of the second session was spent in Dan's office. He had told us we'd be able to go over to Lilly's cottage to say hi for a few minutes when we were done. I think Bruce liked listening to all the academic talk, but I wasn't the least bit interested.

There was a framed picture of elephants on Dan's wall, and I fixed my eyes on it because it was just behind him, and it was a way to zone out yet appear to be listening politely.

After a while, Dan paused and kindly said, "Nealie, I think you've got something on your mind. Would you like to share it?"

"Well, I was trying to count how many elephants are in that picture on the wall behind you."

He looked at me in a most amazed way and blinked twice.

The next instant it was time to go see Lilly.

I knew Dan Wheatley didn't know what to make of me, but I just couldn't help being difficult because he stole my cub. My cub was a wildcat, mind you, but mine nonetheless.

We stood to leave the office and Bruce took my hand to calm me.

Dan led the way out of the building and across campus to cottage twenty-seven. He tapped on the door and a lady let us in. We heard a squeal, and we were almost run down by Lilly as she ran to greet us and burst into tears.

"What took you so long to get here? I don't like it here, and I cry for you!"

I got on my knees to hug and look at her. Her hair was really crazy and wild looking and she had on her own shirt, but I didn't recognize the pants she was wearing.

"Bruce and Nealie, there's a little room over here where we can sit," Dan said as he walked toward a tiny room with two small sofas.

School was out for the day and the other children were watching closely. Two boys had been standing especially close by, so we were glad for the privacy the little room afforded.

We sat down and Lilly squeezed between us on the sofa. She was ten but looked much younger. Mayfair was for kids aged five to twelve.

While we sat there, Dan began to explain to her that she'd be allowed to phone us in the presence of staff once a week for a few minutes. If the conversation was not going well, staff would end it. We knew she wouldn't be able to dial out correctly on her own.

He told her, "Your mom and dad will be here twice a week for family therapy over at my building, and you will be brought over to my office for that."

I spoke up as I patted her back, "Can we send cards?"

Dan tipped his head to one side and nodded, "That's a good idea. The mail gets opened before it gets delivered to the kids, though."

Wow, no privacy with the visits, phone, or letters. We have no control over anything.

Dan said he had another family to meet with and we only had a few minutes left. He seemed genuinely apologetic.

Lilly's bottom lip began to quiver, and I tried to encourage her. "Be good and listen to the staff and teachers. We will see you very soon."

She burst out, "I hate you! You don't care about me! You leave me at this place!"

Dan tried to intervene and said, "I'm sorry you feel that way and that must be a scary feeling. I understand that you miss your mom and dad."

Lilly looked at him and spat out, "Bitch!"

It was time to go.

The next day I drew a maze and wrote my feelings in its paths. I felt we were on one end where it said "Enter," and Lilly was at the "Exit." Only we couldn't get to her because Dan and Mayfair were blocking our path. I sent the maze by mail to Mayfair, Attn: Dan Wheatley.

While all this was going on, two new granddaughters entered our family, and Torie and Hannah were in the midst of drastic life-changes because of the new babies.

Thanksgiving was only a week away and Ann and Marty wanted to take Tina to see Lilly at Mayfair.

I called Dan about our two families visiting her on Thanksgiving, and he said that holidays were less structured and we could have a two hour visitation at her cottage.

I couldn't believe our good fortune.

The Wells family followed us down to Mayfair when the time came, and Lilly was ecstatic that her sister was there. She squealed with delight and hugged Tina, Marty, and Ann. It was like she didn't know what to do or say first, but when she got sight of the lunches we'd all packed to share, she quickly found her words.

"Oh, what's in that? I think it's cookies! Where's little Sarah?"

Tina replied, "She's at Grandma's. We didn't bring cookies. We brought sandwiches and chips and fruit roll-ups."

"Oh, goodie, I love fruit roll-ups! Mommy, what did you bring?"

I smiled and patted my tote. "We brought veggies and dip and cheese and crackers."

Lilly grinned and interlocked arms with Tina as a staff person led the way to an empty conference room where we all went in and settled around a big table and ate together.

For the occasion Lilly had asked a staff person to fix her hair, and she told us she had folded all the clothes in her room and made the bed, too. She was obviously proud of herself and so happy to see all of us.

After we were finished in the conference room, she asked a staff lady if she could show us her room. The answer was yes and we got to see the pitiful room with no hangers in the closet (a danger), and nothing but a little bed and a beat-up, unpainted wood dresser that sat under a window that had double-thick security glass. The walls were tan and some graffiti could be seen under a coat of paint. The door had dents, as did the walls, and the floor was brown industrial tile that had seen better days. It was so small we couldn't all six of us stand in there without breathing on each other.

As I looked around I was touched because Lilly had taken some photos that we had mailed to her and affixed them to notebook pages with little stickers. She had them neatly covering the top of her dresser. They were her only reminder that she had people who cared about her.

On the way home, I was thinking. She did seem better already and had only been there a couple weeks. Since she'd been admitted, I'd gone to bed each night thinking about her lying in the ugly little bed at Mayfair all alone and the distance between us, and it would make me sad. Maybe after Thanksgiving Day I would be thankful for the relatively uncensored two hour visit, and for the papers with the photos on her dresser. Yes, I decided that night I would be thankful.

Christmas was fast approaching. We had our twice-weekly trips to Mayfair, new babies to see, and holiday plans and shopping to do. We also had a teen girl with a cast on her leg staying temporarily with us.

We had heard through the grapevine that Roger and Mary Stevens had been given an award for being outstanding foster parents, and we were happy that they had been recognized. They had adopted two of their foster boys and had another foster boy as well.

I wondered how all the other foster parents that we knew would be celebrating Christmas that year, and what their particular challenges were. I wondered if any of them had children in a residential placement.

In the meantime, we were beginning to realize that Dan Wheatley really wasn't so bad. He seemed to take his job very seriously and printed out papers for us that summarized his observations after a few weeks of therapy.

His several-page work up about her was very insightful and accurate and included things we could say to help her. A couple were, "You must be feeling terrible," and "I bet that makes you feel great!"

We were familiar with these types of conversations because of our training classes, but reading over his assessment was a good reminder for us to use therapeutic talking. It wasn't as easy to remember to do as you might think, especially when Lilly had just bitten or spit on us.

By her fifth week, she had begun running out of offices or buildings, and had gone AWOL four times. She was also running out of one room in a building only to hide in another room. People were being forced to chase her down and retrieve her from different buildings, rooms, woods, bushes, and ravines. Because of this, she was put on "supportive touch," which just meant her hand had to be held everywhere she went.

Dan told us Lilly was urinating on items in her room, as well as down her heating and air-conditioning vent. She'd also succeeded in cutting up her hair after she ran into an office and found scissors.

Christmas was coming, and I hoped she would be able to come home for the day but she was not allowed, and we could only get her two gifts.

Mayfair was letting each child look at catalogs and choose what they wanted as a gift from them, up to $100. Lilly said she was getting a handheld game player that cost all of that, but we doubted she'd get it.

We thought it would be good for her to see little Pete who was three, so we took him the day after Christmas. Snow was piled five feet high and it was windy and cold. We knocked on the door and as soon as they recognized our faces, we were allowed inside. The television was on and the kids were watching cartoons.

Lilly was sitting on a couch with two other girls, and when she saw us, she jumped up and ran to us yelling, "Merry Christmas! Happy Christmas!" She squealed, "Pete, Pete, Pete!!" and tried to pick him up.

He was a very dignified child, and after she set him down, he said, "I like green."

She burst out laughing. She wanted to start in on the presents that we brought but too many eyes were on us, and we were still standing in the entry.

I said, "Wait, we need to sit in your room to open presents."

We stamped snow off our boots and walked across the common room to her dreary little room. Bruce and I sat on the edge of the twin bed with Pete between us.

Rules required that we had to keep the door open.

She showed us what she had received from Mayfair, and it was indeed the expensive electronic game.

Bruce and I exchanged looks. We both thought that maybe the place wasn't so bad. We looked on as she made short work of opening her presents on the brown tile floor.

I had stretched the "only two present" rule and got her slippers and matching pajamas as one gift, and for the second one, two music CDs and a small battery-operated CD player. (No plug-in of any type was allowed.) She was happy and grateful for everything.

Bruce lifted Pete up and went to ask staff where we might be able to go to visit outside of the cottage. I pulled Lilly over to me and gave her a hug. It was pretty standard for her to pull away quickly, and she did.

"I'm so sad to be here. These kids are mean. We're having Christmas cookies today!"

I looked around the room and listened and smiled as she talked. There was scribbling on the door and walls that hadn't been there before. The room certainly smelled strongly of urine, and I wondered how register vents were cleaned?

Bruce and Pete returned, and he said a man would escort us to the gym. It was empty but there were some balls so we played for about forty-five minutes and had a great time, but then we could tell she was getting restless.

We found a maintenance man in the hall outside and told him we were done in the gym, could we go somewhere to sit and color?

He pointed down the hall and said, "There's nobody here. Just go down the hall here and make a right. First door you come to is the employee cafeteria. Sometimes families sit in there."

The four of us soon arrived at a well-equipped but rather plain lunchroom. I had brought coloring books and markers in a tote bag, which I placed on the central table. We piled our coats on top of a nearby chair and I wearily sat down.

Going to Mayfair was stressful. Winter weather made the drive sometimes close to two hours. Then because of the snow piles everywhere, a parking spot near cottage twenty-seven was hard to find. That usually meant trudging through snow until we found a traveled path that must've been a sidewalk in the summer. Add to that wondering what her mood might be and if we would have to fend off the advances of other lonely children who had no visitors. Those kids would try to join in or follow us around, and it made us feel terrible (and made Lilly feel like punching them).

So bleak cafeteria or not, there we were on December twenty-sixth, trying to be happy. Bruce pulled money out of his pocket after he saw three vending machines and handed some to Lilly.

"Oh, boy! I saw those machines. How did you know, Daddy?" She looked slyly at him (as if he wouldn't have known she'd want something from them). She grabbed Pete's arm and away they went to the vending area.

I watched the two of them standing and looking at the different selections. She was wearing a plain white mock turtleneck and a pair of blue jeans. Her chopped-up hair was parted in the middle and hung loosely around her shoulders. There were no glasses on her face.

Pete stood almost up to her armpit, and she looked down at the little guy and said, "So, Petey-boy, what do you want? See, there's Snickers! And there's granola bars -they are more healthy. I'm getting Snickers and Dr. Pepper!"

Pete chose M&Ms. She awkwardly lifted him up to let him feed a dollar bill into the slot, and then she held the bar open at the bottom so he could reach his hand in and pull the candy out. She was being very motherly with him and I knew she was so grateful to see someone from home.

The table where we were seated had the room's only holiday decoration. In the center of our table stood a two-foot-high, metallic blue Christmas tree. I looked all about the unfamiliar room again, then at the four of us around the tiny blue tree. Yes, things were kinda blue. Everything had a surreal feel to it, and I tried hard not to be sad on the way home.

CHAPTER FORTY-SIX

Lilly called me a couple days later and said angrily, "Mom, somebody stole my game! They looked all over our cottage and it's NOT here!"

I asked, "When did it disappear?"

She huffed, "I only had it two days, Mom, and somebody stole it already!"

I was disappointed for her, but not surprised at the theft.

"Honey, I'll talk to Dan Wheatley. This isn't right."

I did tell Dan the next day when we were in his office for our appointment. He was concerned, and said he'd do some checking.

When we heard back, he said, "They did a room by room search, and it wasn't there. I'm sorry, and told Lilly I was sorry. We'll see about getting her a replacement."

I wasn't quite satisfied with that and pressed on, "If each room was searched and the kids are supervised and locked in, how did it vanish? Could a staff person have taken it? That only makes sense, right? I mean, a new and very concealable expensive toy that they could give to their own kid, or sell?"

Dan answered, "I wouldn't go so far as to accuse anyone here. But yes, that's a possibility."

Then I asked him if he could get it replaced quickly and he responded by saying, "Yes it will be replaced soon, but I'm not sure it won't happen again, though."

About three weeks later she received a new game and was tickled pink.

She told me in hushed tones, "Mom, I hid it so nobody can find it in my room. I don't trust nobody."

Within two weeks her "well hidden" game was taken from her tiny room while she was in school. We were steamed and Dan was frustrated, but there wasn't a single thing that could be done. There were various adults going into each cottage to clean, empty trash, do wash, and bring in food. And then there were the house parents that did round-the-clock shifts.

Lilly felt twice-betrayed and the situation only fueled her anger and mistrust of people. The urinating, going AWOL, and room destruction continued.

Then Dan told us she had broken her right hand and it was in a cast.

"There were some conflicting reports. Staff said she had been tearing up the cottage and violent, and her hand got caught in a door. Lilly said staff did it on purpose, but I just can't see that."

When she talked to us, her version of the story was: "I was acting up and I hit Miss B. She shut my hand in the door on purpose, Mom." (Seven years later, she still talks about it. I believed her then and I believe her now.)

We decided to take Pete again for a visit. The day we went was an all-out blizzard, and we shouldn't have gone out in it, but we were concerned about letting her down if we didn't go.

We had a nice visit with her, and Bruce went out in the blizzard to uncover the car and bring it closer to the building when it was time to leave. Pete and I put our parkas on and stood in the common living area of the cottage talking to Lilly and waiting for Bruce.

About that time a nurse was making rounds in cottage twenty-seven and stopped to talk to me about the medications. The next thing I knew, I heard a commotion and shouting, and quickly turned to see that Pete had been grabbed by the neck from behind by an apparently CRAZY eight- or nine-year-old boy. He had him in a neck-hold, and Pete's feet were about six inches off the ground. Pete and Lilly were both screaming, and she was beating hard on the attacker.

I ran over as fast as I could and fought extreme panic as I managed to pry the boy's arm from Pete's neck. There was a mark on his cheek but he was okay.

Lilly was all over that boy beating on him, and several staff had to literally pry the much smaller girl off of him. She and I both got the feeling he had intended real harm.

I was so shook up that after I made sure he was okay, I picked him up and escaped with him into the white-out without waiting for Bruce or the car. (Though crying, Lilly had seemed to know what I needed to do and didn't prolong the goodbye.)

I had Pete bury his face in my open parka to keep the driving snow off him while I trudged through deep snow to our Jeep. I was very thankful that we had our parkas on at the time of the attack because the padding had cushioned his neck.

As we were driving the car slowly out of the campus, I shivered and said, "These driving conditions are dangerous but it is safer *out here* than where Lilly is in that bright, warm cottage."

After that, we agreed Pete would always be held in Bruce's arms for safekeeping when we visited. We also decided that any time other children were within one hundred yards of him he would be up by Bruce's shoulder for safety.

Never again would we underestimate any of the troubled children at Mayfair. From then on we saw each one as a potential danger.

Wonder of wonders, Pete himself seemed unaffected by the attack. He told us that the boy was "wrestling" with him.

Although we went to family therapy twice a week, it didn't seem like we were actually visiting with Lilly because Dan was present. Thankfully, it wasn't long before we were allowed to go a third time each week for Mayfair's 1:00-3:00 p.m. weekend visiting hours by ourselves.

During those two hours we still had staff supervision but it was from a distance. We could walk on the grounds, play in the gym if it was empty, or staff would unlock an empty classroom for us to sit in. Once inside, we usually played checkers, and Lilly actually became a decent checker player. Sometimes Bruce would read to her, we'd color, or play with Play-doh.

When we weren't there, the shenanigans continued at Mayfair. She became more dangerous and daring, and before we knew it she ended up with a cast on her foot. We never really did know what had happened. She had been limping for a while, so an x-ray was taken and it showed a fracture. Bruce and I asked her about it but she did not know how she did it.

After three months and two fractures at Mayfair and very little behavior improvement, we realized her stay would be much longer than the three months that Doris had originally mentioned.

February brought more snow and her eleventh birthday, and it was celebrated much the same as Christmas had been, with limited gifts in the employee cafeteria.

After four-and-a-half years of abnormal living, I felt a desire to live a more normal life but wasn't sure how to go about it. Then one day a good friend called, and offered to help me get an x-ray position where she worked. That encouragement was just what I needed, and I started on a very limited part-time schedule in a small clinic. Although it was challenging after being so long out of the field, the timing couldn't have been better.

When I told Lilly about it, she looked at me strangely and put her thumb in her mouth. I knew she was wondering if my employment might be a betrayal to her, and was trying to understand what it might mean to her for me to work part-time. I didn't even know. But she did seem to mind that the girl with the cast on her leg was at her house, and she was not. Her way of dealing with these was to not bring them up, so we spoke very little about it. We assured her the temporary guest would be moving on as soon as the cast came off her leg.

Lilly did ask, "How did she get a cast on her leg? Did she get hit by a car?"

I saw a learning opportunity and said, "No, she wanted to run away, so she tried to climb out of her bedroom window on the second floor of her house. As she was holding onto the edge of the window frame, it broke and she fell all the way to the ground."

Lilly had been listening closely. "Did she cry?"

"Oh she must have, because she broke her leg very bad."

Lilly was intrigued and asked, "Why did the window break?"

I said, "Well, she's a pretty big girl and it couldn't hold her."

Lilly let out a loud burst of laughter.

So much for a learning opportunity.

Speaking of learning, at that time, I felt driven to write and illustrate a simple picture book specifically for Lilly, so one afternoon I drew pictures of her doing things that had gotten her into trouble in the past. Below each picture were words describing how she was still loved regardless of whatever trouble she got into. She adored the book, and I think it was the catalyst that helped her improve enough to be discharged from Mayfair. (See pictures.)

I'd Still Love You

If you cut your clothes to ribbons
and run naked in the park,
I would feel embarrassed for you
and would hope you'd wait 'till dark.

But I'd still love you.

If you took off out a window
and you ran and ran and ran-
I'd make a 911- call, and ask the policeman
to please catch her quickly;
I do not want to lose her-
I love her very much.
I will be so glad when you are found,
but you'll be on supportive touch!

And I'll still love you.

Nealie Rose

**If you ran into an office
and cut off all your hair,
I'd look at your bald head and
wonder why you went in there.
Did you hate yourself so much
that you wanted your head bare?**

But I'd still love you.

If I walk into your bedroom,
And it smells just like a potty,
I will try not to yell at you
And tell you that you're naughty.
We will talk about how you feel today,
And you will have to scrub the stink away...

But I'd still love you.

If you get angry at me later,
And yell nasty words because you're MAD:
I know that you don't mean it
And it doesn't mean you're bad.
You will have to pay your quarter, though.
That will probably make you sad.

And I'll still love you.

I'll still love you when you're nasty,
I'll still love you when you stink,
I'll still love you when you run away,
And I'll try to make you think,
Why do you feel this way today?
What is happening inside?
It's OKAY to feel this way
You don't have to run and hide.
I will tell you that you are okay;
My heart will be open wide.
We'll work through this together

...and I'll still love you.

Nealie Rose

CHAPTER FORTY-SEVEN

A glimmer of light came in March, sort of a gradual turning around. Funny thing was, it seemed like the little book had encouraged not only Lilly, but Bruce, myself, and Dan Wheatley. We all tried a bit harder to try to see the light at the end of the tunnel, and she tried harder not to go AWOL, which was her biggest problem.

Dan showed renewed determination to help her in therapy sessions. He started doing a very engaging play therapy with little stuffed cats that was very similar to what Kathi Beadle had done with her. There were differences though, because Kathi had never leapt through the air from an overstuffed chair to a sofa, or hidden behind a chair and made a stuffed monkey talk. Dan was pulling out all the stops, fervently wanting to help her, and as ridiculous as his actions may have seemed, our respect for him grew with each passing week.

The next month Lilly was able to start coming home for short visits, and that continued for four more months. Life became even more grueling because we drove over an hour to pick her up and then over an hour back to our house. She'd stay with us for four hours and then we would make the drive to take her back, and then immediately we'd drive back home.

She was so happy those days, and although she had her slipups at Mayfair, she was heading toward a discharge in August if everything continued well enough.

During one session in Dan's office, he pointed out that Lilly had never had the opportunity to progress in normal developmental stages from infancy on. Her parents did not demonstrate loving eye contact, warmth and love, hygiene, manners, or engage her in nursery rhymes and simple games as a baby or toddler. He went on to say that he felt Lilly was about four years old developmentally, and at that age a child might assume that because he can't see you, you can't see him.

He said, "What I want you to do is play hide-and-seek with Lilly. Let her hide several times and go find her, and then you hide and let her find you. Don't make it too hard, though, and after a little while when it's your turn to hide, cover yourself with something sheer so that she will be able to see you through it."

I studied him and tried to picture what he was talking about. I couldn't figure out what sense it made for me to hide under something sheer.

He noticed my puzzled look because he asked, "Do you have a sheer curtain or something similar that you could use?"

Anything to help Lilly. "Yes," I replied. "I'll give it a try."

I went home from that session determined to be the best foster mother in the world. I found a sheer, cream-colored curtain in the attic and brought it down and put it in a closet while I waited for an opportunity to play the game with her.

On one of her visiting days I asked her, "How would you like to play hide-and-seek?"

She happily exclaimed, "Yes!"

We played a normal game of hide-and-seek for a while and then when it was my turn again, I grabbed the see-through curtain out of the closet and curled up in the middle of the living room floor, pulled it over myself, and waited.

When she finished counting, I heard her hurry up the steps from the basement as she said, "Ready or not, here I come!"

I felt so silly but trusted that Dan must know what he was talking about. I heard her walk down the hall toward the living room and stop not far from me.

She paused and then said, "Helloooo. Mom. I can see you. Helloooo." She giggled, and I suddenly wanted to hurt Dan Wheatley.

Bruce and I were celebrating our twenty-fifth anniversary that summer and we decided to take a break from all the therapy and traveling back and forth to Mayfair. We set aside eight days and flew to see the Grand Canyon. When we returned we were refreshed and ready to take on her care.

She was discharged August first, after almost ten months away. We had put fourteen-thousand miles on the car and had become friends with Dan Wheatley. (Imagine that.)

Dan would continue as her therapist because the discharge plan said we would take her to Mayfair for weekly therapy. She would also be seen monthly by their psychiatrist to prescribe her medications.

We still had Delsie Whiteleather, Kathi Beadle, and Doris Champion all ready to get back in the saddle to help. CHC was enrolling Lilly in a new school for the upcoming year because she had become much too difficult for Eastland to handle. She didn't have many choices, but we found a charter school for behaviorally-challenged kids, and they agreed to take her when school started at the end of the month.

Life returned to "normal" with her back home in her bedroom off the kitchen. She still loved being outdoors and still didn't like being told what to do. She definitely trusted us more than ever, and would hug us more often. At the same time, she was also more independent and autonomous.

At eleven, her understanding in most areas was about the same as an average six-year-old. She had grown the previous year and actually looked like a tween. Her body was not six, though, and her interest in boys was evident everywhere we went. She'd usually tell me, "Mom, he keeps looking at me. I know he likes me." She'd say that even when I knew for a fact that the particular boy mentioned had not even given her a glance. Some did though, and the future made me nervous.

Lilly still had a penchant for clothes that had a leopard or tiger-stripe pattern, and when she wore those outfits she strutted as if to say, "I am way too cool!" The hair she had lopped off at Mayfair was growing out and we had it cut in a layered bob that made her look more grown up.

All that said, you could still hear her singing as she rode her bike on the sidewalk, trying to engage strangers walking by. The same old, "I like your hair! I like your bike! What's your dog's name? He's too cute!" Her verbal articulation had improved, though. The repertoire of bad words had multiplied considerably, and she was just as quick as ever to use them.

Baler and Peek were still pretty much off-limits and put away. She had been gone ten months but they had not forgotten *her*. When she was around, they were not.

We told Dan one thing had definitely become a huge problem, and it was that she was stealing things —lots of things. It seemed her ten little fingers wanted to take souvenirs from each store we visited.

That caused a lot of tension, and angry outbursts from her when we demanded to check pockets and purse before leaving a home or store. August was one very long first month home because of that. Once again, we were SO looking forward to school starting.

The new school was called Advance and had only been open a couple years. She would be taken to school in her own chartered van, and the woman who would be driving her was named Mrs. Ivan. She was probably thrilled to have such a cushy part-time job —all she had to do was drive one special-needs girl to school and back each day.

You could tell by her huge smile that she had not been told everything she needed to know.

Advance was housed in a small building with an office and six classrooms and the enrollment ages were from ten to eighteen years old. Administrative staff consisted of what looked to be ex-football players – huge men with rippling muscles showing under their polo shirts.

This is good, I said to myself as I passed through a metal detector on my way into the building. They introduced me to Lilly's class, and there were only ten students, eight of which were boys. She later informed me angrily that the other girl was not at all nice to her.

The school didn't have much of a female presence. Her teacher and assistant were men. I left thinking how perfect it all seemed and was elated.

When she came home that day I went out by the curb to retrieve her from the van.

Mrs. Ivan said, "Have a nice evening, Miss Lilly. See you in the morning."

Lilly stepped out and I reached in to get her backpack. I thanked the driver and we went inside. I began to look through the backpack for school papers and dirty lunch containers.

She wanted to take a box of raisins outside and eat them, and I said okay. After changing clothes she headed out while I finished emptying the backpack and went into her room to hang it on a wall hook.

As I was leaving the room, something caught my eye. *What was sticking out from under her pillow?* I went to check and lifted the pillow to find bandages, white medical tape, aspirin, ointment, and latex gloves. *What?* Then it dawned on me –Mrs. Ivan must have had an emergency kit in her van, and Lilly had unloaded it into her shirt or pants.

I gathered it all up and replaced the pillow. All of the items went into a plastic bag, and in the morning she would give it back and apologize.

When she came in, it didn't take her long to discover that her stash had been confiscated. "Grrr!" she growled and threw a shoe up against her wall.

From the kitchen I calmly said, "You will return that emergency kit to Mrs. Ivan when you get on the bus in the morning. And you need to tell her you are sorry. She's a nice woman and she really seems to like you."

The next morning she and I went out to the van when it pulled into the drive. Lilly got in the back and I handed the backpack and the clear bag containing the emergency items to the driver.

"What's this?" she asked, puzzled.

I replied, "Ask Lilly, Mrs. Ivan."

She looked again at the bag, and turned to look at Lilly.

"You take my stuff from that box back there?"

Their eyes met and Lilly said, "I'm sorry, Mrs.Ivan."

The woman shook her head, "*Tsk ,tsk, tsk.* Now you ought to know better than that. If you ever got hurt we'd need that kit." She spoke softly and kindly, but with authority. She was not smiling as she hit the lock button and started the drive to school.

That is only the beginning of what may make you unhappy, Mrs. Ivan.

CHAPTER FORTY-EIGHT

Hurricane Katrina hit New Orleans. We read about the horror of it all and watched news footage talking about people that died, no food or water; buildings, jobs, and homes all gone.

I wondered about the children in foster homes in New Orleans. Were their foster families able to keep them? Would they keep them if paychecks were stopped by the catastrophe? What was happening to those kids whose lives had already been filled with loss and destruction?

I have a thought about people who work with those kids. They are either sheep or goats. Sometimes it's hard to decide. The goats are the bad people and the sheep are the good people. Goats shouldn't foster children because their highest motive is some kind of gain or benefit for themselves. Nobody is perfect, but on the way into training classes for fostering, people should have to walk through a "goat detector."

People who want to adopt children should. Sometimes the adoption push isn't always the best for the kids in foster care, and often they have no say in who gets them, just like a dog or cat being given or sold. Older children fare better, unless they are developmentally disabled.

I remember CHC being abuzz with concern over two little brothers about five and nine years old, who were in foster care with a CHC family and doing well. A couple from a major city in another state found the boys on an adoption website and decided they wanted them. The couple followed procedure and traveled from where they lived across the country to meet the boys. They came back a month later for a visit, and on their third trip, they took the brothers home with them. The people at CHC felt that the boys should not be adopted by them, or taken out of state, but nothing could be done, so the brothers left their familiar surroundings, friends, foster family, school, aunts, uncles . . . everything, and were just gone.

The special-needs children who cannot talk or speak out, as well as the youngest children are the most at risk in this arrangement. Unfortunately, it would take a lot more funding to provide long-term, frequent follow-ups on adoptions.

Having Lilly back home and doing well in school was very encouraging. It was amazing that she was not acting up at Advance, and we felt it was mostly due to the presence of power and unspoken intimidation from the mostly male administration and teachers. Most days she said she *liked* school. As long as she wasn't threatened or harmed, that was fine with us if that's what it took for her to succeed in the school setting.

Mrs. Ivan continued to greet her with a smile in the mornings. One day after school her van pulled into the driveway and Lilly was sitting up front in the passenger seat.

I opened her door and she got out. I needed to speak to the driver about it but couldn't let Lilly go into the house alone, so I told her to get her bike out of the garage. While she happily ran to do that, I stood at the open van door and accepted the backpack from Mrs. Ivan, as usual.

"Mrs. Ivan," I said urgently, "Lilly can't sit up front with you." I looked over my shoulder and continued, "She may unbuckle and try to grab the steering wheel while you drive."

Her eyes popped open wide, and her head jerked a bit at that news. "What? She does that? Why would she do that?"

I answered, "Well, because she sometimes gets out of control in vehicles. That's why she has her own driver and van instead of taking the bus."

I didn't mention that Lilly may at some point also bite, pull hair, and knock her glasses off while she was driving. I didn't want to overly

SCARE the woman. Someone along the line must have had the same fear as mine because she really hadn't been properly briefed at all. Shame on us.

"Well, okay," she said. "We've really been having a good time. I've been letting her listen to the radio and sometimes we sing."

I smiled and said, "That's wonderful. I'm so glad that things are going well, but she has to be in the backseat for safety."

She nodded and we parted. I had the backpack in my hand as I trudged thoughtfully up the drive, wondering how Lilly was going to take the news in the morning.

I spoke to Bruce about it that evening and he said, "We will tell her it is a CHC rule and we and Mrs. Ivan do not have a choice in the matter."

That announcement still made her angry but at least she had no one in particular to blame.

The next day was Friday and she sat in the back each way. After school I went into her room to hang the empty book bag in its spot, when I noticed a Band-Aid wrapper on her floor. I bent down to pick it up. "Lilly, come here please."

She came, and I think she thought a treat was coming.

I sat on the edge of her bed and asked, "What's in your pockets?"

Surprised at the question, she shrugged and said, "Nothing. I didn't take nothing."

I bent over to empty them myself and said, "Let's see." I pulled out most of the contents of the first aid-kit again.

She narrowed her eyes at me and muttered threateningly, "I'm leaving this place. I'm going out my window when you are asleep!"

Alarms went off inside me but I faked a confidence I didn't have and said firmly, "You just try it, Sister, you just try it. You are staying here with us because we are your parents, and you will apologize to Mrs. Ivan on Monday morning."

She grabbed her backpack off the wall and flung it across the room with all her strength.

What I had said was not very therapeutic. (Dan Wheatley would have said to her, "How could you say that? You must be feeling terrible.")

It was so hard to be therapeutic when you were afraid or angry. Lucky for me she was there the next morning, which was a Saturday. I wanted it to be a good weekend from the get-go. We had talked about extending her sidewalk limits a little, and if I gave her that announcement in the morning, it would help with the previous night's attitude. It worked, and the day went well.

We also produced a good set of working walkie-talkies, which she had never seen before. We bought a navy blue fanny-pack so she could put her walkie-talkie inside. I had mine with me in the house. I worked and worked with her on how to use it, and she loved the thing because it made her feel very important.

I set it on "monitor" so I could hear every sound coming from her end of our connection, but she didn't understand that.

If I heard her talking to someone I'd press "talk" and say, "Lilly who are you talking to? Over and out."

Then a click and crackle could be heard before she'd reply, "I'm talking to Ingrid. How come you hear everything? Over and out."

And so it went. It was easy to tell if she was on the move, going through our grass or down our sidewalk because the monitor would transmit the sounds of her feet making little thuds on the ground and I'd hear her accelerated breathing.

She never went AWOL when the walkie-talkie was on her waist. Maybe she felt it was impossible to try anything, and it never occurred to her to take off the fanny- pack.

It didn't keep her totally out of trouble though. (What could?) One day, she was out riding her bike on the sidewalk by our house, when two teenage boys came walking down the center of the street. They were talking to each other and one evidently used the expletive, "Mother F-" as they talked.

Lilly has never been able to mind her own business. My radio crackled on.

"Mom! Two boys are *cussing you out*! Come out here fast! Over and out!"

I did go out fast, but only to keep her from getting throttled by two ignorant boys who were in an escalating shouting match with a busybody little girl. I went to her and grabbed her wrist and pulled her toward the house.

Although I hadn't uttered a word, the boys started yelling at me, as if I were responsible for whatever Lilly had said. I was so glad to get into the house and shut the door behind us.

That incident was the turning point in deciding to start looking for a more Lilly-friendly neighborhood. A place with no neighbors and in the middle of nowhere, with a mile-long driveway.

CHAPTER FORTY-NINE

Things started to get rocky toward the end of Lilly's third month home from Mayfair. She decided she didn't want to go to school some mornings but once she got there, they were able to work with her. It was the process of getting her there that was becoming tougher. She wouldn't get up in the morning, or she'd drag her feet, miss the breakfast-time deadline, throw her shoes and glasses, kick the walls, and run to various rooms in the house.

One morning in November I called 911, figuring the CHC on-call person wouldn't be able to do anything because at that time of the morning they were probably trying to get their own kids off to school.

A policeman came and immediately got her attention by saying, "You need to get ready for school right now. You need to listen to your mother. Come on, get moving." He stood in the kitchen with his own radio crackling and arms crossed over his chest.

Maybe he reminded her of the men at her school, or maybe she thought she might have to go live at Mayfair again if she didn't listen. She got ready right away but because she had missed her van ride, I had to put her in my car and take her to the school late.

She had grown too big for the car-seat vest that I'd made for her over eighteen months before. I had considered making another bigger one, but I would've had problems making her put it on if she didn't want to.

After we got on the road heading towards school, she unbuckled and started swearing at me and threatened to run away once we got to the school. I called the school and told them that we were pulling in and they needed to send out people to safely escort her into the school.

As soon as my car stopped in the parking lot, her teacher came out and took charge. She complied, but not without her typical expletives.

He stopped and looked at her, and she became quiet.

Wow, that's impressive, I thought as I drove away. I knew we couldn't have police continue to come, so how were we going to get through future similar mornings?

Delsie and I spoke frequently, and we saw her often after Lilly came home from the months at Mayfair. She felt Lilly might benefit from a short readmission to get her regulated again. We were trying to circumvent this by taking her to the community center to swim, and we enrolled her in a Christmas kids' choir.

I was working then but it didn't interfere much, because the very few days I worked were covered by Bruce or a respite. Lilly liked choir and swimming and became more peaceful going into December.

Whenever it was time for choir practice, I would go in the class with her and sit off to the side just in case I was needed. Sometimes other kids her age didn't want to sit near her, so she would keep changing her seat to be near the others until the practice actually started. Then she would get into the music and forget who didn't want to sit with her.

The night of the program, an excited girl kept her glasses on and wore a gorgeous black and red satin dress with red tights and black shoes. I was pretty nervous though, because parents were to be seated in the gym for the performance while the kids were behind the stage in groups, depending on the song each age-group was singing.

Lilly backstage with a hundred other children terrified me. If Bruce was nervous he didn't say, but he did stand in the hall near the stage just in case.

Her choir sang, "Hark! The Herald Angels Sing!" She smiled as she sang loudly along with the rest of them, but we left just as soon as we could with her in tow, because we didn't want to press our luck.

All the way home she sang about three hundred more "Glorrrrrrria's." It was a happy memory for all of us because her successes were glorrrrious!

During the break from school she went to the Joneses for a respite, and on the second evening she ran out into the wintry night without a coat, shoes, or socks.

They found her by following little footprints in the snow. The prints led to a garage, where they came upon her half-frozen and trying to get into the attached house.

She gladly returned to the respite home with them, but her attitude returned as soon as she was thawed out, and before the night was over, she had bashed out a bedroom window with a chair. That was the last respite with Gertie's foster family.

Lilly turned twelve in February, and we celebrated at a children's party center and invited the Well's and my own family. She chose to wear all pink and was starting to look like a tiny young adolescent with that awkward-age appearance that so many twelve-year-olds have as they go from child to teen. She was happy and very sweet to everyone at the party, and we were glad we had taken the risk and done it.

The birthday happiness was short-lived though, and her tradition of falling apart the last few months of school began to hit head-on.

We must have been crazy, but we decided to take her along on a trip to Oklahoma to see Grandma. If you have ever been to a rest stop between Illinois and Oklahoma and saw a man sitting outside restraining a little girl who was SCREAMING at the top of her lungs, "GET OFF ME!," then you saw us. It was miserable. She had tried to run away and Bruce caught her just in time. If she took off from a rest area and someone picked her up, she could have ended up anywhere in the United States. The struggle and scuffle caused such a scene that I expected the State Police to get at least three or four calls about it. We didn't stay one second longer than we needed to before hurrying on.

Once safely back home, CHC said they had located another respite family. We would need to take her to meet them.

"Here we go again," I said to Bruce, but what choice did we have? We had to have respite. The family was about an hour away and had four children Lilly's age and younger.

The first stay was fine and without incident. The second time, everything seemed to go very well until I received a call after we got home.

"Nealie, this is Jane. I'm sorry to call you but we discovered that after you left here with Lilly, she'd cut every wire and electric cord in my oldest daughter's room!"

Frowning, I asked, "Cords on what?"

"Well, she cut the cords on the karaoke machine, the clock radio, the Atari, Nintendo, and the little television."

CHC reimbursed the family for the damages, or at least some of them.

I couldn't believe the family would have her back but they did. The next respite went well until Sunday at their church, when Lilly sneaked into an office and stole the offering. It was missing, and she was the most likely culprit.

The whole church had to be searched and the money was finally found.

Also, the post-Mayfair shoplifting continued in stores and everywhere else. We were reduced to "pocket checks" and handholding (supportive touch, as Dan had called it) wherever we went.

Then we went to a class at CHC that gave us an idea for dealing with stealing. We got the navy blue fanny-pack and took the walkie-talkie out.

Lilly watched, dumbfounded, as I filled it with about fifty caramels.

I handed it to her and said, "Put this on. You don't need to take things, because you have a family who loves you and gives you what you need."

She burst into a big smile and said, "Thank you, Mommy!" She immediately began unwrapping them and stuffing the caramels into her mouth.

That had certainly made her day and I was feeling very good about it, too.

Bruce took her to Walmart later on, and before leaving the store, he found a stolen keychain in her pocket.

I thought wryly that maybe we should have filled the fanny-pack with key chains?

Then there was the white correction-fluid heist.

I went in her room to get her up for school and immediately saw "white" on her rug, the front of her dresser, and the wall.

A Barbie doll lying on the floor looked up at me with open eyes and hard white hair on her head. *Toy Story* could have used that.

"Good morning, Lilly. It's time to get up now."

She rolled, over still kind of sleepy, and that's when I saw she had on blue winter gloves. She may have been twelve, but seeing those gloves on her hands reminded me her true age was much younger.

"Do you think I don't know you've got white-out all over your hands?"

Her eyes widened and her gloved hands threw back her covers. She yelled, "How do you know? How do you *always* know? That's why I'm *not* glad God gave us mothers!"

CHAPTER FIFTY

Even though she had been home from Mayfair seven months, we still made our weekly drive to have therapy with Dan. We discussed the many thefts and that we were putting our house up for sale. We told him Lilly had written her name in large letters on the top of her dresser, "So when we move my dresser won't get mixed up with everything else."

I had to laugh when I thought about what the dresser looked like with dents, pen marks, white-out, and scratched paint. That thing stood out like a sore thumb, and there was no chance it would ever get mixed up with anything. It was funny that she thought it might get lost among all our other belongings.

Lilly was always anxious about things, and it was a big deal to be considering a move to a new house. How could she know the house was being chosen with her best interests at heart? Dan tried to alleviate some of the apprehension and anxiety in therapy.

Spring usually proved to be a difficult time for her even without an upcoming change of homes. During one particularly obstinate therapy session, she ran out of the play therapy room and took off into the huge three-story building. Bruce went down one hall and Wheatley went the other way looking for her. I stood near the doorway of the therapy room in case she ran back past.

It felt like forever before they finally found her.

Sometimes chasing Lilly has had me near a breaking point where I've felt like saying, "Fine, go. I'm DONE." But I could never, because I know Lilly Angel is somehow connected to my heart, and although the hunt for her can be exhausting, it's forever.

Mrs. Ivan was such a nice woman, and I began to feel sorry for her because Lilly became crankier as time went on.

The last week of May, Lilly was in the van after a bad day at school, and during the drive home on a busy double-lane highway she started demanding that Mrs. Ivan pull over and let her out or, "I'm gonna jump out while you drive!"

The driver was very scared so she came to a stop alongside the road to try to calm Lilly down. As soon as she stopped the van, Lilly jumped out and took off running north along the edge of the southbound lanes of highway traffic.

Mrs. Ivan shouted at her, pleading for her to get back inside the van where it was safe.

Lilly responded to the pleading by stopping long enough to pelt the poor driver with small rocks from the roadside.

After Mrs. Ivan retreated, Lilly began throwing the stones at the cars whizzing by.

Once back in the safety of the van, Mrs. Ivan called the police and told them to hurry up. She also radioed her dispatcher, who called me to report what was going on.

The report was terrifying, and Bruce told me to stay by the house phone as he jumped in our car to go to get Lilly.

Mrs. Ivan called the police again and said, "She ran for a quarter mile, and it looks like she just jumped over a guardrail, climbed up an embankment, and disappeared over a hill!"

By then, Bruce and five police cars were hunting for her a good eight miles from our home. A few of them got off a nearby exit to search, while others climbed the same embankment to follow in the direction she'd gone.

Two sheriff's deputies that Bruce knew finally found her.

Do you believe she had joined a party of people grilling at a park and was sitting with them eating a HAMBURGER?

Little did they know who was in their midst . . .

In the meantime, Mrs. Ivan's van pulled into my drive and she got out and came to my door with the backpack. "Here, you'll need this, because I'm done driving her." Her hand held out the bag for me to take, then she turned and marched back to the van. She didn't know if Lilly had been found and didn't ask.

Why do angry people keep coming up my driveway?

I guess we all have our limits as to what we can take. I really didn't blame her but was so sad to see their good relationship end like that.

When Bruce got home with Lilly, I heard her shouting before they were even inside.

She threatened, "I'm going to press charges on you guys!"

Bruce returned loudly with, "For what? Being good parents?"

"Yes!" I heard her yell back.

They came in the back door and she started screaming at me as soon as she saw me.

Bruce interrupted her with, "Cut the attitude. You're in my house now!"

She settled down and I thought, *We live an absolutely nutty life. Nobody would ever believe all this. I don't believe all this.*

That was the week before school was out, and after it ended we contemplated taking her to a young cousin's birthday party.

I told her that we couldn't stay for the whole party and did she understand that? We'd have to leave after the cake and presents were opened and we wouldn't be able to stay and play. (I was getting warier about her behaviors.)

"It's okay, Mom. I still want to go."

I looked at her and wanted to believe her, so we went ahead to the party. When it came time to leave, of course she was mad and never would have gotten into my car if Bruce hadn't been there to help me.

Once we got back home, her mood continued to darken and obscenities and toys began flying through the air.

We bagged up everything she threw from her room and called CHC and told the on-call person that things were not looking good. We tried a blanket-wrap as well but she was not to be settled down.

After the window blind was torn down, we decided we'd had enough for one day and called the police. When the agency person and the police got there, Lilly was strapped to a gurney and taken to Columbia Children's. She hadn't been there in eighteen months, so we hoped she'd be admitted, and to our relief they accepted her.

She ended up staying there eight days, and during that time we packed much of our stuff to take to the new house. We wanted her room set up ahead of time so she would have less to be agitated about. The house was on a quiet street that was not as close to the road as before, and the huge backyard was fenced and had a big swing-set, and a slide with a little playhouse. We really hoped the new location would help keep her out of the public eye, and lessen potential interactions like what had happened with the two teen boys and the walkie-talkie in the street.

When she came home from the hospital to the new house, her thumb was in her mouth when she got out of the car. She had known that would be our house because she had been at the open house and a follow-up visit with us.

But it was her first time as an occupant, and that changed everything. I took her upstairs to her new room, and she smiled and looked around.

"Do you like it? And see, we didn't lose your dresser!"

She walked from room to room looking, looking, looking, and occasionally had a comment such as, "Where did you put my bike?" or "What's in here?"

After the tour, she asked excitedly, "Can I go out and play?"

"Sure, but you have to stay inside the fence in the backyard."

I watched out the kitchen window as Lilly ran out to the swings. She sat on one and started to swing. Higher and higher she went until she abruptly put her feet down and dragged them to a stop. She hopped off and began scouring the grass for bugs.

I felt relief because it seemed like everything would be okay. I was so glad we had moved, and thankful she liked the place, and I couldn't have imagined what was coming.

We had a week of peace and happiness, and she couldn't wait to go out and play each June day. I set up a lawn sprinkler for her to run through, and she actually caught a chipmunk with a little dish turned upside down. I convinced her to let it go after a few hours.

Then one afternoon I made brownies. I still can't make brownies without the memory of what happened coming back to me.

Lilly smelled them and came running into the kitchen all excited. "Can I have some?"

I responded to her question by saying, "I made them for after dinner tonight, and you'll have to wait until then. Besides, they just came out of the oven and are very hot."

She glared at me as if her "look" could get me to give in.

Undaunted, I said, "Go on now. I said they are for later."

She kicked a cupboard and ran up to her room.

I heard things hitting her walls, and for some reason, I felt afraid for my own safety. Until that point, I had been afraid that my actions might be misinterpreted by others, but this was different. This time I considered that Lilly could physically injure me.

I called Bruce on his cell phone to come home from getting coffee nearby. Then I heard what sounded like her dresser hitting the floor above me with a boom.

When Bruce arrived, she was still shouting and banging things around loudly. I told him it sounded like she had pushed over her dresser. He took the steps three at a time and tried to open her door, but she pushed on it from the other side to keep it shut as she screamed profanities.

His strength finally got it open and she dashed to the other side of her room and grabbed a jewelry box and threw it at him. There was a struggle and after he had gotten her restrained, he felt his mouth and realized it hurt because a crown had been broken off. It took a long time for her to finally give up, and he was hot, tired, and fed up.

After he let her go he asked loudly, "Why are you acting like this, young lady? Speak up, because I want to know!"

I heard her snarl back, "'Cause I wanted brownies!"

"What? You wanted brownies? Is that it? Brownies?"

Lilly answered a little less intensely, "Yes!"

"Well," Bruce said, "that is the wrong way to act if you want them, and now you won't be getting any. You are grounded to your room and I want it cleaned up before dinner."

We came downstairs while he held his mouth and spoke to me in low tones so she wouldn't be able to hear. "I'm going to call CHC and see if she can go to Mayfair for a couple weeks, then I'm going to see if the dentist can get me in." Bruce seemed rattled, which was unusual.

The dentist's office was only about a mile from our house and they had time for him.

He checked in on her before he left for the dentist, and she was quietly stewing in her trashed room.

After he left, I could hear her walking around upstairs while I worked in the kitchen. There was no way I was going up there. She was a small twelve but she packed the strength of a huge twelve when she was mad. I thought it would be best to just let her cool down anyway, and hopefully Bruce would return within the hour.

I heard water running upstairs and thought maybe she was using the bathroom and didn't think anything of it. Then I smelled smoke.

Oh, dear Jesus, did Lilly have matches or a lighter?

I ran upstairs to her room but she wasn't there, so I dashed down the hall to the bathroom and saw smoke pouring out of a supposedly disconnected electric wall heater.

Lilly had a large plastic glass filled with water and was trying to splash it up against the smoke pouring out of the heater.

I screamed, "No, Lilly *no!* You'll get *electrocuted!*"

She tossed the glass of water at the smoking heater anyway and swore at me as she turned back to the sink to refill the glass.

I was so scared. I yelled, "Put that down! Now! Get out of this bathroom!"

She ignored me so I grabbed her arm and tried to pull her out before she could pour more water on the heater, but she pushed me down hard and ran out of the bathroom.

When I fell, I caught my breath at a sharp pain in my ribs. I had to hold my side as I struggled to my feet and went back down the stairs to see where she'd gone.

The front door was open.

I dialed 911 while looking out windows for her. I soon saw and heard her shouting obscenities at a skinny blonde CHC woman. Bruce must have called them again on his way to the dentist and told them they had to come, and I was so relieved.

Police and an ambulance arrived a few minutes later. We had barely moved in. What did our neighborhood think of their new neighbors? I could well imagine.

After much cursing and commotion, Lilly was put in leather straps and carted off to Columbia Children's. They kept her only on the condition that a bed at Mayfair was immediately pending. Actually, all of the Mayfair red-tape took five days before they took her there by ambulance.

The county would only approve a fourteen-day stay in an "Intensive Therapy Unit" (ITU) at Mayfair. It was a building with a high fence surrounding it and a courtyard. A single small room inside served as a school, and food was brought in on carts with wheels.

The ITU plan was intensive treatment, which included daily therapy. We traveled to Mayfair twelve times during those fourteen days for family therapy and visits. It was grueling for us not only because it took up four hours each day, but because Bruce still had to work full-time and all the sitting was painful for my ribs.

But we did it. You can do anything for fourteen days, right?

During a visit to see Lilly at that time, she handed me a picture she'd drawn.

I thanked her and began to study the simple drawing of a face that took up the entire piece of paper, edge to edge.

I looked at her and asked, "Who is this?"

She looked back at me and quietly answered, "God. God is a big God."

I studied her and said, "You are right, Lilly. He is. Thank you for this."

As Bruce and I drove home, we talked about the picture I still held in my hand. We had needed that reminder, and it came from a most unlikely source.

CHAPTER FIFTY-ONE

After the two week stint in ITU, she came home with five weeks to go until another school year would start at Advance. CHC and the county were scrambling, trying to figure out how she would be transported to school now that Mrs. Ivan was gone.

The month of August was a roller coaster for Bruce and me. We walked on eggshells all the time and never knew what would happen next.

One Sunday, Lilly's conscience was bothering her, and she came to me. She was barefoot and wore a wrinkled lime-green shirt with a rainbow on the front, and a pair of black shorts. Her shoulder length hair was combed and she had placed a barrette neatly on one side.

I could tell she wanted to talk, but seemed a little hesitant, so I stayed nearby until she was ready.

A few minutes later, she asked, "Mom, can we talk? I mean, I got to tell you something that you'll be mad at."

I looked at her and said, "Yes, of course we can talk. Let's go sit down on the sofa."

She sat on the edge of the cushion and announced, "Mom, I hate to tell you this, but I got drunk."

I studied her and thought, *Lilly hasn't left our property and we don't have any alcohol here.*

Curious about what kind of a story was coming, I asked, "How did you do that?"

She took in a breath and said, "Well, I went in the neighbor's house and took their beer. Then I went by the garage and drank it."

My eyes widened with alarm. That was no story –it rang of the truth. "Lilly, you went in the neighbor's house? Which one?"

She looked scared and answered, "The ones with the two dogs. One dog has a blind eye."

The back of my shoulders and neck tingled with dread. Their house sat right beside ours. "How much did you take and how much did you drink?"

She swallowed and confessed, "I drank a half a can. That's all there was. It was sitting on their porch –you know, inside the sliding glass window. It was on the table." She pulled the shirt's neckline up and put it between her lips, as her eyes held mine in anticipation of my reaction.

I didn't really know the neighbors, and all they knew of us was the huge scene out front before the police carted Lilly off. Not sure what to do, I sighed, and said, "Lilly, thank you for telling me the truth. When we see the neighbor lady, you can apologize, but not until then. And don't you ever go into anyone's house again!"

A couple days later she ran in from the backyard all excited. "Mom! She's outside! You know -the lady I took the beer from!"

I went out with my stomach in a jumble and walked her over to the woman. "Hi. I am sorry but Lilly has something to tell you."

Lilly hung her head for a moment then looked up at the lady and said, "I took your beer. I'm really sorry, and I won't do it again."

The pretty woman's eyebrows went up and her jaw dropped a bit as she cocked her head to one side. She asked, "How did you take my beer?"

Lilly smiled at her own sneakiness and responded, "I went in your porch when you weren't there."

My neighbor's eyebrows were still up and she appeared to be trying to take it in. Her facial expression hadn't changed but she nodded her head slowly.

I could tell she wasn't pleased at the news, so I assured her it wouldn't happen again and said a quick good-bye.

As we walked away, Lilly turned back to her and said breezily, "I like your dogs. They are so cute!"

I was so thankful when Lilly returned to Advance. The transportation issue had been a huge obstacle, and the agency and the county decided she would ride a regular school bus.

My shock at first hearing the news was lessened when Delsie said, "But there will only be two other kids on the bus, and they go to Advance, too. One is in her class at school."

In my mind the only workable possibility was an *airlift*. We could have Lilly stand on the sidewalk as a hovering helicopter lowered a harness. She could slip it on and the chopper would make its way to Advance with her swaying gently in the breeze. Then when it arrived, they could let her down through a hatch in the roof, right next to her desk. Problem solved.

The first week went very well on bus 63. Lilly had a huge crush on a boy who rode the bus, and beamed as she held out a scrap of paper after school one day. "See, Cory gave me his phone number!"

I looked at the scribbling on a little piece of paper and read, "704-21-Cory."

"Lilly, there are numbers missing, and I need to ask your dad if you are allowed to call boys. We'll have to talk about it." The fact was, we had never considered she would ever actually have a boy to call.

"Mom, don't worry. If he calls, it'll be okay."

I questioned, "Did you give him your phone number?"

She smiled knowingly as she sauntered out of the room with her chin up. "Yes, I did."

We had a new phone number and address because we had moved, and with all that had been going on, we hadn't told her the phone number had changed. I suppose we should have, but she had caused so much trouble since we had moved that it never even crossed our minds.

Lilly's body was twelve and a half, but her cause and effect reasoning was sometimes around five or six. The thought of her and boys was alarming. How were we going to navigate those waters?

A few days later, she came home from school in a very foul mood and threw her backpack on the floor in the entryway. I could tell she was in an unreasonable state of mind.

"Lilly, how was school today? Is everything okay?"

She clenched her fists and growled, "No! It's not okay, and I don't want to talk about it. Stupid, stupid school! I'm going to go ride my bike."

There was no way she would stay on our street's sidewalks in that mood. She'd take off for sure. "Not now," I said. "Not until you settle down and I feel you can be safe."

She glared at me and said, "You bitch! You damn bitch! I wish I wasn't here. I wish I was back at the hospital!"

She ran up to her room and slammed the door. Within seconds, there was a boom, and I was sure the dresser had just been knocked over again.

I cringed and dialed 911 and then CHC for help. While I was on the phone with the on-call person, I heard the glass from a window breaking upstairs, and I dropped the phone.

I ran up two steps and saw her removing a chair from the broken window opening, so I turned and ran down to the front door to lock both locks in an attempt to keep her from running. I knew she could just turn the locks to unlock them, but thought there was a chance she wouldn't be able to figure it out because the house was still new to her.

She started to hit me, but I backed away from the door and tried to dodge her. The thought crossed my mind that I might have to run into a room and lock myself in for safety until the police came. At that point, with my ribs still sore, I knew she could really hurt me. If I were to be injured again, it wouldn't have been premeditated, only that I got in her way. I wasn't going to endanger myself any further by trying to stop her.

Our house was close to the police station, and they pulled in with lights and sirens as she was running down our drive. A medic truck was right behind them. By then the police were somewhat familiar with her.

She screamed threats at them and the world in our front yard. A bit later a caseworker's car pulled up and she tried to reason with Lilly to no avail. Soon she was once again loaded into the medic truck and driven to Columbia Children's. They refused her admittance, so she went to the old

CHC house for the night and was to be taken to school from there in the morning.

Bruce and I suddenly found ourselves free and decided to go out for a relaxing evening. Boy, did we need one. We were trying to leave worries at the door and not let them consume us.

Lilly was Lilly. We had help in many forms: CHC, police, respite, therapists, and our faith that God was watching over Lilly. It was time for us to distance ourselves emotionally more from her problems, and the deciding factor for that was the day we were both injured. She had become more than we were equipped to handle safely. We knew that she would have to go back to residential sooner rather than later. We could no longer keep her safe, and realized as well that we could never be everything she needed. But we could love her and stick by her.

The next day, Torie brought over a big black tomcat while Lilly was in school. She said he wasn't declawed, and that he had lived for a couple years outside their apartment building. She'd fed him during that time but they were moving to another apartment, and she was worried he might starve and wondered if we could let him live in our new big backyard.

"Johnny Cash" didn't look like he would starve. He was one big cat, and we hoped he would stick around and keep Lilly in the yard. Bruce put a swinging cat-door on the side of our shed so Johnny Cash could have shelter, but he avoided it like the plague.

Lilly was still obsessed with animals but after sizing up the big black cat with claws, we decided they would be a good pair.

After she got home from school she seemed glad to be home instead of at the CHC house, and I told her we had a new pet.

"What?" she asked excitedly.

"Well, remember Torie talking about a cat named Johnny Cash? She brought him over here, and he has stayed inside our fence all day scoping out the yard."

Lilly almost danced and declared, "I am going out to see him!"

I looked at her and said, "Not so fast. You need to clean up your bedroom from yesterday first. And I have to warn you that he has sharp claws."

She scrambled up the steps and put her room in reasonable order. She knew I would have to look at it when she was done, and say it passed inspection. What she didn't know was that I wasn't going to nit-pick that particular afternoon, so I gave the okay after seeing she'd made a reasonable attempt.

She hurried out to try to make friends with the cat but he wouldn't let her get close to him. She never gave up and spent the evening fuming about it until bedtime.

I knew that I had better help out a bit, so the next day I went out with her to demonstrate that he might not come to me either and to be patient. But he came right to us and followed us like a dog all over the yard while Lilly laughed and petted him. He would not allow her to pick him up, which was good.

After a while I said, "Lilly I need to go in and start fixing dinner. Just be nice to him and he'll be your friend." As I turned to leave the yard, I saw her doggedly following him around and saying, "Here, Johnny, here, big buddy . . ."

I went inside and watched out of the window over the kitchen sink. It was obvious she was trying to force the issue with a cat who would not be forced. She was becoming agitated, so I decided to throw a sandwich together quickly and call her in for dinner. She usually loved to eat but refused to come when I called.

An hour went by and I went out on the deck and announced, "Last chance to eat before tomorrow at breakfast!"

She quickly came in and wolfed down her food. "Can I go back out again?"

It was a request, but I knew there'd be consequences if I refused her.

Johnny Cash can go under the deck where she can't get him if he wants to hide. Maybe she won't be able to find him when she goes back out and she'll give up?

"Okay, you can go out for a little while if you get your pajamas on first."

She complied and went back outside wearing mismatched pink and blue pj's.

Our yard had some privacy because of the four-foot fence, and every few minutes I'd watch her through the kitchen window. Soon she was standing up against the fence, obviously talking to someone beyond our yard, so I decided to go out and investigate.

Her chin just cleared the points on the fence, and while she was standing there oblivious to her attire, she yelled, "Can I come over to your house?"

I came up beside her and looked two yards over and saw a twelve-year-old girl that I had met once, heading into her house.

Lilly's eyes were lit up and she excitedly said, "Mom, her name is Tiffany. Can I go to her house?"

My heart sank. I only wished it would be that easy, but nothing with Lilly ever was.

"You have your pajamas on, and it will be bedtime soon. We don't know them well, but maybe you can play with her here in our yard soon. I'll give you ten more minutes and then you must come in."

I went into the house and looked out in time to see her climb over the fence and disappear in the direction of Tiffany's house. I remembered the last name and found their number in the phone book and called them to ask if they could try to convince her to come home.

About fifteen minutes later, Tiffany and her mother walked up the driveway with Lilly. We talked by the side door for a few minutes, and I thanked them as they left. As soon as they did, Lilly jumped on her bicycle and took off down the middle of the street.

I watched in disbelief as she pedaled with bare feet toward the main street wearing the satin pajamas.

I called 911 and heard the sirens wailing within five minutes. *Good, that will teach the little stinker.* The police treated our runaway, young, special-needs child as a priority. I waited for them to pull in with her in tow, and prayed they would do it quietly. I knew our reputations were shot in the new neighborhood but still held hope that the police would keep it low-profile.

The phone rang. "We have your little girl in the parking lot of The Baker Motel. Please come and get her."

Please come and get her? That had never happened before. I hurriedly called CHC and was advised *not* to bring her home if she could be taken to Columbia Children's, because they knew that Lilly would most probably run again at the first opportunity.

My car slowed before pulling in to The Baker Motel, and I noticed her bike lying on the parking lot pavement. I figured that must have been where she deserted it to flee the police cars on foot. I stopped my car beside the bicycle and paused, not wanting to get out in front of the many onlookers.

Scanning the scene, I saw a watering can on the pavement and knew Lilly must have used that as a weapon. I was getting very good at figuring things out. I knew her whereabouts when I saw the open back doors on the EMS truck.

Still sitting in my car, I inhaled deeply, exhaled, opened my door, and got out.

Lilly was handcuffed to the inside of the truck, and a uniformed woman was talking quietly to her while a man wrote on a tablet. The lights on the vehicles continued to blink and folks lining the sidewalks gawked.

I approached an officer and said, "I am Nealie Rose, her foster mother. I got a call that you wanted me to come, but I don't know what to do with her even if I can get her home."

The officer kindly said, "Well, based on all that has gone on here today and recently, the medics can take her to Columbia again if that's what you'd like." He looked sympathetic.

I nodded, and glanced across the street to see if all of the people had stopped watching. No such luck. I glanced over at Lilly, who had two paramedics talking to her. I decided not to go near the truck lest the sight of me set her off.

A caseworker met me at the hospital, and Lilly was refused admission again. By then, it was one a.m. and the whole scenario was getting very old. The social worker decided to take her to the CHC house because it was fully staffed that night. She could once again go to school from there the next morning.

I still had to drive home and get needed medications and school clothes. I delivered them to the house at 2:30 a.m. and Lilly was asleep.

Instead of her coming to our house after school, our CHC team decided she had to go back to the old CHC house as a consequence. It sounded reasonable, but just minutes after she got there, she ran out the front door and across the drive to a nearby house where she snatched a garden shovel. She ran back to where the social workers' cars were parked, and went to the front of one car and started bashing it. She got in about five good hits before workers grabbed her and the shovel.

After several phone conversations between the manager-on-call and the staff who had Lilly, a plan was devised for what to do next. They decided that Bruce and I should leave our house for a few hours while a lady that Lilly liked brought her to our house and did the bedtime routine. Nice. Hopefully Lilly would fall asleep and the next day would be better. Bruce would be home the next morning to help get her on the school bus.

That ONE child would need so many people working to make things a success was absolutely amazing.

After school, the second part of the plan transpired as we drove onto the Mayfair campus for a twofold purpose. One was for an emergency family therapy session, and the second was for an emergency consult with their psychiatrist.

Each time we were at Mayfair for our sessions with Dan, it was a reminder to Lilly that at one time her behavior had sent her there. She didn't exactly become fearful whenever we'd pull into Mayfair, but she would be a little more guarded or cautious.

We met with the doctor first, because he had agreed to see us before closing shop at four thirty. He was a creepy-looking guy with no personality but we had sort of gotten used to him. He listened as we recounted as gently as possible the recent tantrums and activities.

We didn't like to bring up all the dirt in front of Lilly while she sat looking at pictures in a magazine.

He nodded and wrote down some things and cleared his throat. He said there would be some medication adjustments that "should help."

Lilly listened to him talk as her eyes darted up from the pictures. As usual, she showed some relief that a doctor was trying something else to help her manage.

The medication adjustments normally had to be gradual, but often her behavior would improve overnight. I think those times she just rose to the occasion because it was more of a mental decision, like taking a placebo.

CHAPTER FIFTY-TWO

The good effects from the medication change lasted ten whole days, and ended colorfully when Bruce and I had conflicting work schedules. Normally one of us would have had her while the other was working. Torie had been a backup but her life had changed, and she had a little baby to take care of.

I called Delsie and explained the problem. She considered it legitimate, and because it had never come up before, said Lilly could go to the CHC house after school, and stay there for an hour and a half until I got off work and picked her up.

I explained to Lilly that she'd go there after school for a very short time and it was not a consequence. She seemed to understand so I'm not sure why she ran out of that house after school. CHC called the police and reported that she was wearing a pair of jeans and a leopard print top.

A policeman located her after checking all the streets surrounding the old house. He spotted her trying to hold onto a heavy chain that had a large, ugly dog at the other end of it. When he caught her, she had mud on her shoes and hands, and the dog-walking wasn't going so well.

The dog probably hadn't been off that chain in years and she was lucky she hadn't been attacked by him. Maybe he sensed that he better not mess with her.

The following day after school she went out back to play, and I soon heard her screaming and cussing. I went quickly to investigate and found she had left the backyard and gone to the front.

"Lilly, what are you yelling about?"

She was irate and pointed across the street. "There was a white cat in our driveway and I chased him out!"

I had never known her to want an animal *out* of our yard before. "Okay, just leave it alone. He won't come back. You need to go in the backyard, though, and not come out front."

She silently obeyed but had her thumb in her mouth and her shoulders hunched, which had always been a sign of being "disregulated," as Dan called it.

My thoughts raced as I considered the options. With her already outside and wound up, I couldn't do much. I was afraid of her now, too, and unwilling to get injured again. She was too big and too strong. But she needed to be kept safe, so I hurried inside to get the dinner meds, thinking they might help calm her.

I was only inside a couple minutes but when I went back out with the meds, she was nowhere. I looked in the shed and in the car, as well as up and down the street. Not seeing her, I called 911 and CHC. I had my phone with me and was standing in my drive when the neighbor who'd had her beer taken walked quickly over to me.

"Your daughter stole my dog." She was not happy and proceeded to walk quickly down her drive and crossed the street. She went between two houses and disappeared.

She must have seen Lilly go that direction.

I felt awful. The dog was a nice, old, one-eyed yellow lab that just plain didn't need to be stolen.

The police arrived, and then the on-call social worker came.

Soon my neighbor appeared with her dog on a leash and stalked to her house. (I wished I'd had a chance to get to know her and explain some things about Lilly *before* all this happened, but we eventually found her to be a wonderful neighbor.)

The police scoured nearby yards and returned with Lilly struggling to free herself. Once they released her, she wouldn't allow them to come near until the CHC lady finally coaxed her to go inside our house. I think she finally agreed only because she was smart enough to know it was a better option than going away again in an ambulance.

While she was out front, she yelled over and over, "I was just trying to chase that damn cat out of our driveway! It had no business on our property! I needed the dog to chase it away. I don't trust you cops! You can't tell me what to do! You stay away from me!" The bad words followed, and my heart sank because I just knew we were ruined in the new neighborhood. I felt sure the people in at least twenty houses on the once-quiet street heard everything.

Once Lilly went inside, the CHC woman played Barbie dolls with her for about an hour and persuaded her to take evening meds. They usually knocked her out about an hour after swallowing them, but that never happened and about six thirty p.m. she dashed out the front door.

Stunned, I called 911 again. I was drained from the day and didn't know if I'd live through another public round. Maybe the ambulance could cart ME off and I could start life again somewhere else. Yeah.

I knew they'd found her when I heard the obscenities coming from our front sidewalk. Bruce was home by then, and he went out to talk to the poker-faced police who had had about enough of this new little girl in town.

Lilly was strapped down in the ambulance and carted to Columbia Children's. The CHC manager drove her own car and we met there.

Around midnight we were sitting half-asleep in the ER waiting room and got word from the doctor that Lilly would not be admitted, now for the third time in a row.

By that time she was half-asleep herself, and I put her in my car and drove to the old CHC house with the social worker following me. Lilly would go to school from there in the morning, and Delsie would finalize arrangements for her to be readmitted to Mayfair after school.

CHAPTER FIFTY-THREE

It fell to me to put together the things Lilly would need at Mayfair. There was such a feeling of finality as I folded her pants, shirts, and pajamas. I placed small piles of items across the top of her white floral bedspread. The pajamas were significant to me, because without them, she would have been a visitor by day. Needing pajamas signified sleeping in a home and being a part of it. This time when the pajamas left, I felt certain it was final, and she would be gone. I picked up the last set and held them to my chest and looked up toward the ceiling and sighed as tears filled my eyes.

Bruce and I had seen it coming as she grew larger and older. The first time she'd gone away to Mayfair for ten months was exhausting, and we didn't have it in us to go through all that again indefinitely. We had come to the end of the road as far as her need for pajamas at our house. But it was something that her guardian ad litem said that finally made it "okay." She knew us and Lilly well, and was a wise and seasoned guardian.

She said, "Now don't quote me on this, because I NEVER said it. Sometimes –and it is rare –sometimes we need to give a child the freedom to be a residential or institutional child. Some children cannot make it in a family, period, and feel better about themselves when not in one, but still cared for, naturally. These are the most severely damaged and abused kids that can never be what they need to be in a family for any length of time. It is actually freeing for them to be out of one."

Although that was a very politically incorrect statement, I knew she was right, and it helped immensely to hear it. We had reached the place in the road where permanent residential living was the only safe option for Lilly –and us. It wasn't like she was going to shrink in size and strength, and become easier to handle as she got older. No, it was the opposite, and we had been living with this reality. The fact that she was alive after all of her travels alone was a miracle in itself. How long could this go on before she was hit by a car or kidnapped? We'd always be there as parents for Lilly –that was not the question. The question was what were we willing and able to DO for her for the rest of our lives and hers?

We talked at great length about it. We couldn't commit to two or three trips a week, driving an hour each way for family therapy. There was no point, as we knew it was geared toward establishing a future reentry into our home. We had little grand-babies who were often at our house now and could be at risk, as we were ourselves.

What we could commit to was to continue to be her mother and father. We could have regular visits at her facility. We could take her off campus when her behavior merited it, but her pajamas would remain on campus.

Bruce and I pulled into the Advance School's parking lot. Delsie had told her what would be transpiring after school that day. Bruce got out and went in the school to get Lilly for the drive to Mayfair, while I sat in the car with the window down and watched kids and parents coming out of the building.

Bruce and Lilly left the school from a side door near her classroom. He was carrying the backpack which rarely had any books it, and jean-jacketed Lilly walked beside him with her height coming just a few inches above his elbow.

She was smiling and said, "Hey, look at that kid. He's got his coat on backward!" She laughed teasingly at the boy, and he turned his head and shrugged his shoulders at her like he was quite aware that he had put his coat on that way. She flashed her crooked smile at him and said, "You're crazier than I thought you were."

Bruce opened the back door for Lilly, and she got in.

I turned to look back at her and smiled. "Hi, honey."

She didn't seem to hear. Her face was glued to the window where she was looking at all the (mostly) boys crossing the parking lot and getting onto buses.

"There's Cody! He still likes me. That girl there is a brat. You know what she did? She stole my lip gloss but I told the teacher on her."

I asked, "Did you get it back?"

"No. Teacher put it in his desk. It makes me SO MAD!"

We pulled out before the five or six buses, and I realized someone needed to tell her teacher that she wouldn't be back. I was sure she wasn't thinking about the fact that it was her last school day there. She was still in the moment of living out part of the school day, and
I was in awe that she could do that.

As we drove though, and got onto a familiar highway leading to Mayfair, it seemed we were time-traveling backward two years. There we were with Lilly's things neatly packed. Polly had been replaced somewhere along the line by "Sammy," a big, stuffed, white seal that she had begged for when we had been at a zoo gift shop. Sammy had seen some violence and the white fiberfill stuffing was visible from a tear at the base of his tail. His fur was kind of grubby and scuffed and his shiny glass eyes with gray flecks had tiny scratches on them. They had seen an awful lot.

Lilly didn't seem afraid, and her comments as we neared Mayfair were sporadic but didn't convey dread: "I hope that kid that choked Pete isn't there. Will I be in cottage twenty-seven? You remember I told you that woman shut my hand in the door and broke it? I hate her. I hope they are having pizza tonight!" She had her thumb in her mouth off and on between the comments.

We drove into the entry drive and her face scanned the area to see if any people that she knew were walking around. We had been there weekly with her for family therapy since her discharge twelve months before, so it seemed as if that was the reason we were there. We parked and decided not to cart her stuff in until we knew which cottage for sure.

Bruce said, "Lilly, please hold my hand," and she did. We headed to Dan Wheatley's office.

While we were walking, she said to me, "Mom, leave Sammy in our car. Can you take him home and fix his tail?"

I could tell she was being brave, as I looked down at her taking big steps. "Yes, I will."

Dan's door was open and he was at his desk. He saw us in the hall, and his hello was chipper as usual. After greeting us, his smile tightened, and he swallowed.

It dawned on me that this was also hard for him. He had worked with her and us for two years, and now it seemed it was back to square one.

"Lilly, you're in Cottage fourteen. Come on with me to the cafeteria for dinner, (he knew she never refused food), and your mom and dad can drive their car to fourteen and take your things in." He looked at us for approval. "Meet us in the cafeteria in half an hour?"

We liked the arrangement and half-smiled as he led her away, chatting her up. He was pretty good at that.

After doing as we were told, we met up in the small cafeteria where they were finishing. We three walked her to fourteen and showed her the tiny bedroom with her belongings all unpacked. She was allowed to have very little, of course, because the space was limited.

Dan left us in the room to say goodbye. She didn't cry until she saw my eyes water, and then we embraced.

"Lilly, we love you and are not deserting you. We'll be back in three days. The house lady here said your call day is tomorrow night, so call us." I hugged her hard and Bruce gave her a kiss on the cheek.

Lilly cried out, "Mommy! Daddy!"

We left the cottage quickly, and met Dan outside and stood there to talk with him.

He asked, "What days would work best for you for family therapy?"

We had known the question was coming, and Bruce spoke up, "Dan, we are not going to work toward Lilly living with us. It's become too much –and too dangerous. We have little grandchildren that we don't want to see get hurt, and you know that's a possibility. We have done everything humanly possible, but that's the way it will have to be unless a miracle happens."

I added, "We'll come for regular visits, and we can take her off campus if she qualifies. Maybe she can even come for the holidays –we're not walking away from her. We're still going to be her family. She can't live at our house, though."

Dan Wheatley looked from me to Bruce, and he started to cry.

We leaned in for a group hug as the cold wind tousled our hair. We were all three crying as we parted. We told Dan we'd call him soon.

It reminded me of the time protocol was forgotten as Kathi Beadle and I drove to the emergency room together in her car. When you have fought the same war and taken some hits together, a bond forms that blurs the lines of protocol. That bond may seem to fade with time, but it is not erased.

Our drive home was solemn and each of us was lost in our own thoughts. I realized that I had been irrationally hopeful for Lilly many times over the six and a half years. If it hadn't been for that, then cold hard facts would have won out, and she would have had to leave after the initial fourteen days. Whose loss would it have been? I daresay ours as well as hers.

Even though it had been the most challenging thing we had ever done, I was very glad that we had said yes when the phone rang six years earlier. I had, with Bruce's help, done the right thing, and a great peace flooded over me as I remembered.

CHAPTER FIFTY-FOUR

Three days later we were sitting back in Dan's office. He explained to us that Lilly wouldn't be staying in Cottage fourteen for more than a few months because Mayfair kept kids only through age twelve. He said that since she would be thirteen in five months, the county was looking for another residential care center to take her.

I was quite alarmed and asked, "But shouldn't her developmental age be considered? Why put her in with teenagers?"

Dan shrugged and replied, "They go by ages, Nealie, and there's nothing we can do about it. Most all of these kids are behind their age level."

Bruce asked, "Will they keep her in Illinois?"

Dan nodded, "Every effort will be made to make it conducive for you to remain her parents and see her. I doubt they'd move her far away because the county knows how important you've been in her life, and Tina is also in Illinois."

We silently pondered his response and I thought he was right.

Dan tapped a pen slowly in the palm of his hand. He had his readers perched on top of his head and looked down at the pen. "I really think Lilly needs to be told she won't be returning to your home." He said it as if he had given it some thought.

I was incredulous and frowned at him. "I disagree," I said sharply.

Bruce looked over at me and then at Dan.

I continued vehemently, "What's going to change? We'll still be her parents. We'll still be in her life. She knows her behavior is dangerous and why she's here. So why crush her with *that*? What's the point?"

Dan spread his hands palm up and said, "She needs closure. She needs to be able to move on."

"Move on to what?" I almost shouted. "She's not going anywhere except another institution. We're not going anywhere."

I dug my heels in and said, "No, I'm not telling her any such thing, because there is no reason for it."

Bruce had been quiet up until then and cleared his throat. "There's no hurry on it, is there? Let's just see how things go for a while." His statement didn't please me or Dan but it calmed the tension in the room.

I wanted to change the subject. "We'd like to see her once a week. If she has problems, we want to know, okay?"

He nodded. "Certainly. Hey, it's almost time for my next family but I'll go with you over to fourteen."

We walked through fallen red and yellow leaves to the cottage. He let us in with his key and introduced us to the staff who we'd not met three days earlier when Lilly had been admitted.

We heard a yelp and saw her barreling across the room toward us. She flew into our arms and hugged us.

Dan secured the little visiting room before he took off to meet with the next set of parents. I hoped they wouldn't give him trouble, too.

"How are you doing, Lilly?" Bruce asked as he sat on the little brown sofa beside her.

She sputtered, "Not so good. There's this boy who keeps cussing at me, and once he threw a book at me." Her eyes narrowed and she continued with a toss of her head, "You know my dress-up high heels? I put holes in my walls with them –all over and you know why? Because the stupid bitch in the other bedroom kicks her walls and I hate that noise! So, I hit my wall with the shoes back at her!" She had been scowling but then she smiled mischievously.

I pictured the tan wall covered with little holes in the plaster, and I tried hard not to smile too. "What did the staff say?"

She lowered her voice and said, "They took my shoes away, but they didn't do *nothing* to her!" Once again the scowl was back.

At that moment, the door opened a few inches, and two green eyes peered in at us.

Lilly uttered a profanity and sprang from the couch toward the door. "Get out and mind your own business!" she screamed and pulled the door shut. "I hate him."

Bruce wanted to settle her agitation. He asked, "Have you found anyone to play Barbies with?"

She sighed. "No. Yes. Joanna played Barbies with me once."

We sat for a moment in silence. Her dark blue eyes looked angry and her shoulders were hunched forward as she sat. "How long will I be here?" She put her thumb in her mouth as she waited for the answer.

Bruce and I glanced at each other, and he let me take the lead.

"Lilly, Dan said you are getting too old for Mayfair. You are going to be a teenager soon, and teenagers aren't allowed to stay here."

Her eyes darted from me to Bruce, and I hurried on before she assumed that meant a discharge back home. "Dan and the county are looking for a place around here for you to stay. We will come to you wherever you are," I added, desperately hoping to reassure her.

"Why can't I go home?" Her eyes locked on mine.

Bruce gently responded, "Lilly, you have to learn to be safe. You have to learn not to be violent and not to run away. Those are things that have to happen first."

She narrowed her eyes and with the thumb stuck to the roof of her mouth, quietly said, "I hate you. You aren't my real parents."

I had had enough and our time was about up, so I rose and said very matter-of-factly, "Sorry you feel that way but we're the only parents you've got, and we love you."

She spat out, "No you don't!" and started to get up. She was at the door in three steps and before she slammed it behind her, she growled, "I don't care about you! You hate me! Damn you! Don't you ever come see me again!"

We got up and stood and looked at each other. Bruce shrugged his shoulders and I sighed. We saw an older man on the way out and I said to him, "Tell Lilly we'll be back the same time next week, please. Tell her she can call us on her call-day if she wants." I spoke these things kind of loudly, figuring she was in her room listening for our departure. I was right, because she immediately began screaming profanities in her room and we heard the sounds of things being thrown.

We left the cottage and stepped outside into cold semi-darkness. Crunchy leaves broke under our footsteps. The coldness felt so good, and by the time we walked to our car, the oppressiveness we had felt was gone.

I didn't feel Bruce had lied to her when he had responded to her question about going home. If a miracle actually happened and she became totally safe with herself and others, then we could revisit that question. At that moment, though, we weren't even her foster parents anymore. CHC had relinquished their role with Lilly when her team of people agreed she couldn't be kept safely in a home environment. Their contract with the county had ended, as well as the funding to CHC to manage her case.

Anything that we did with (or for) her from then on was totally on our own. We had committed to being her parents, with or without compensation. Whether or not Lilly wanted to claim us on any given day didn't diminish the moral obligation we would always feel for her.

CHAPTER FIFTY-FIVE

 Dan's prediction that Lilly would have to leave Mayfair at age thirteen came true. A religious charity in Kankakee, Illinois had room for her. We would continue to have about an hour drive from our house, and we were relieved it wasn't going to be any farther.

I made it clear to Dan that I definitely planned to be with Lilly the day she was moved. We three adults realized we were parting company professionally and saying goodbye wasn't easy.

For Lilly, she was leaving a place where she was one of the oldest and knew the grounds, staff, and rules inside and out. She had made a reputation for herself at Mayfair. Staff there (especially Dan) had become like family to her, and she was frightened about the move.

We were concerned because she would be one of the youngest in a teen lockup environment for "special situation" kids. That meant self-harmers, suicidal, violent, mildly mentally retarded kids, or kids too young and violent to be a candidate for a typical juvenile detention center. Some of them were admitted by their parents at the advice of medical experts.

We wondered how anyone was able to pay for residential because we had heard the cost was well over $200 per day and stays were typically three or more months.

Lilly was headed to Blair Village, and the first part of her stay was supposed to be in an all-in-one securely locked building. The school-room, therapy room, lunchroom and bedrooms were all under one roof, and there was no leaving except for escorted doctor or dental trips.

The hope was that after she made progress, she would be moved to a step-down building. In step-down, kids practiced the coping skills they had learned during their initial stay in the first building, with the goal being reunification with their families. Those without a family lived out their teen years in places like Blair Village as wards of the state.

That's what Lilly was –a ward of the state. There was no other way to say it, and it sounded awful. How could she ever live in our home without something happening to her from running loose in town, or harming us or visitors when she became out of control?

At that time she had a very good county worker who told me she would be transporting Lilly to Blair Village, and I could meet them and facilitate with the admission process. There was no way I would have missed that, given her apprehension about the move.

I had a difficult time locating her building on the new campus and was a nervous wreck worrying about her. When I finally found her, she was in an office with the worker, surrounded by four pathetic-looking large black garbage bags that held all her belongings. She was wearing a hot pink shirt and blue jeans and stood sucking her thumb.

She burst into tears when she saw me. "Mommy! I didn't think you'd find me!"

"Lilly, it's okay. I will always find you. I'll get you settled in here."

I looked at the county worker and asked her, "What can I do?" I was still frazzled from the drive and trying to find the right building on time, but I put on a game-face for Lilly.

The county lady had experienced the admission process many times before for other children, but I could tell from her expression she still felt compassion for us.

She said to me, "A Mrs. Booth is checking on an empty room where we can sort all the stuff in these bags." She motioned to the four large beat-up garbage bags.

Just then the door opened and a cheerful woman said, "Hi, you must be Lilly's mom. I'm Mrs. Booth and I found an office where we can sort her things." She led the way and we each had to drag a bag as we went down the hall.

I noticed the last two doors required a key for us to enter. Once in the room, the county worker said her goodbyes and Mrs. Booth unlocked the doors to let her out while I waited momentarily with Lilly.

She returned and looked at Lilly, took in a deep breath, and said, "Okay, we need to sort these into four piles: dirty clothes, clean clothes, toys, and a pile for things that you really don't need." She bent over and opened the bag nearest her.

Lilly looked suspiciously at the woman and objected, "You can't throw my stuff away."

Mrs. Booth paused and said, "I'll ask your permission first. See this dirty green sock? If it doesn't have a mate can we toss it out?"

Lilly shrugged.

I spoke up, "Let's open another bag. You can look at the piles when we're done but we really need to get this over with." I opened the bag and knelt on the floor and began sorting. A faint bathroom odor wafted up as I looked at a menagerie of clothes, stuffed critters, papers, and three Barbie dolls with magic marker scrawled on their faces. I wished there were rubber gloves to wear and glanced over at Mrs. Booth, who showed little hesitancy or aversion to the rummaging task.

Lilly began to relax a little as we sorted because she felt she had a say in what we were doing. The office kind of stunk by the time we were done. Mrs. Booth wisely re-bagged and tied shut the discard pile before Lilly had a chance to change her mind.

After hand sanitizer was passed around, Mrs. Booth looked at me and said, "Lilly has to get settled in before mealtime. She's probably hungry. Wait here for me to let you out and I'll take her to meet her unit manager."

Lilly started to whimper and cry, "Mommy . . ."

If I didn't act strong it would make parting worse, so I forced a big smile.

"Okay Lilly, time to give me a hug. Daddy and I will be here to see you soon." I hugged her, and she looked resigned.

Mrs. Booth opened yet another door and led her away.

When Mrs. Booth returned to let me, out she said, "We have very good staff in this unit. She'll be okay. She's small for her age, but quite a handful from what I've read."

I looked at her and grinned. "Oh, yeah. By the way, her closest companion is that stuffed seal. His name is Sammy."

The door clicked shut behind me as I headed toward the parking lot. Halfway to my car I turned to survey the area. I had been too nervous getting there to really pay attention to the surroundings. Lilly's building looked newer than the many other buildings, and there were some deer standing near it that caught my eye.

They didn't seem afraid, and I hoped they would hang around long enough for her to get a glimpse of them from wherever she was inside. It would help take her mind off her troubles, at least momentarily. That was one thing my little waif had going for her. She vacillated quickly from one thing to another, which at times enabled her to temporarily forget everything troubling.

After that, Bruce and I visited her weekly in a room that served as the school during the day. It seemed that our arrival was the high point of her week because she made us feel very special, and she would try to introduce us to kids and staff before being let into the school room to eat the snacks we'd brought with us and to play games.

It was difficult to focus in the room because we could sometimes see and hear the other kids and staff through a window. It was common to see running or hear angry shouts and screaming. More than once we had to go to our car while staff tried to safely secure the building during some particularly violent outbursts of other teens.

We felt that we weren't removed just for our safety, but also because the less witnessed by visitors, the better. I knew firsthand how people could look at a situation and make a judgment-call about what was taking place. It was tricky for staff in these places to practice safety and the proper reactions when confronted with the craziness and violence typical of some kids' behaviors. We hoped the staff response would always be above reproach because our daughter was in there.

Overall, we felt Lilly was being helped, but it was a scary place to me because the teens were all very disturbed and unpredictable. We had to remind ourselves her behavior put her there, and she could definitely earn her way out into a step-down unit.

CHAPTER FIFTY-SIX

Bruce brought home a newspaper some months after Lilly went to stay at Blair Village. "You're not going to believe this, but it says in here that Roger Stevens was arrested for sexually abusing their foster boys." He sadly shook his head and placed the paper down in front of me.

I looked up at him from my chair, confused. I asked, "Roger, as in Roger and Mary from our training classes at CHC?"

Bruce replied, "Yes."

I kept my eyes fixed on his and didn't look down at the paper. "I don't believe it."

Bruce pointed to the newspaper and said, "Well, I don't know. Read it."

I read the article, and it said a boy was being transported by car to the Stevens' home for respite when he opened his car door and tumbled out in an attempt to avoid arriving at the Stevens' home. Upon questioning, the boy said Roger had sexually abused him during his previous respite stay, and he didn't want to go back there.

"There is no way, Bruce. Roger is a nice grandpa. He loves Mary and treats her great. He helped Mary watch Lilly when they did day-respites. He helped fix up the CHC house and adopted two boys. They won a fostering award . . . he goes to our church. I don't believe it."

Bruce shrugged his shoulders and said, "I hope you're right. It doesn't make sense."

I looked at him and frowned. "Maybe that kid set Roger up on purpose. Some of these kids are pretty devious."

Bruce looked thoughtful. "Well, jumping out of a moving car seems more desperate than devious."

That thought sank in and I had to agree. The last thing I said was, "One thing we have learned by now is that the newspaper doesn't always tell it right, and I still don't believe it. I'm going to send them a card."

Roger and Mary Stevens were living every foster parent's worst nightmare, and I cringed inside. Every allegation made by a foster child had to be investigated by law. Lesser accusations such as bias or favoritism did not involve police. Most gripes leveled by kids against foster parents could be resolved or dismissed during talks with their case managers, often in the presence of the foster parent. Those were similar to a family meeting. If a foster child asked, they could have a private meeting.

I prayed justice would be done and the truth come out, but it really disturbed me.

After three months of being locked up, Lilly started to improve in some areas that were prerequisites for being considered for step-down. Those areas were fighting with other kids, self-harming, threats of any type, and attacking staff. Of course, the AWOL or running away issue couldn't be tested because there was no opportunity to run when all the doors were locked.

She would improve and then regress. All in all, it took six months in that building for her to reach the desired goals. By then we felt she had become much more inhibited and less confident than we had ever seen her. I supposed anyone incarcerated for six months would come away with a more subdued personality.

Lilly was excited as well as reserved when Mrs. Booth told her, "You have been doing so well, and your county worker and I agree you are ready to move into one of the step-down houses here soon."

Lilly's excitement at the news was tempered with, "But what if I'm not ready? I don't trust myself. What if I run away? No, I won't do that and mess up. I don't want my butt put back in here!"

She had about a month where she knew the step-down time was approaching, and toward the end, it was all she could do not to get into violence and aggression just because of the anticipation.

The move occurred one day out of the blue, and we didn't know she'd actually been relocated on campus until several days later.

When we went to see her for the first time after the building transfer, it was apparent the inhibitions had fled. Lilly's swagger was back.

Bruce and I were happy for her, but concerned at the same time for a number of reasons. It was basically a house with a "family" of messed-up kids. Her building housed only girls and so the workers were all women. Some of them were top notch staff who showed professionalism and concern. A couple of them were morbidly obese and rarely left their chairs, so communication might be by cell phone or shouting, but we tried not to judge them for this unusual method of communicating. Fat or skinny, we just never knew who the goats might be and were on guard for Lilly because she needed us to watch out for her.

Another concern was the unlocked front door. Who would stop Lilly from leaving when she got mad? The facility was only twenty minutes from the heart of good-sized city. We wondered how long she would stay safe living in the house.

She had been in her new place for a few weeks when I went to visit her by myself at one point, because Bruce was working. Staff told us we could walk the grounds and as we went out the front door together, Lilly pulled out an eye shadow compact. No cosmetics had been allowed in the previous lockup unit.

"What do you have there?" I asked.

She answered me in a ghetto groove, "Ooh, yeah, uh-huh... I've got some eye shadow that this girl gave me." She opened it as we walked, and I looked over at it. The two colors in the compact were very dark blue and black.

We walked a little farther and then I said, "Lilly, you're only thirteen."

She started putting it on and said with an attitude, "Mom, I'm thirteen and a half. And we're allowed to wear make-up in step-down."

She noticed a couple of teenage boys who were hanging around a nearby boys' house. I jumped when she yelled out, "Hey, Dave!"

I was very uneasy about the close proximity and seeming availability of those teen boys. I cautioned her, "Those boys are here because they have huge problems, and you are not old enough to be around them, either."

"Well," she sneered at me, "I'm wearing this eye makeup and you can't tell me what to do!"

I stopped walking and turned to look intently at her. "I'm your mom, Lilly, and you need to listen to me because I care about you."

She suddenly threw the compact on the ground and stepped down hard, cracking it into pieces. "I'll do what I want, you bitch!"

She had not talked to me like that in the ten months away from our home, so although I had heard far worse in the past, that one nasty word was like a rock thrown at me.

As soon as it was out of her mouth, she turned abruptly and took off running toward her house, but didn't go inside. She darted between it and another one and disappeared.

I could hear her cursing me as she went. I called the phone number at the house. "Hello, this is Lilly's mom. She got mad at me and took off behind the house, and I'm leaving."

It wasn't my job to physically chase her anymore. If I did run after her to try and tackle her, I'd probably get arrested because I wasn't even her foster mother. It was daylight and I knew they'd find her before she could get off the huge grassy acreage.

I was mad as I drove the hour home because it had been a long while since she had treated me like that.

Staff found her after I left and convinced her to go back to the house, but she was angry at the world and proceeded to tear up her room and bash the glass out of her large bedroom window. I think she may have been angry, too, that I didn't stay around for the chase. She also knew she wouldn't see me again until the following visit seven days later.

I hate to admit it but I did not go the following week. There were times I felt used and abused myself and would be angry. When that happened, distance between her and I was the best remedy.

Bruce went alone to the next visit, and Lilly anxiously asked him, "Where's Mommy? Is she sick?"

"No, she's not sick. You treated her pretty bad last week, and she needs some space."

"Oh." The thumb went in her mouth and she hung her head a bit. Then she took it out and asked, "Can we walk over the bridge? I saw deer over there."

He answered, "Sure."

He told me they had a nice time and she didn't talk a whole lot.

The next week when I arrived with him, she gave me a hug. "Mom, I was afraid you didn't want to see me. I'm sorry. You were right. You are my mom and need respect. I mean, I don't like it when people don't respect *me* –I want to punch them in their face!" She giggled and hugged me hard.

One week, Bruce and I asked for permission to take her in our car to a McDonald's and it was granted. That marked the beginning of her behaving well in the car. Maybe the change came because she had only been in a vehicle four or five times during the previous eleven month period. Or maybe she finally understood the dangers. We don't know, but from that day on, Lilly didn't hit, kick, spit, or try to get out of the vehicle.

I wish I could tell the reader that everything turned around from there. Not so in most areas, and in other areas, things became more dangerous.

One afternoon a girl in Lilly's house gave Sammy the Seal a swirly in the commode. A fist-fight broke out and Lilly ran out the door after getting in some punches.

She ran off the grounds and came upon a group of firemen involved in a training exercise where they were preparing to burn down an old house. She was outraged that they would start a fire, so she picked up bricks and began throwing them at the firemen while she damned them to hell.

Police came and carted her back to Blair Village.

She turned fourteen while she was there, and that particular birthday fanned her ego. She felt entitled to more respect and privileges by all, but it didn't happen in her group of peers.

Each girl had her own issues, and that had to be a hindrance to any real friendships being forged. Her friendships were reserved for the deer and geese on the property. I doubt they felt safe around her but she nonetheless oohed and ahhed over them daily.

One day she noticed a skunk at the edge of the woods. She didn't include skunks in her group of friends and took off out the door after it. She scooped up a stick and pursued the evil beast as fast as she could. The skunk didn't react until she whacked it with the stick and shouted, "Get out of here, you devil!"

As soon as it sprayed her, she yelled some more and dropped the stick and ran fast toward the Blair houses. She tried the door of the first house she came to, and it opened.

"Lilly –whoa!" The door slammed shut in her face.

She ran to the next door and they wouldn't let her in, either.

The third door was her own house, and they decided to let her in only after thinking about what could happen to them if they didn't.

CHAPTER FIFTY-SEVEN

Roger Stevens pleaded "not guilty." Five months later he changed it to "guilty" and was sentenced to nine years in prison. It did not go to trial. He was convicted of sexual battery, gross sexual imposition, and rape. Roger was labeled a sexual predator.

I still had my doubts about his guilt. How could things be so messed up? Maybe he had been a goat all along. Only he and that boy knew the truth.

Bruce and I talked about his conviction almost the whole hour we drove to Blair to see Lilly her twelfth month there. He believed Roger must have been guilty. Someone told me that he changed from "not guilty" to "guilty" when it looked like his dear Mary would have to testify if he didn't. Anyway, we ended up lost in our own thoughts on the matter during the last ten minutes of the drive.

We had been notified that Lilly had to stay on campus that particular trip because she'd run away a few days before. But we already knew she was grounded, because a few nights before at 2:10 a.m. a phone call woke us up.

Bruce picked it up immediately. He whispered, "Nealie, it's the Greenville police."

I could hear Lilly screaming in the background while he held the phone.

"Yes, this is Bruce Rose." He listened momentarily. "No, she doesn't live with us. She lives at Blair Village." He listened some more and then spoke louder, "I'm sorry, officer, but I can't hear you very well with all the screaming. We were her FOSTER PARENTS. Her name is Lilly Angel and she lives at BLAIR VILLAGE."

From my side of the bed, I could hear radios clicking and Lilly cussing.

"Okay, thank you for calling. Goodbye." Bruce set down the phone and climbed back into bed. "The officer said she had a lot of black stuff covering her face and hands. They found her after someone at a gas station called them, and she gave them our phone number."

I was wide awake and rolled onto my side to look toward him. "She was at a *gas station*? In the middle of the night? Bruce, how did she remember the phone number? And black stuff? That's so bizarre."

A few days after that happened, we were knocking on the door of her step-down house.

We heard her excitedly yell to us as she ran towards the door, "Mommy! Daddy!"

We both did a double-take when she came into sight. Her hair was Gothic black, but we didn't put two and two together until she was seated across from us in the visiting room.

"I suppose you noticed my hair is black." She smiled sweetly.

Bruce smiled and said, "Yeah, we noticed."

Lilly took in a breath and said, "Well, I'm going to tell you the truth. I already got big consequences from it. But you are my parents, and I'll tell you the truth." She put her thumb in her mouth and looked from Bruce to me. We noticed the cuticles around her nails were black.

"Okay . . ." I prompted.

She spoke in a wee little girl's voice and softly said, "I ran away to a drugstore. I stole hair dye."

We were starting to get it. I couldn't imagine the mess she'd made in that bathroom.

She continued, "I went to a gas station and put it on my hair in their bathroom. Then someone called the F-_____ police (Oops! Sorry Mom!) cops on me."

We looked at her white-as-a-sheet skin and the blacker-than-coal hair sticking out all over her head. *Would Lilly ever be safe out in the community?*

I spoke first. "You could have been kidnapped. That was late at night."

Bruce nodded his agreement, and she hung her head.

"I know. Someone could have taken me and hurt me." There was a pause.

I shrugged and said, "Your hair doesn't look so good. Was it worth it?"

"No, but now I don't have to wait until you say I'm old enough. But I know it was bad to steal it." Her blue eyes twinkled and she gave me a mischievous grin. She clearly didn't understand the dangers lurking in the outside world.

Once her grounding ended, I was granted permission to take her to a Taco Bell in town for dinner. It was just me that visit, and she was very excited because she hadn't left Blair for three weeks.

It was late August, and she was wearing a brown, long-sleeved shirt under her blue jean jacket. She also had on wide black gaucho capris and fuzzy gray ankle socks. The ensemble was completed by neon pink flip-flops wedged between the toes of the fuzzy socks.

We went in and sat near a front window at the restaurant. When I was with Lilly, I would always try to choose an isolated spot because she was continually in everybody's business. There was no one near us when we sat down.

While we were opening our food items, a group of five girls and boys walked in.

Lilly's antennas went up as she watched them order at the counter.

They were probably about thirteen years old. Luck would have it that they sat only two tables away, giggling and acting cool.

Her eyes had been glued on them and she was not eating her food.

"Lilly, eat and quit staring at them please."

She dipped a nacho in cheese and put it in her mouth. She and I both heard a swear word come from the kids' table.

She put her palms flat down on the table in front of her and looked at me and hissed, "Did you hear that, Mom? They are cussing!" She turned to glare at them but the junior-high kids were only interested in themselves and continued the language as they talked on.

Suddenly Lilly sprang up from her seat and marched up to the counter.

I sat helpless and watched as she spoke to a young girl behind the cash register. I concentrated and could barely make out what she was saying as she pointed toward the group, "Those kids over there are being inappropriate. They are cussing and my mom shouldn't have to listen to that!" (Thanks, Lilly.)

I was grateful the kids were so into themselves they didn't see her talking at the counter.

I saw the employee put her hands on her hips and say something to Lilly, but I didn't hear what. She smiled at my oddly-dressed girl and motioned for her to go ahead and sit back down.

Lilly came back to our table and took her seat with me. Her expression showed satisfaction as she started back in on her food. She ate a few bites and glanced over again at the teens.

What neither of us saw coming was what happened next.

The Taco Bell employee strode quickly up to the table of talking kids and bellowed, "Shut the f--- up and get the hell out of here!"

I froze.

The kids became quiet, gathered up their stuff, and stood to leave.

As they did, Lilly picked her jaw up off the floor and put her hand over her heart. She smiled her crooked smile at the employee in admiration and said, "You told THEM!" She looked at me with her eyes still wide, "Mom, did you hear that? She told them, didn't she?"

Lilly turned back to the employee and nodded her head up and down approvingly and said, "You go, girl!"

I could have fallen face-down in my nachos.

The next AWOL chilled me to the bone. Evidently two of the girls in Lilly's house were familiar with the nearby city and planned to run away after dark for some fun, and she naïvely went with them. They ended up at the home of somebody's relative for a while, before walking the streets until they got to a park. The two girls met some other guys and girls there, and then the teens played in the lake at the park.

Lilly didn't want to get wet because it was dark and she was afraid, so she left on her own. She later told me, "I didn't want to be with those boys and my friends. I didn't trust them, so I left. I walked to a gas station and got some candy. A man in a car asked me, 'Do you need a ride young lady?' I said yes and got in and we drove all over. He let me use his cell phone for a while, and I tried to call people but their numbers wouldn't work. I couldn't remember them. He wasn't nice. He was actually BAD. I told him I was calling the cops if he didn't let me out. So he let me out."

I sat and listened with every alarm bell in my brain going off. She had to be behind locked doors for her own safety. How else was she going to live to see age fifteen in a few months?

Her county worker felt the same and started looking into other residential options. Nothing opened up until October, and then it happened fast.

One day Lilly was in her eighteenth month at Blair Village, and the next day she was in a ranch house in the middle of nowhere.

The new place was also a religious charity, but not of the same religion as Blair Village. The drive to see her went in the totally opposite direction from Blair, but amazingly it was still about one hour from our house.

"The Taylor Home" was far from everywhere. It was set in the middle of vast cornfields and was a sharp contrast to the populated areas at Mayfair and Blair Village. We were asked to wait one week before visiting, to allow Lilly to adjust.

When Bruce and I arrived the first time, we found her very happy with the new situation.

The Taylor Home was run as a family with live-in house parents, a dog, an outside cat, family cooking, meals, and laundry. The house parents actually showed us Lilly's room. (Blair village never allowed us to see where she slept the entire eighteen months.) She was pleased as punch that there was a real live dog in the house, and that she could help herself to food when she liked, as well as eat seconds at mealtime.

Bruce and I toured the friendly place wondering if this was "it" – what she needed to succeed in life and be happy.

The house parents had an hourly staff person come in every eight hours around-the-clock to support them. The situation and set-up seemed ideal.

The house also had a safe room just like the one that had been at Lilly's Eastland School a few years before. The parents said the room wasn't used much but it was there if a kid needed a safe place to go to vent. We marveled that it even existed but felt it was a more suitable option for those special kids than to be taken away in handcuffs.

As Lilly spent time at Taylor, she would go in the room and shut the door at times herself. Once inside she'd go nuts. After she was done screaming and carrying on, she would sit on the floor for a while. House parents would check on her and eventually she would feel safe to come out and rejoin the others. She was never locked in the room, although the door did have that capability.

Lilly would sometimes run away, but there was nowhere to go except muddy and freezing cornfields. We happened to come for a visit once while they were out looking for her, and waited an hour until she was found. We were very concerned because it was freezing cold out, and relieved when the sheriff brought her back half-frozen and covered with mud.

When we saw her, we told her that we had waited almost an hour and knew it would probably take a long time for her to get cleaned up and presentable, so we were going to have to leave. We said we were sorry she missed our visit and left.

We felt that was another way for her to learn consequences. The world wouldn't stop turning because she decided to run away again.

Little more than two months after she moved to Taylor Home, we heard media reports about an investigation back at Blair Village following the death of a teenage girl there. We immediately wondered if it had been one of Lilly's housemates.

We followed the news and learned that the girl had acted up after privileges had been taken away from her. A struggle with the staff women ensued, and ended when two women in the employ of Blair Village turned the girl face-down on the floor and sat on her. That caused the girl to vomit, and she eventually suffocated while lying there.

We thought it might have been some of the staff we remembered from Lilly's house, and it turned out that our suspicions were correct. Not only had this occurred in the same house that she had lived in, but it happened to a girl she had known. What a tragedy.

We shuddered at the thought that it very well could have been Lilly who died such a miserable death. We had been learning that staff could certainly make or break a facility.

In Lilly's world there were very few media or news reports, and in this case, it was just as well because she wouldn't have been able to handle the news.

At Taylor, the "school part" had us concerned because Lilly was riding a public school bus. We knew it was only a matter of time until she wouldn't be able to keep it together in the public school setting, but it was out of our hands.

She hadn't been at Taylor long and seemed mostly happy, and the house parents were great. The other five kids there weren't teasing her either, and it seemed mostly peaceful.

Lilly's fifteenth birthday was approaching, and I asked her what she wanted. She told me about a doll she had seen advertised on TV. It actually drank a bottle filled with water and wet her diaper.

We got her the doll for her birthday and she named it Jasmine, after her favorite pretend character.

Around this time, I finally admitted to myself that Lilly was mildly mentally challenged. Maybe she was born with it, or maybe her brain had been damaged from the horrific early physical abuse and neglect. I don't know, but she had made a lot of progress in bonding with and trusting us. It was a miracle, actually. She behaved in the car all the time, which was another triumph for her. She still had very poor cause and effect reasoning abilities, though.

She looked grown-up, but still adored her dolls and still wiped her mouth at meals on the neckline of her tops. One day as I was leaving her, Lilly was saying goodbye to me at the front door, and a visiting mother walked past us to leave.

When the woman saw the stains on Lilly's shirt, she stopped and looked at her and said, "You know, OxiClean will take those stains out. You should try it."

Lilly looked blankly back at her.

"Try it," the woman encouraged with a nod as she left through the front door.

Really? I literally laughed most of the way home, thinking about that goofy comment to a girl who used her shirt for a napkin.

CHAPTER FIFTY-EIGHT

I got a call from the Taylor Home house mother about a month after the birthday.

"Nealie, this is Donna. I'm so sorry to call, but our dog was hurt pretty bad and we think Lilly did it."

My feelings all crunched inside. It was awful for the dog and it was awful for Lilly.

She continued, "We don't have proof, and nobody saw anything. She is denying involvement and seems very upset about it, but we still suspect her. We aren't sure what to do. I think he'll be okay, but . . ."

I found my voice and said, "Donna, I am so sorry! What are you going to do to protect him from now on?"

"Oh, we are going to keep him in our bedroom unless the kids are in school."

I knew the county worker would get the report about the dog, and I also knew that it was a huge setback for Lilly. Somehow I was certain she had been the culprit. Then I was angry, because hadn't those wonderful people been told of her past problems with animals? Probably not. Nobody ever got the whole story with these kids.

Was it the county worker's fault? Maybe in part, but most likely the files on Lilly could have filled a five-drawer filing cabinet. The worker must have had dozens of kids and oodles of papers and couldn't know everything.

Then I looked inward. Why hadn't I warned the house parents? I guess I felt that all the bases had been covered, and we had managed to keep Peek and Baler safe. But Bruce and I had been forewarned with detailed stories.

Four days later, I pulled into Taylor Children's Home. I was there to celebrate Lilly's ninth anniversary in our family. We had taken to treating her every spring with dinner out and a gift, if she was allowed.

Donna greeted me when I went in the house, "Hi, Nealie. Lilly will be coming down from her room in a minute. She wants to take her birthday doll along."

I looked around and asked, "How is Bingo?" I didn't see him anywhere.

"Oh, he's much better and doing fine. He stays in our room."

I was so relieved.

Just then, Lilly came into the room. She was wearing blue jeans and a white hoodie, and would have looked like a million other fifteen-year-old girls except she carried a large green bundle.

"Hi, Mom!" She shuffled toward me, trying to see over the huge green bath towel that was wrapped around her doll.

I smiled at her and asked, "Watcha got in there?"

Lilly lifted one end of the towel covering the doll and replied, "Jasmine. See, here's her bottle. Can we go now?" She put her thumb in her mouth and waited.

I hesitated, but figured she would leave the doll in the car when we got to the restaurant.

"Okay, let's go!" I said acting happy, but inside I was disturbed about the lack of closure on the dog incident.

As we drove the miles towards town, I asked her, "Where do you want to eat?"

She enthusiastically said, "Bob Evans!" Then she said, "Mom, did you hear what somebody did to Bingo? They need to pay for that! I wish they'd be put in jail." Her voice trembled as she spoke.

"Yes, I heard. It was so sad. Do you know anything about it?" I was really pushing into dangerous territory. What if she went off in the car, or ran away once we were in town?

She answered, "No, but I hope they find them. That poor, innocent dog." She was emotional as she spoke, and put her thumb back in place and looked out her window.

I decided to drop it, because I was alone with her.

When we reached our destination, she picked up her green bundle and we walked into Bob Evans.

I could tell the hostess was trying to figure out the teenager with the doll wrapped snugly in a big bath towel.

"Table for two?"

Lilly jostled her bundle and replied, "No, for three."

The girl looked at me and said, "Okay . . . follow me."

We sat down at a table with four chairs, and a heavyset man came up and said, "Hi, I'm Benjamin, and I'm going to be your waiter. What would you like to drink?"

Lilly raised her eyebrows and asked, "May I have a booster seat for Jasmine?"

He said, "Of course, let me go get one." He disappeared and returned with a booster seat and placed it on the chair beside her.

"Thank you, Benjamin," she said and began to place the doll in the booster.

He tried to resume where he had left off. "So, what would you like to drink —pop, milk, coffee, tea, juice?"

Lilly ignored the question and said, "Benjamin, I think Jasmine needs a high chair instead, because she's not sitting up right."

"Okay," he said and quickly dashed away. When he returned, he had a heavy wooden high chair and placed it at the end of the table.

Lilly placed Jasmine in it and propped her up with the bath towel.

Benjamin looked at me and tried a third time. "Drinks?" That time his eyebrows were raised.

I smiled at him because I was slightly amused, and a little embarrassed that he had the bad luck to be our waiter. "I'll have iced tea with lemon, please. Lilly, do you want a Sprite?"

"Yes, Mom."

Benjamin left, and when he returned, he had our beverages.

Lilly smiled at him as he set them down. She said, "Thank you sir. You are so nice."

We gave him our order, and as he turned to leave, Lilly held out her already-drained glass and asked, "Could you please get me a refill?"

"Yes, I can," he replied good-naturedly.

He did, and then Lilly accidentally knocked it over, so he had to run and get us a pile of napkins to wipe it up, then a big wet washcloth to keep the table from being sticky. After it was all cleaned up, he had to get her a new paper placemat and silverware.

She inhaled her meal and then sent Benjamin off to get her pie for dessert. She leaned forward towards me and whispered, "Mom, I'm really worried about Benjamin. Did you see how much he is sweating?"

Eventually Lilly told the therapist at Taylor that she had hurt Bingo, but didn't think she had, because it was like she hadn't been herself when she did it. That rang true because she had never explained anything like that before, and she had never before shown real remorse.

That's hard to explain, but part of her did not believe she had hurt the dog –it must have been someone else, and they deserved to go to jail. She was exceedingly distraught about it, which demonstrated to us that Lilly's conscience was developing more.

After that revelation, we all knew she still needed to be away from animals, so the county worker started looking for another place for Lilly. It only took a few weeks for her to secure a place at Holbeck Home, another religious charity's facility on a beautiful campus near a big city.

It was now Lilly's third religious charity whose mission had been to extend help to troubled or abused kids. We were grateful for all three. It was also a lockup and had step-down living when a teen qualified for less restriction.

Once again the drive was a little over an hour for us. By that time, we realized we must have been located in the center of the Residential Universe.

Our girl did well at Holbeck, and I gave their uncommonly personable staff credit for that. They were as wonderful and professional as we could have ever asked for, and Lilly liked them.

She did well for six months, and we thought the step-down might be possible after a few more months there. Things were looking good for her, and she seemed mentally and emotionally more stable.

And so, one beautiful July day, Bruce and I were driving the hour trip to have our weekly visit with fifteen-year-old Lilly. As we drove, I hoped she had been having a good week so that we could spend our time visiting in the sunshine on the grounds of the facility.

We went to her red brick building and used the outside phone to tell the staff that we'd arrived.

Several minutes and three security doors later, Lilly was escorted out to us, and yes, we could sit at a picnic table.

We exchanged hugs and greetings as Lilly gave my tote bag her usual once-over glance to see if we'd brought anything for her to eat.

Pleased to see the peanuts in the shell, she grinned and said, "Peanuts, yeah!"

We found a picnic table with not too many bird droppings on it and sat down.

Lilly began cracking open and eating peanuts faster than a squirrel.

As I sat across from her and cracked open my own pile, I said, "Lilly, people keep telling me I need to write about you and your life with us. I'm thinking about writing a book about it. What do you think?"

Lilly popped more peanuts into her mouth and chewed more slowly. She thoughtfully replied, "I think you should. There's a lot of kids who think they're the only one."

Imagine our surprise when the county lady called to say that Lilly was going to be moved again. She would be going to a secure residential hospital to live, and it was over two hours from our house. It wasn't an ordinary hospital, but one for severely mentally-troubled kids.

We were so, so bummed about the news, but could do nothing.

Had Holbeck felt Lilly wasn't a good match for their program? Or maybe the county felt that the residential hospital would be a better place for her? It just didn't make sense considering she had been doing so well, and I was fuming about it. To this day, we do not know why.

She was going to be moved within five days, and I needed and wanted to see her first. Bruce was working a sixty-five hour week so I decided to go by myself. When I got home later that night, I wrote this in my journal:

"I went to see Lilly this morning because she's going to be moved soon. This was my last trip to Holbeck Home. Staff there has been great. I had missed my exit for Holbeck a few times in the past because it always seemed to sneak past me. Today I was alert for landmarks before the exit, so next time I wouldn't pass it. Then wait! I sadly thought, this was the last trip, and it didn't matter. A few days ago I went to Walmart and purchased an overnight organizer bag for Lilly. It looks very much like a Coach bag, but she's never heard of Coach. I also got her a pair of purple pj's with a cat on them. I thought those items might help ease the transition of packing and moving. We haven't been in on any of these last three moves; the social workers do it during the day while Bruce and I are at work.

"I got there today at one o'clock p.m., and she was so pleased to see me and the presents. She found pretzels and gum inside the travel case and immediately opened up the pretzels. She looked pale today. Her brown hair was mostly clean, but combed. It's always crowding her face. I love it in a headband but she breaks or loses them. Her gray-flowered top had what looked like macaroni and cheese sauce at the neck where she'd wiped her mouth. I remembered the nutty woman who once told her to use OxiClean, and chuckled inside.

"It's clear to me after all these years that only a few will ever really love her. But I think it's the same way with each of us. We are blessed if we have a few who love and stick by us. Lilly is blessed because she deserves to be. I take comfort in that without saying to myself that I am her only blessing. No, her blessing has been her sense of humor, the ability to live in the moment, and the prayers and help of hundreds of people who didn't understand her, but did what they could. She is on a new leg of her journey in life. I don't know what the days ahead hold for her or for us, but it has been an amazing journey so far, with some hard-won progress for her.

"Our commitment to her holds fast because I believe very much in hope and love, and the goodness of God. We all have our futures to live day by day, as does Lilly. I love what Mother Teresa said, 'Yesterday is gone. Tomorrow has not yet come. We have only today. Let us begin.'"

EPILOGUE

I started writing this story in 2009, at the urging of a friend. He felt very strongly that I could help people by telling the story. I had heard "You need to write a book!" many times over the years, but until the reason-to-write became to help (rather than entertain), I could not do it. I finished the story in 2012, and have not added to it, nor do I plan to.

Everyone on Lilly's team of caregivers and decision makers always looked for better ways to help Lilly. If you didn't walk in our shoes, it may be easy to say that we didn't handle issues or behavior the right way. Some things have changed since then in the way things are done, but at the time, we all honestly did our utmost to help her. The teachers, schools, doctors, therapists, CHC, Children's Services, support service workers, family and friends who prayed –we all did our best (sometimes out of desperation). Nothing was implemented without the knowledge and help of the many involved in her case.

We tried everything possible to save and change her life. And though our best sometimes fell short, her life has changed because she can *feel*. She feels her conscience at work and feels regret for poor decisions. She feels love!

Her life may not look like yours, but Lilly is a survivor –and she and I and everyone involved can remember, shake our heads, and smile, for Lilly *knows* she is loved.

And that's what really matters.

Nealie Rose

Notes from Lilly and conversation clips from ages fifteen to eighteen:

About my Life. BY: LILLY
It is a true story
Once there was a girl
Her name was Lilly
She was abused by her Family
Then she got taken away from her family.
but that was a long
Time o go.
Now I'm 16-teen.
And have a new Family that loves me.
When I think about my past I see
Myself dying Day By Day.
By Day.

Hi Mom, Was up with you? i miss you.
i Love you so much.
You have been A good Mommy
to me. School is going good.
You were there for me when I felt down

Dad, You are the best DAD
You Did so much for us
You rock
Best wishes
God is with you. By Lilly

_____

We were sitting in traffic.
Lilly said excitedly, "Hey, that looked like Miss Kline!"
I asked, "The blond?"
"No, that brown-haired dude in the truck."

_____

Hi Mom was up with you? I miss you?
I wish I can see you. But the good
thing is I can see you?
P.S. I Love You.

_____

I was talking to Lilly on the phone one evening.
"What are you learning in school?"
"About the President."
"And who is the President?"
"Uh, I don't know."
"What?!"
"Uh, Oh yeah, Barak Obama. We're going to write him letters."
"That's great! What are you going to say in your letter?"
"I'm going to tell him we watch his show all the time."
"What show, Lilly?"
"You know, the Barak Obama Show."
"He doesn't have a show."
"Oh."

Hi dad, was up with you?
I miss you.
I love you so much.
I wish I can Be with you guys.
But I know I need help.
And you guys need help too. (*We probably do!*)
But one of these days I will
come home. And I will be your
little girl
For the rest of my Life.
And I will be there for you when
you need me. P.S. I love you guys

We were sitting in a restaurant during an off-campus visit.
Lilly said, "Guess what? Me and Miss Kline is cool. I didn't attack her since Sunday. I didn't attack her Monday, Tuesday, Wednesday, or Thursday!"

Lilly was talking on my cell phone to Torie during a visit at her facility. I had taken her some pistachio nuts and she was prying them open and eating them as she talked. I whispered, "Don't eat while you're talking on the phone." An unopened nut fell on the floor under the table. Lilly ignored me and kept prying the nuts open, eating and talking. I watched her chubby little toes feel around under the table for the nut that had dropped. Her toes found it and grabbed it. She continued chewing and speaking into the phone as she bent down to retrieve the nut from her toes. I blinked and asked, "You're not going to eat that are you?" Lilly started to howl with laughter. "No!" she giggled.

---

happy memorial - Day
Mommy And DADDY
You rock.
I love you guys
Mom, was up with you?
I miss you so much.
I wish I can go home with you guys.
I feel sad for the soldiers who die for us.
I bet you that they have Family.

"Mom, I just want to tell you that when you and Daddy die I'm going to live in your house. So don't sell it."

We were in an Italian restaurant and beautiful music was playing from the sound system. Lilly commented, "Do you hear that music? That's what rich people dance to." I said, "It's beautiful music and you could dance to it if you wanted." She slurped her fettuccine Alfredo and responded, "No, I'm not like rich or anything."

Nealie Rose

Run Away Love
by Lilly
once there was a girl
her name was Lilly
She was abused by her Family and
She had a sister who was abused too.
And they put me and my sister
through hell.
But we got taken away
from each other.
Now I can see her once a month.

The McDonald's had lots of people in it, but Lilly still noticed a gorgeous teenage girl come in and sit down near us. The girl was wearing all black and had waist-length blond hair. Soon a manager came over to the girl and handed her an employment application. Suddenly Lilly's admiration turned to sympathy as she loudly exclaimed, "Ahhh, she's trying to get a JOB!"

Lilly and I were talking and she said, "I was about to smack this kid, but I didn't want to get slammed on the wall by Mr. Ped."
"What do you mean, 'slammed on the wall'?"
"You know, picked up and *slammed*!"
"He does that?"
"Oh, yeah. We don't mess with HIM. But he's a nice guy."

We were wrapping Christmas presents and Lilly asked, "Dad, did my eyes just see that?"

"See what?"

"Did I just see you smack Mommy on the butt? How disgusting is that? I can't believe you did that, Dad."

Lilly was with us in the car and the national anthem could be heard on the radio. She started singing weird and making fun and I said, "Hey, that's the Star Spangled Banner, our national anthem." She stopped goofing around immediately and respectfully said, "I didn't know it was the Star Bangle. There's guys who risked their lives. I wouldn't laugh about that."

We were at Shake'n Steak, and Lilly had ordered a gigantic hamburger, French fries, and a hot fudge milkshake. After eating the hamburger and milkshake she sat looking at the pile of French fries. She said, "I feel really bad. There's all these people in Africa that don't have any food. I wish I could give this to them." I nodded sympathetically and asked, "And how would you do that?" She shrugged and replied, "That's the problem."

Nealie Rose

(Over the phone) "Mommy, guess what? I got new glasses."
"Do you like them?"
"Yeah, they're really nice."
"What do they look like?"
"Let me take them off and look." (pause) "They're black."
"Are you going to take care of them?"
"Yeah."
"Do you suppose John still has your old ones?"
Lilly erupted into laughter as she answered, "Yeah, he's probably wearing them right now!"

"Mom, you won't believe this but there was this kid who kept saying to me, 'My dead girlfriend is following me around, my dead girlfriend is following me around…' He was really getting on my nerves."
I asked her, "How did you get him to stop?"
Lilly held up two fingers and said, "I told him, 'OKAY!! PEACE-OUT!!'"

"You know, I protected your identity in the book about you and changed your name."
"What did you call me?"
"Lilly."
"Lilly! Oh, I love that name!"

Resources

Recommended Books

The Connected Child
co-authored by Dr. Karyn Purvis
*www.*empoweredtoconnect.org

Sometimes God has a Kid's Face
by Sister Mary Rose McGeady (Covenant House)
www.covenanthouse.org/

The Whole Life Adoption Book
by Jayne Schooler and Thomas Atwood
www.jayneschooler.blogspot.com

Parenting with Love and Logic
by Foster Cline, MD and Jim Fay
www.loveandlogic.com

Parenting the Hurt Child: Helping Adoptive Families Heal and Grow
by Gregory C. Keck and Regina M. Kupecky

When Love is Not Enough, a Guide to Parenting Children with RAD
by Nancy L. Thomas
www.nancylthomas.wordpress.com/

Lighting Mary's House
by Lori Mitchell
This was a book a friend gave to us, and Lilly has requested that it be read
to her many times

Nealie Rose

Resources

Foundations and Agencies

Okey's Promise
okeyspromise.com/
This is an initiative that seeks to raise awareness for the safety of animals and children through artistic projects.

Making it Happen Foundation
with Leigh Anne Tuohy (Author of *The Blind Side*)
www.makingithappenfoundation.com/

Covenant House
www.covenanthouse.org

Manufactured by Amazon.com
Columbia, SC
08 April 2017